GUIDE TO THE PERFECT LATIN AMERICAN IDIOT

GUIDE TO THE PERFECT LATIN AMERICAN IDIOT

Plinio Apuleyo Mendoza
Carlos Alberto Montaner
Alvaro Vargas Llosa

Introduction by Mario Vargas Llosa

Translated by Michaela Lajda Ames

MADISON BOOKS
Lanham • New York • Oxford

Published by Madison Books
4720 Boston Way
Lanham, Maryland 20706

12 Hid's Copse Road
Cumnor Hill, Oxford OX2 9JJ, England

Distributed by National Book Network

Library of Congress Cataloging-in-Publication Data

Mendoza, Plinio Apuleyo.
    [Manual del perfecto indiota latinoamericano–español. English]
    Guide to the perfect Latin American idiot / Plinio Apuleyo Mendoza, Carlos
Alberto Montaner, Alvaro Vargas Llosa; introduction by Mario Vargas Llosa;
translated by Michaela Lajda Ames.
        p.   cm.
    ISBN 1-56833-134-7 (cloth : alk. paper)
    1. Latin America—History. 2. Latin American—History—Errors, inventions, etc.
I. Montaner, Carlos Alberto. II. Vargas Llosa, Alvaro. III. Vargas Llosa, Mario,
1936– IV. Title.

F1410.M57313 2000
980—dc21

                                                                                    99-055248

⊗ ™The paper used in this publication meets the minimum requirements of
American National Standard for Information Sciences—Permanence of
Paper for Printed Library Materials, ANSI/NISO Z39,48–1992.
Manufactured in the United States of America.

*In memory of Carlos Rangel
and for Jean François Revel,
one on each side of the Atlantic, together they
have relentlessly fought political idiocy*

CONTENTS

TRANSLATOR'S NOTES

A work of this type imparts a great deal of challenge and enjoyment to the translator. Its unique "part literary/part academic" approach, blending the scholastic with workaday vocabulary, demanded that its playfulness and rhetorical wit be maintained in order to whet the reader's palate for the meatier factual and statistical data embedded within. Although no effort was spared in retaining the delectable wordplays, with heavy heart I must acknowledge that some of these linguistic gems were lost due to the particularity of the language.

Certain personalities, and even some of the political and religious references appearing on these pages, will probably be unfamiliar to the average "Anglo" reader. But it didn't seem necessary to specifically point out, for example, at each and every reference to "liberal" and "neoliberal" that it is nearly opposite to our current English usage of these words, being more synonymous with what we would describe as a "classical" or "Jeffersonian liberal"; that is, a "libertarian." Yet such considerations are fundamental, since the ideology of the entire book rests on them.

Quoted in the *Guide* are also numerous other works, which are addressed in two ways: First, texts originally appearing in English or with published English translations are listed only with their English title. Second, foreign works without published English translations are first cited in the original language, followed by my translation of the work in quotation marks and parentheses. In addition, all quotes from foreign-language sources are my own translations of the originals, unless otherwise noted.

But enough of these minutiae, our idiot awaits. . . .

TRANSLATOR'S ACKNOWLEDGMENTS

Let me here recognize and truly thank the following contributors to this translation: Dr. Leland D. Wright Jr. for his meticulous proofreadings and consultations; Alvaro Vargas Llosa for his invaluable assistance with (and feedback on) details of the translation; my dear friends and family who indulgently served as audience readers; and especially my husband, Justin, for his encouragement, enthusiasm, and support.

FOREWORD

Mario Vargas Llosa

He believes that we're poor because *they* are rich and vice versa, that history is a successful conspiracy of evil against good, where *they* always win and *we* always lose (he is always among the poor victims and the noble losers). He has no objection to surfing through cyberspace and being on-line, while at the same time—without realizing the contradiction—loathing consumerism. When he speaks of culture he boasts, "What I know I learned from life, not from books, so my culture isn't academic but pragmatic." Who is he? He is the Latin American idiot.

Three writers (Latin Americans, of course) quote, dissect, describe, write biographies about, and immortalize him in a book—*Guide to the Perfect Latin American Idiot*—which is written in the way a skilled matador fights a Miura bull: drawing the creature in ever closer, fearlessly taking him by the horns in each performance. But the ferocity of the chafing criticism is softened by the guffaws awaiting on each page and by a relentless self-criticism that leads the authors to include their own idiocies in the delightful anthology of stupidity, by way of an appendix, at the end the book.

I know the three authors very well, and their credentials are among the most respectable that a contemporary writer can boast of. For years, Plinio Apuleyo Mendoza has been stalked and threatened with death by Colombian terrorists linked to crime and drug trafficking for ceaselessly denouncing them in his reports and articles. Carlos Alberto Montaner fought against Batista and later Castro and for more than thirty years has been fighting in exile for Cuba's freedom. Alvaro Vargas Llosa (my son, by the way) has three pending trials in Fujimori's Peru as a "traitor to the country" for condemning the inane Peru–Ecuador border squabble. At one time or another in their youth, all three have been leftists

(Alvaro says he wasn't, but I found out that when he was at Princeton he belonged to a radical group that, sporting Che Guevara berets, demonstrated against Reagan in front of the White House). Now all three are liberals, like myself, belonging to that unveiled, simple ideological variant that in some regions verges on anarchy and that is referred to as "ultra-liberalism" or "liberal fundamentalism" by some of the book's protagonists—the aforementioned idiots.

The idiocy pervading this guide is not congenital, not the cerebral or spiritual phenomenon, nor that state of mind that fascinated Flaubert (the French *bêtise* or what we in Spanish have clothed in beautiful and mysterious euphemisms, such as the anatomical "halfwit" in Spain or that meandering "village idiot" in Peru). This type of idiot arouses affection and sympathy or, even worse, commiseration, but not anger or criticism. At times he even inspires secret envy; there is something that resembles purity and innocence in those simpletons of nature and in their spontaneous idiocy. There is also the suspicion that they possess nothing less than that terrible thing believers call "godliness." The idiocy documented in these pages is of another kind. In fact, this idiocy exists not just in Latin America—it runs like quicksilver and spreads its roots everywhere. False, intentional, and chosen, it is consciously adopted because of intellectual laziness, ethical sluggishness, and social opportunism. It is ideological and political but above all frivolous, because it reveals an abdication of the ability to think for oneself, to compare the words with the facts they claim to describe, to question the rhetoric that replaces thoughts. This idiocy is devoted to the prevailing trend; always carried away by the popular tide, it worships stereotypes and is defined by clichés.

No one is immune from succumbing to this type of idiocy at some time in life. (I too appear in the anthology with an atrocious quote.) The sufferers possess ontological lunacy like the official of Franco's government who, on a trip to Venezuela, defined the regime he served thusly: "What is Francoism? It's socialism with freedom." With such transient and almost stealthy idiocies and a stroke of literary genius, they suddenly explain, like Julio Cortázar in a burst of lyrical innocence, that the Gulag was only "an accident on the road" of communism. Or like García Márquez in his report on the Falkland Islands war, they document with mathematical omniscience how many castrations the savage British *Gurkhas* performed on Argentina's armies, by the minute. Contradictions of this type are easily forgiven due to the brevity and cheerful manner in which they were emitted. The stifling ones wrap themselves around baroque theological treatises that explain that the "choice for true Christian poverty" is experienced in class struggle, democratic centralism, guerrilla warfare, Marxism, or economic quagmires that, by using a bombardment of statistics and inventive comparative tables, show how each dollar recorded as profit by an American or European company confirms the success of the Shylock business model since those profits were amassed with the blood, sweat, and tears of Third World peasants.

There is sociological idiocy and idiocy derived from historical science; from political science and journalism; from Catholics and Protestants; from the right and left; from the social democrats, the Christian democrats, the revolutionaries, the conservatives, and—oh, dear—even the liberals. All appear here, mercilessly treated and mistreated, although always with a truly spicy and exhilarating humor. What this book really outlines in its thirteen witty chapters (and its priceless anthology) is something that binds and explains all those aberrations, equivocations, distortions, and raving exaggerations accepted as ideas: *intellectual underdevelopment* (a phenomenon that, although weakened, is still alive and kicking).

The book's great merit lies in cloaking its conceptual seriousness beneath its funny bone: to show that all doctrines that make an exaggerated attempt to explain grim realities such as poverty, social inequalities, exploitation, ineptitude in producing wealth and creating jobs, and the failures of civil institutions and Latin American democracy are primarily a result of an obstinate and ubiquitous irresponsibility. Playing ostrich in their own misery and defects, they refuse to acknowledge and therefore correct them, rather looking for excuses and scapegoats (imperialism, neocolonialism, multinationals, unfair trade terms, the Pentagon, the CIA, the International Monetary Fund, the World Bank, etc.) so as to take comfort, all in good conscience, in the position of an eternal victim and dwell endlessly on the problem. It appears that Mendoza, Montaner, and Vargas Llosa have in their research on intellectual idiocy in Latin America unintentionally arrived at the same conclusion as the U.S. economist Lawrence E. Harrison, who many years ago confirmed in a polemic essay that underdevelopment is "a mental illness."

Here this idiocy appears, above all, as a weakness and cowardice in the face of true reality and as a neurotic propensity toward avoiding this reality by replacing it with a fictitious one. It is no wonder that a continent with such tendencies embraced surrealism, the distorted beauty of dreamlike states and intuition, and distrust for the rational—a place where military satrapy and authoritarianism proliferated at the same time and attempts to establish a tradition of consensus and reciprocal concessions through tolerance and individual responsibility (these being the food of democracy) failed over and over again. Both situations appear to be the consequence of the same cause: the profound inability to distinguish between the truth and falsehood, reality and fiction. This explains how Latin America has produced great artists, distinguished musicians, outstanding poets and novelists, and thinkers who are so far removed from reality; how it has raised up such shallow doctrinaires; how it brought forth innumerable ideologues who place a perpetual ban on historical objectivity and pragmatism. It is also where the intellectual elite religiously and piously adopted Marxism (more or less like it had usurped the Catholic doctrine as its own), the twentieth-century catechism with prefabricated answers for every problem, which exempts thinking or questioning situations and oneself, dissolving its own conscience in a cacophonous chorus of dogma.

The *Guide to the Perfect Latin American Idiot* belongs to a rich tradition of satire, with Pascal and Voltaire as its masters, later continued by Sartre, Camus, and Revel in the contemporary world. This is a militant and polemic text, provoking and seeking intellectual confrontation in the arena of ideas, not anecdotes, using arguments, not insults or personal attacks. It balances its light-hearted expressions and dialectic virulence against the strength of its content, its serious analysis, and its expository coherence. So, although it is riddled throughout with humor, it is the most serious book in the world. After having read it (just as with Vallejo's verses), the reader is left thinking—and then is immediately overcome by sadness.

Will we Latin Americans always be like this, creating so freely and theorizing so slavishly? There is no doubt about it—Latin America is changing for the better. In almost every country, military dictatorships have been replaced with civilian governments, and everywhere you look a certain resignation to democratic pragmatism seems to be infiltrating old revolutionary utopias. Stumbling and tripping along the way, issues that only a while ago were considered taboo (internationalization, markets, privatization of the economy, the need to reduce and discipline governments) are now being accepted. But all this is being done reluctantly, without conviction, because that's just how it is and nothing can be done about it. Aren't some of these reforms that are being carried out with such unwillingness, foot-dragging, and muttered curses destined to fail? How can such policies bring forth the expected fruits—modernity, jobs, rule of law, higher standards of living, human rights, and freedom—if no conviction and ideas are present to support and perfect them, ceaselessly vivifying and rejuvenating them? Latin America's current paradox is that its governments are beginning to change, its economies are being reformed, and civil institutions are being born or reborn. But its intellectual life continues to be largely stagnant, blind and deaf to the world's great historical changes, unchanging in its routines, myths, and conventions.

Will this book shake up Latin America? Will it awaken it from its deep slumber? Will the throng of idiots open their eyes and respond with opposing ideas and arguments to the challenge presented by the *Guide*'s three musketeers? Hopefully. There is nothing we need more than a great debate for Latin America's changes to endure, giving this long and sacrificial modernizing process an intellectual foundation—the ideological stew from which freer and more prosperous societies will emerge and a cultural life with no idiocy or idiots, or at least hardly any.

Paris, January 1996

❶

THE FAMILY PORTRAIT

The perfect idiot's political tutelage included, in addition to connivings and resentments, a mixture of the most varied and confusing ingredients. First, of course, there is a lot of the Marxist Vulgate from his university years. In those years, various introductory-level Marxist brochures and leaflets provided him a simple and complete explanation of the world and history. All was duly explained as class struggle. History advanced according to a preordained script (from slavery to feudalism to capitalism and then socialism, the threshold of a truly egalitarian society). Those guilty of our countries' poverty and backwardness were two disastrous allies: the bourgeoisie and imperialism.

Such ideas of historic materialism provided him a stew in which he could later brew up a strange mixture of Third World theses, outbreaks of nationalism and populist demagogy, and one vehement reference or another to compassion, almost always comically quoted from some emblematic strongman from his country: José Martí, Augusto César Sandino, José Carlos Mariátegui, Víctor Raúl Haya de la Torre, Jorge Eliécer Gaitán, Eloy Alfaro, Lázaro Cárdenas, Emiliano Zapata, Juan Domingo Perón, Salvador Allende, Simón Bolívar, or Che Guevara. All were served up in a boiling rhetorical cauldron. Our perfect idiot's political thinking resembles those extravagant tropical stews where you can find anything you're looking for, from chickpeas and slices of fried bananas to parrot feathers.

If we could put this character on a psychoanalyst's couch, in the most intimate crevices of his memory we would discover ulcers from some social complexes and resentments. Just as does most of Latin America's political and intellectual world, the perfect idiot comes from the lower middle class, very often from a rural background and somehow now rendered penniless. Perhaps he had a wealthy grandfather who fell into financial ruin, a mother widowed at an early age, a professional, businessman, or civil servant father pressured by daily trials, yearning for better times for the family. His world is almost always marked by social fractures, common to the vanished rural environment that is now badly entrenched in the new urban reality.

It could be that he grew up in the capital or a nearby city; his house could have been one of those that the rich scoff at when they inhabit the more elegant and modern part of town. His was a modest estate in a middle-class neighborhood or one of those old, damp, dark houses, with courtyards and flowerpots, tiles and rusty pipes, a Blessed Virgin image at the end of the entry, and exposed light bulbs in rooms and hallways. That is, before rampant urban development confined him to a tiny apartment in a multifamily dwelling. His friends since childhood would have been Scott's Rub, iodine-tonic cough syrup, radio soap operas, Pérez Prado's mambos, rancorous tango and Mexican *ranchera* tunes, end-of-the-month hardships, and relatives always fearing the loss of their jobs with every change of government.

Below this dusty social stripe, which we all probably belonged to, were the "people," that great anonymous and destitute mass pervading the streets, market squares, and churches during Holy Week. And high above, always arrogant, were the rich with their clubs, their enormous mansions, their debutantes and exclusive parties; from the heights of their elite surnames they looked down disdainfully at the middle-class people, who, depending on their country of origin, were called "social climbers," "half-breeds," "*nouveaux riches*," or some other derogatory name.

However, our man (or woman) was not awarded his "idiot" title for coming from a social caste, as if he could be the pastrami rather than just the rye. Nor was it earned as a pimply-faced teenager, in search of explanation or retaliation in Marxism. Almost all of us Latin Americans have suffered from Marxism, like from childhood measles. So experiencing such silliness is not what's alarming, but rather continuing to repeat it or, even worse, to believe it without having tested it against reality. In other words it isn't having been an idiot that's so bad, but persisting to be one.

And so it is with a great deal of tenderness that we too are able to share like memories and experiences among our friends, whether having belonged to a communist organization or to some small leftist group, having sung *Internacional* or *Bella Ciao*, thrown stones at police, plastered antigovernment posters on walls, distributed pamphlets and flyers, or chanted in chorus "a united people will never be defeated" with yet another multitude of blossoming idiots. Those first twenty years are our age of innocence.

It's probable that while suffering from that common-to-many bout of measles, the Cuban revolution, with its bearded-legend images deliriously entering Havana, surprised our fellow. And here is where his idolizing of Castro or Che Guevara came not to be ephemeral but perennial. This idolatry, which convinced some of that generation's youth to run to the hills and to death, will have become somewhat concealed in our perfect idiot by the time he's no longer a militant radical leftist but a delegate, senator, ex-secretary, or leader of an important party in his country. In spite of this, however, he will still gyrate in excitement like a dog seeing a bone if during a visit to Cuba he finds before him the hand and the bearded, exuberant, and monumental presence of the "Maximum Leader." And naturally, being a perfect idiot, he will find plausible explanations for the worst disasters created by Castro. If there is hunger on the island, the cruel U.S. embargo is to blame; if there are exiles, it's because they are traitors incapable of understanding the revolutionary process; if there are prostitutes, it isn't due to the poverty on the island but rather because Cubans now have the freedom to use their bodies as they wish. The idiot, as we all know, goes to lofty extremes when interpreting the facts so as not to lose the ideological baggage that has accompanied him since youth. You see, he has no change of clothing.

Since there is no chance of our perfect idiot being a follower, his participation in small leftist factions will not survive past his student years. After completing his university degree and beginning his political career, he will search for a comfortable refuge in a party with some tradition of and option for power, transforming his Marxist capriciousness into an honorable relationship with the Socialist International—or if he is of a conservative breed, with the so-called social doctrine of the Church. He will be, to use his own words, a man with a social conscience. The word "social," by the way, fascinates him. He will speak of social change, social politics, social platforms, social trends, social vindication, or social drives, convinced that that word blesses everything he does.

A few things from his childhood ideological measles will stay with him: certain oppositions to and criticisms of imperialism, plutocracy, multinationals, the Monetary Fund, and other *octopuses* (various zoological metaphors from his militant Marxism remain with him). He will probably stop using the term "bourgeoisie," instead designating it an oligarchy or "the rich" or using the evangelic title of "the powerful" or "those chosen by fortune." And obviously everything will be from a Third World point of view. If there are guerrilla fighters in his country, they'll understandably be called "the insurgent army," and he'll ask to have patriotic dialogues with them even though they kill, abduct, rob, extort, and torture people. The perfect idiot is also, according to Lenin's definition, a useful idiot.

At the age of thirty, our chap will have suffered a prodigious transformation.

The pale student from the Marxist cell or small semi-clandestine group will now have the robust appearance and the flourishing, matured personality of a professional politician. He'll have inhaled road dust and sweated under the burning sun in the town squares while embracing *compadres,* shaking hands, drinking beer, *pisco,* rum, tequila, *aguardiente,* or any other native liquor in the village and neighborhood *cantinas.* His disciples will call him Boss. He'll be a copious and sensationalist orator who is overcome by orgasmic quiverings whenever he sees a microphone. His success will essentially depend on his ability to demagogically exploit social problems. "Isn't there unemployment, poverty, a lack of schools and hospitals? Aren't prices rising like balloons while salaries are meager starvation wages? And why?" he'll suddenly ask as he happily listens to the sound of his own voice, dispersed by loudspeakers, filling the plaza grounds. "You know why," he'll say. "We all know why. Because," and at this point the veins in his neck pulsate violently behind his menacing fist, "the wealth is badly distributed, because the rich have everything and the poor have nothing, because as their privileges increase, so do our people's hunger! Therefore, a true social policy is needed, and the state should intervene to defend the disinherited people. So everyone should vote for candidates (like him) who represent the people's aspirations."

This is how the perfect idiot, when he chooses a career in politics, will harvest votes to become elected as a delegate, a house representative or senator, governor or mayor. And so, from speech to speech, balcony to balcony, he'll almost without effort go about selling his populist ideas. His ideas are pleasing; they elicit applause. He will blame not only the rich (who have everything and give nothing), but also the unfair trade conditions, the International Monetary Fund's demands, free-market policies that blindly expose us to disastrous competition in international markets, and neoliberal ideas responsible for poverty.

In addition, he's also a true nationalist. He'll profess to defend national sovereignty against the conspiracy of foreign capital and that great international bank that continually subjects us to debt and then strangles us, leaving us without any social investment. So instead of handing over our natural wealth to the multinationals, he'll reclaim the country's sovereign rights to administer its own resources. "Privatize state-owned companies? Never!" our perfect idiot will shout, trembling furiously. "We will not hand over our people's, our nation's entire inheritance to a handful of private capitalists. Never that," he will repeat with his face redder than a turkey wattle. And his enthusiastic crowd will also say never, everyone will return home inebriated, excited, and happy, without even asking how many times they had heard the same speech and yet their condition hasn't changed a bit. In this story, the only one who prospers is the idiot.

He prospers, yes indeed. At the age of forty, our perfect idiot, involved in politics, will hold some leadership position in his party and will already have access to some good bureaucratic office, whether in Governorships, Ministries, Institutes, or Secretariats. This will be very convenient since his town-square and balcony speeches will probably have begun to fade. What is certain is that the poor will still be poor, prices will continue to rise, and public services, education, transportation, and sanitation will remain as inefficient as before. Since his proposals have now lost their meaning through useless repetition, his electoral strength will from now on have to depend essentially on his ability to award public positions, grants, aid, or subsidies. Our perfect idiot is by necessity a political power broker. He has an electoral clientele that may have lost hope in the promise of the great social change, but not in their leader's influence and what little benefits he can get with it. Something is better than nothing.

Of course, our fellow is not alone. In his party (of the social elite), his congress, and his government, he is accompanied by other politicians of the same ilk and a similar path who fight with him over power quotas. And since they swarm to public administration like bees to honey, fattening their political résumés, very soon the government offices begin to suffer from bureaucratic obesity, inefficiency, and labyrinthine "procedures." From state-run companies there emerge voracious bureaucratic unions. Our perfect idiot, who never stops campaigning, adulates the unionists, giving them whatever they ask through disastrous collective bargaining agreements. This is another expression of his social conscience. In the end, the money is not his but the state's, and the state's money belongs to everyone; in other words, to no one.

With these types of practices, it's no wonder that state-run corporations end up with deficits and in order to pay their expensive operating costs they must increase rates and taxes. This is the bill the idiot makes us pay for his social efforts. Increased public spending, characteristic of his welfare state, frequently results in serious fiscal deficits. And if it ever occurred to some unfortunate soul to ask to sell off an incredibly expensive monopoly or to privatize the electric power company, the telephone companies, the ports, or pension funds, our friend would react as if stung by a scorpion. He would ally himself with union bureaucrats in denouncing such a proposal as the path toward savage capitalism, as a neoliberal tactic used to discredit the noble social role provided by public service. This is how he will side with the unions against the huge, silent, and helpless consumer majority.

Our politician and his nationalizing policies will be aided and supported by other perfect idiots, such as economists, scholars, leftist columnists, sociologists, anthropologists, vanguard artists, and every member of the varied array of leftist factions: Marxists, Trotskyites, adherents of the Shining Path, Maoists, all who have spent their lives smearing walls with graffiti or preparing armed conflicts. All will mobilize in favor of public monopolies.

Another higher battle is fought by the economist of this vast fringe where ideological nonsense reigns. This person may be some forty-year-old man, a professor at some university, the author of some essays on political and economic theory, perhaps bearded and bespectacled. Maybe he enjoys chewing on a pipe and on theories inspired by Keynes and other mentors of social democracy. Father Marx is always present in some part of his heart and mind. The economist will fervently talk about "structuralism," a term that will surely perplex our friend the populist politician, until he understands that the bearded economist is proposing to unabashedly rev up the little money-making machine that emits bills to revive demand and finance social investment. It will be the happy meeting of two perfect idiots. The economist, using loftier terms, will impugn the Monetary Fund's recommendations as a new despicable form of neocolonialism. But his fiercest criticisms will be reserved for those called neoliberals.

The economist, to the joy of the populist, will say that the market inevitably creates unrest, that it is the state's responsibility to correct inequalities in income distribution, and that opening the economy only serves to blindly and excessively increase imports, leaving local manufacturing industries at a clear disadvantage or provoking their demise by the inevitable consequences of unemployment and an increase in social problems.

Of course, "I've said it all along," the populist politician will say, thoroughly impressed by the appearance of erudition his thesis is given by the economist and his well-documented books: books published via some funded university press. Paging through the books, the politician will find numbers, charts and graphs, and memorable quotes in order to demonstrate how the market cannot abolish the state's regulatory role. There he will read that Alan García was right when he said that "the law of gravity does not imply that man should give up flying." And naturally the two perfect idiots, united in their common admiration for the brilliant metaphor, will forget to tell us what the concrete results were of Mr. García's lucubrations and catastrophic government.

At the age of fifty, after having been a senator and perhaps a minister of something, our perfect idiot will begin to think about his options as a presidential candidate. The economist could be a wonderful minister in his Department of Finance. He will also have by his side noble constitutionalists of the same ilk, professors and illustrious essayists, perfectly convinced that solving the country's problems (instability, poverty, administrative chaos, violence, or drug trafficking) requires a profound constitutional reform, or a new Constitution that would finally recognize new and noble rights: the right to life, free and mandatory education, a decent house, a well-paying job, breast-feeding, privacy, virginity, tranquil old age, eternal bliss. Just four or five hundred articles of new laws and legislation and the country will be like new. Our perfect idiot is also a dreamer.

He's certainly not a man of great intellectual schooling, although in his speeches he may frequently quote Neruda, Vallejo, or Rubén Darío and use words like telluric, symbiosis, synergy, programmatical, and conjunctural. However, his ideas are best received by the leftist cultural world, comprised of academicians, indigenists, folklorists, sociologists, vanguard artists, authors of protest works, protest songs, and propaganda films. He gets along with these people very well.

He shares their views. How could he not agree with the essayists and academicians who exalt those so-called autochthonous and telluric values of national culture and popular artistry, opposing importers and producers of foreign, decadent art? Our perfect idiot, along with all of them, thinks that the Latin American indigenous races should be saved by following in the steps of Mariátegui or Haya de la Torre, whose books he quotes. He supports those who denounce cultural neocolonialism, and those who promote works of real "social" content (this ever-enchanting term) and those who include pre-Columbian forms and references in their pictorial art.

Our idiot, finally a congressman, has probably proposed (and at times imposed through some law, decree, or resolution) the obligation to replace foreign music (including the Beatles, which he considers decadent) with native music. This way he has probably driven his unfortunate compatriots crazy or will be at the point of driving them crazy with a deluge of Caribbean joropo tunes, Colombian bambucos, Peruvian marineras, Andean huaynos, Mexican rancheras, or Chilean cuecas. He has also required a quota of performances by local artists and has censured the excessive presence of foreign technicians and artists.

With this same nationalist litmus test, he encourages the formation of folk artist groups, giving them all forms of subsidies regardless of their quality, all in order to banish destructive cultural elitism, which in spirit can include Rossini's operas, Bach's concertos, Pollock's and Andy Warhol's art, Ionesco's (or Molière's) plays, Bergman's films, all in order to further works full of sociopolitical diatribes, horrifying *costumbrismo* or deplorable folkloric localisms.

The paradoxes: negotiating or receiving scholarships or subsidies from American officials or universities does not seem repugnant to our perfect idiot of the cultural world. Thanks to them he can, from within the imperialist monster's own bowels, denounce in books, essays, and conferences the neocolonialist's role carried out not only by the Chicago Boys and Harvard economists, but also by figures such as Donald Duck, Inspector Columbo, and Alexis Carrington. In this case the perfect Latin American idiot becomes an astute fifth columnist eroding the political and cultural values of the empire from within.

Thus, our friend moves in the vast universe of politics, economics, and culture all at the same time, where each discipline supports the others and idiocy is propagated prodigiously as an expression of a continent wide subculture, blocking for us Latin Americans the road to modernity and development. A Third World theorist, the perfect idiot leaves us in Third World poverty and backwardness with his vast catalogue of dogmas presented as truths. Such sublime stupidities circulating freely in Latin America are those which are collected, once and for all, in the following pages in this guide.

THE FAMILY TREE

*"We Latin Americans are not happy with ourselves, with what we are.
But, then, what are we? And what do we want to become?"*
—*Carlos Rangel*, The Latin Americans: Their Love-Hate
Relationship with the United States (*1977; translated by Ivan Kuts*)

Our revered Latin American idiot didn't originate by spontaneous generation, but is rather the result of a long gestation, which took almost two centuries. It's also possible to confirm that the current Latin American idiot's survival has been possible only by maintaining a lively intellectual debate involving some of Latin America's best minds. Indeed, this is how our idiot has come into being.

Everything began at a time when, at the onset of the nineteenth century, the ties between the Spanish colonies and Madrid were severed, and our countries' forefathers immediately asked the inevitable question: Why are our republics—which almost immediately entered a period of chaos and impoverishment—worse off than the neighboring thirteen North American colonies?

As long as our compatriots do not acquire the talents and political virtues that have characterized our northern brothers, I greatly fear that our completely traditionalist systems, far from being favorable for us, will be our demise. Unfortunately, the requisite level of these characteristics seems to be far from us; and, to the contrary, we are dominated by the vices acquired under the direction of a nation like Spain, which has

excelled only in cruelty, ambition, revenge and greed. (Simón Bolívar, "Letter to a gentleman showing great interest in South America's republican cause," 1815)

The first response that flourished in every corner of the continent had the liberal trademark of that period. Latin America—which had already begun to stop calling itself Hispanoamérica—was becoming worse because it had inherited Spain's inflexible, obscurantist, and dictatorial tradition, aggravated by the harmful influence of conservative Catholicism, an accomplice to the restlessness of the times: It was Spain's fault.

A prime advocate of this anti-Spanish sentiment was the anti-Catholic and antidogmatic Chilean Francisco Bilbao, a formidable agitator, whose work *Sociabilidad chilena* ("Chilean Sociability") earned the paradoxical distinction of being publicly burned by civil and religious authorities in a couple of Latin American countries dedicated to ideological pyromania.

Bilbao, like any good liberal and romantic of that time, went to Paris and there participated in the shocking revolution of 1848. As was to be expected, in the City of Light he received the esteem and support of the liberal revolutionaries. According to Zum Felde, Michelet and Lamennais called him "our son" and they carried on extensive correspondence with him. Naturally, once in France, Bilbao reinforced his conclusion that in order to progress and prosper it was necessary to *de-Hispanicize* oneself, a thesis that was presented in a much-read pamphlet at that time: *El evangelio americano* ("Gospel of the Americas").

Once back in Chile in 1850, he founded the Society of Equality and put up a commendable fight to abolish slavery. However, reunited again with Latin America he incorporated another, somewhat contradictory element into his analysis, which was later picked up by Domingo Faustino Sarmiento and countless essayists: "We must not only *de-Hispanicize* ourselves but also *de-Indianize* ourselves," a thesis that the author of *Facundo* had just defended in his previous book: *Conflicto y armonía de las razas en América* ("Racial Harmony and Conflict in the Americas").

The much-cited postcolonial hypothesis of our relative failure, put forth first by Bilbao and later by Sarmiento, already appears established by the second half of the nineteenth century: The reason we are faring poorly is not only because of our Spanish blood but also because of our Indian blood. Because of our Negro blood we are, of course, backwards, unable to live free, and, as Francisco de Miranda once despondently said, predisposed to "complete disorder"—the never-ending Latin American chaos that so many of our restless contemporary idiots are addicted to.

Throughout the entire nineteenth century, the *ruling class* posited this belief, in one way or another, as the reason for our misfortunes, and one doesn't have to be too bright to comprehend that this view brought about an understandable and growing admiration for the different and promising scene developing in the America of British origin. Hence, the two most important thinkers of the second half of the nineteenth century, the aforementioned Sarmiento and Juan Bautista Alberdi, enhanced Bilbao's judgment with a concrete proposition: Let's imitate the Anglo-Saxons within our own uniqueness. Let's imitate their pedagogy, their social structures, their economic model, and their Constitution, and from that miraculous *facsimile* there will arise a vigorous and indestructible Latin America.

We imitate what we believe to be superior or prestigious. And this is why the vision of an America de-Latinized of its own will, without threat of conquest, and reconstituted in the image and likeness of the North, now looms in the nightmares of many who are genuinely concerned about our future. This vision is the impetus behind an abundance of similar carefully thought-out designs and explains the continuous flow of proposals for innovation and reform. We have our USA-mania. It must be limited by the boundaries our reason and sentiment jointly dictate. (**José Enrique Rodó,** *Ariel,* **1900, translated by Margaret Sayers Peden**)

Only at the end of the century did this faith in U.S. progress, this confidence in the pragmatic, this amazement for material achievements begin to fall apart right in Alberdi's and Sarmiento's homeland when in 1897 Paul Groussac (an oracle to the Plata River's intelligentsia of that time) published a travel book, *Del Plata al Niágara* ("From the Plata to Niagara"), in which he was already sharply outlining the spiritual confrontation between a materialist Anglo-Saxon America and a Hispanic America weighted down by the ethical and aesthetic burden of Latin spirituality.

Groussac was not pro-French, yet he was French through and through. An adventuresome Frenchman who arrived in Buenos Aires at the age of eighteen, unable to speak a word of Spanish, he succeeded in mastering the language with such surprising perfection that he became the great dispenser of intellectual honors of that time. He became the director of the Public Library of Buenos Aires—it was said with exaggeration that he had read all its books—and from that position he exercised a great deal of authority in the Southern Cone countries.

It's quite likely that the Uruguayan José Enrique Rodó had read Groussac's papers before he published, in 1900, what would become the most read and influential political essay of the first half of the twentieth century: *Ariel*—a short book in syrupy modernist prose—Rodó "captured prose on India paper," as Blanco Fombona once said—and clearly written under the obvious influence of Renan's work *Caliban* (a drama in which this French author of the famous *Life of Jesus* used the same symbols as Shakespeare in *The Tempest* and which were later used by Rodó).

What, however, did Rodó's famous little work reveal? Essentially, three things: the natural superiority of the Latin humanist culture over Anglo-Saxon positivist pragmatism; the goal of Comte's positivist influence over Latin America; and the implicit rejection of Sarmiento's and Alberdi's anti-Hispanicism. Rodó, just like the Arielist generation that followed, which included even Rubén Darío (drunk on swans and alcohol), who actively engaged in the crusade through his anti-imperialist poems, believed that the Spanish heritage should not be rejected but rather embraced as part of the Latin legacy—of France, Italy, Spain—exalting Hispanic-Americans.

As is evident, Arielism signified an important split in the old debate to find the origin of Latin America's misfortunes, surfacing exactly at the right time to capture the imagination of the century's numerous politicians and writers, since two years earlier, in 1898, the Spanish-speaking continent had witnessed the Spanish-Cuban-American war with a mixture of admiration, stupor, and caution. Within a matter of weeks, the United States destroyed the Spanish fleet and occupied Cuba, Puerto Rico, and the Philippines, humiliating Spain and almost entirely eliminating its 400 year-old colonial empire.

The United States, before Latin America's nervous glance, was no longer an archetypal social model, but rather had transformed itself into an active international power that competed with the British on the economic market and with all the European powers in the military arena. The United States ceased being the admired republic and became another empire.

The first conquerors, with a primitive mindset, used to appropriate inhabitants as slaves. Those who came later appropriated territories without regard to inhabitants. The United States, as we have implied in the preceding chapters, has unveiled a system of appropriating wealth without regard to inhabitants or territories, thereby shunning appearances in order to get to the heart of domination without carrying the dead weight of administering colonies or controlling the masses.
(Manuel Ugarte, *La nueva Roma* ["The New Rome"], 1915)

Armed with this geopolitical and philosophical vision, a very effective and extraordinarily popular creature began to proliferate in our continent, someone we now call a *political analyst:* the ardent anti-imperialist. The most outstanding of this species was undoubtedly the Argentine Manuel Ugarte, a good journalist of lively prose, a speaker always capable of inciting the masses, and a satirist who uselessly screamed to exhaustion trying to explain that he wasn't anti-American but anti-imperialist. His work—a collection and summary of articles, discussions, and conferences, published in various volumes—had an immense impact on the entire continent, especially in Central America, the Caribbean, and Mexico (the Yankees' own backyard). Ugarte, therefore, could possibly be considered the first professional Latin American "progressive."

Curiously, Ugarte's basic idea and the work he had assigned himself were traditionally more conservative and inspired by Spain rather than progressive. Ugarte saw *anti-Pan-Americanism* (Pan-Americanism was the imperialism encouraged by Washington at that time) as a way to restrain the U.S. imperialist appetite, just as the Spanish Crown had done when it placed the delicate responsibility of preventing Protestant Anglo-Saxon penetration into Hispanic America on "the antemural of the Indies" 400 years earlier.

That outdated argument, dressed up as something new, had experienced a recent revival shortly before the appearance of *Ariel* and Arielism. In fact, in 1898, before (and during) the Spanish-American War, there was no shortage of Spanish voices asserting Carlos V's and Felipe II's old geopolitical reasoning by stating that the war between Spain and the United States—just like the battle fought against the Turks in Lepanto during the previous era—would spare decadent Europe from falling victim to the agile claws of the new imperial power arising from the other side of the Atlantic, albeit by sacrificing Spain.

As was expected given his tremendous influence, Ugarte produced a large number of disciples, including the picturesque Colombian Vargas Vila and the equally extravagant Peruvian José Santos Chocano. But his sermon brought forth its greatest fruits in Havana, the city where a serene, moderate, and serious thinker, Mr. Enrique José Varona, published in 1906 an essay entitled *El imperialismo a la luz de la sociología* ("Imperialism in the Light of Sociology"). Varona, a man respected by many, established for the first time on the continent the hypothesis that the growing U.S. influence was the result of an exploding capitalism, impetuously driven by a deluge of American banks and industries, finding their most fertile soil in Latin America's weakness. For Varona, a skeptic, a positivist, and therefore receptive to certain deterministic explanations of history, the U.S. imperial phenomenon (Cuba was being taken over by Washington at the time when the pamphlet appeared) was a consequence of the relative economic strength of its neighbor. Capitalism is simply that way. It takes over.

Since the vast majority of the Mexican people in towns and cities no longer own the land they walk on, nor are able to improve their social position or own an industry or farm, given that the mountains, hills and water are monopolized by only a few; therefore, a third of those monopolies will be confiscated from the powerful landowners as a compensation to the peoples of Mexico so that they will have common lands and colonies, and the Mexican people's lack of prosperity and well-being will be improved. (Emiliano Zapata, *The Ayala Plan*, 1911)

Ugarte's incendiary speech and Varona's reflections were the prelude to a much more elaborate conceptual mechanism that begot two movements, existing even today, firmly rooted in political activists' thinking. The first was agrarian reform, which appeared at the beginning of the Mexican revolution of 1910. The second was the emergence of Marxism, which very directly influenced our most outstanding thinkers and was present since the victory of the Russian revolution in 1917.

The Mexican revolution left behind the mariachi-like myth of Pancho Villa (more hummed than heeded), as well as the rousing agrarian vengeance affixed to the popular, vague persona of Emiliano Zapata. Likewise, there was the 1917 Querétaro Constitution, severed from the liberal groundwork Juárez had laid in the previous century, and the emergence of the formal commitment from the State that from that moment on it would be responsible for administering happiness and prosperity to all citizens through a fair redistribution of wealth.

From this era of Marxist adulation and expectations for the Bolshevik experiment, the most illustrious representative was undoubtedly Dr. José Ingenieros (1877–1925). Ingenieros, an Argentine and a psychiatrist (two words that have over time become almost synonymous), never belonged to the Communist Party, but voluntarily and deliberately launched the devious tradition of the intellectual Latin American fellow traveler. He was never a member of any communist party, but he supported all of its causes with the precision of a deadly sharpshooter.

For the first half of the century, Ingenieros's books, well reasoned but written in wretched prose, were found on the bookshelves of all Latin American intelligentsia. *El hombre mediocre* ("The Mediocre Man"), *Las fuerzas morales* ("Moral Forces"), and *Hacia una moral sin dogmas* ("Toward a Morality without Dogmas") were read as much in Buenos Aires as in Quito or Santo Domingo. His activities as a lecturer and debater, penetrating sense of humor, and irreverent red tie (not much different from the crimson umbrella that Azorín, hardly an "anarchist," used to wave around Spain) not only put Ingenieros at the apex of the debate but endowed him with a certain air of socialistic dandyism, so attractive that even today it's common to see his trivial trademark on some Latin American intellectuals more enamored of symbolism than substance.

*Now, with the emergence of a new ideology that translates the interests and aspirations of the masses—who are gradually acquiring a class consciousness or esprit de classe—there is surfacing a national tendency or movement that is expressing solidarity with the Indian's fate. For this movement, the solution to the Indian's problem serves as the foundation of a program to renew and rebuild Peru. The Indian problem ceases to be, as in the time of liberal and conservative dialogues, of secondary importance. It is now the Main topic. (*José Carlos Mariátegui, *Seven Interpretive Essays on the Peruvian Reality,* 1928)

After Ingenieros, the response to our eternal and pressing question—"Why do we Latin Americans have it so bad?"—shifted from Buenos Aires to Lima, where two important thinkers gave it their own special interpretation.

Curiously, these two thinkers, José Carlos Mariátegui and Víctor Raúl Haya de la Torre, both Peruvians, embodied the two political movements that were already appearing on the horizon: one, a Russian Bolshevik Marxism, and the other, Mexican nationalism.

José Carlos Mariátegui (1895–1930) had a brief and unhappy life. His father was practically a stranger to him, and an injury to his leg that left him lame from childhood later had to be completely amputated, a misfortune that bitterly affected the remaining years of his brief existence. He was a poor, brilliant student (educated by priests) and a good writer almost from adolescence. Possibly his only time of happiness was the four years he spent in Europe, paradoxically and a bit opportunistically with a scholarship from his enemy, the dictator Augusto B. Leguía.

In 1928, Mariátegui wrote the book *Seven Interpretive Essays on the Peruvian Reality,* which fecundated the Latin American idiot's promiscuous muse for several decades. The work is a mixture of indigenism and socialism, although, as the brilliant essayist Eugenio Chang-Rodríguez once pointed out, it contains certain racist anti-Chinese and anti-Negro statements. For Mariátegui, the Indian problem (now analyzed from the Marxist perspective) was more than a racial problem. It was a conflict that revisited the issue of land possession. The exploitation carried out by large estate owners was responsible for the backwardness and the horrible slavery of the Indians. But the problems of the Peruvian farmers did not stop there. The subservience of local producers to foreign needs also weighed heavily on them. In Peru, only products that were consumed abroad were grown.

Probably, many of these ideas—the good and the bad—truly belonged to Víctor Raúl Haya de la Torre, since Mariátegui's first political activism began with this compatriot and founder of APRA (the American Popular Revolutionary Alliance). But shortly after having met each other, they began to move to differing positions. In 1929, in the midst of a failed attempt to create a party with Marxist leanings in Lima—the Socialist Party of Peru—Mariátegui presented a short list with six objectives that would later be reproduced over and over again in practically every country on the continent, although in differing degrees:

1. Agrarian reform and forced expropriation of large estates.
2. Confiscation of foreign companies and the major industries controlled by the bourgeoisie.
3. Denial and denunciation of foreign debt.
4. Creation of worker–farmer militias to replace those armies that served the bourgeoisie.
5. An eight-hour workday.
6. Creation of soviets in municipalities controlled by worker–farmer organizations.

Despite its radical stance, Mariátegui's Marxist effort was not supported by the USSR, basically for ideological reasons. The Peruvian writer wanted to establish a classless party, a worker-*campesino*-intellectual alliance, resembling one that the old patriarchal anarchist, Manuel González Prada, had proposed to his fellow countrymen in the previous century; but Moscow only trusted the work of the vanguard, as defined by Lenin.

As long as the capitalist system rules in the world, Indo-American people, just as all those economically underdeveloped, have to receive and live off foreign capital. These pages show quite clearly that APRA is situated on the realist level in our time and in our place in the history and geography of humanity. Our economic Time and our economic Space show us a position and a path: as long as capitalism endures as the dominant system in the most advanced countries, we will have to deal with capitalism. **(Víctor Raúl Haya de la Torre, *Anti-imperialism and the APRA*, 1928)**

Víctor Raúl Haya de la Torre (1895–1981), born the same year as Mariátegui, not in Lima but in Trujillo, was a natural leader, capable of inspiring unity in practically every sector that made up the country's social spectrum. White and from the impoverished aristocracy, he did not alarm the Peruvian oligarchy much, but mysteriously succeeded in establishing a connection with the lower classes, the mestizos, and the Indians as probably no politician before him had been able to do.

Haya de la Torre's life has two parallel histories. On the one side, there is the story of his political battles, failures, long exiles, and imprisonment; on the other is the noteworthy account of his intellectual education. At a young age, Haya de la Torre was heavily influenced by communism and the 1917 Russian revolution. But at the same time other friendships and readings of a philosophical and political nature caused him to distance himself from communism and brought him closer to positions that today would be called social-democratic, although he interpreted these ideas from a radically different viewpoint, which included a certain fascination for fascist aesthetics: parades with torches and the notable presence of thugs ("buffaloes") in a party that fostered what Spain's Falangists called "the fists and guns dialect."

Haya lived in exile during the dictatorships of Leguía, Sánchez Cerro, and later Odría, but he didn't waste time in the Colombian Embassy in Lima during those long periods overseas or in exiled residency. His impressive list of friends and acquaintances included people as different and distant as Romain Rolland, Anatolio Lunasharki, Salvador de Madariaga, Arnold Toynbee, and Albert Einstein. In addition to Spanish, which he wrote with elegance, he mastered other languages—English, German, Italian, and French—considering himself, perhaps rightly so, as the original thinker that had succeeded, since Marxism, to surpass the doctrine and establish a new interpretation of Latin American reality.

Haya de la Torre arrived at this conclusion with a political thesis he called *Espacio-Tiempo-Historia* ("Space-Time-History"), a cross between Marx and Einstein which included Trotsky's previous reflections on Russia. In fact, at the beginning of the century, Trotsky, faced with the obvious disparity of degrees of civilization found in Russia (from the very refined St. Petersburg to the Asiatic villages scarcely beyond the Paleolithic age), concluded that within Russia there existed different "historical time periods." Haya de la Torre reached the same conclusion regarding the mountain-dwelling Incas, contrasting them with the white, mestizo (although very European), coastal people of Lima. Within the country of Peru there existed two historical time periods, whereby he concluded that Marxist theories could not be applied equally to these two very different realities.

This is where Haya de la Torre alleges that he transcended Marx, and he finds support for his assertions in the Hegelian dialectic of negation. If Marx refuted Hegel and Hegel refuted Kant, then by using the theory of "Space-Time-History" (to which Einstein's relativity was added, applying it to politics), the APRA doctrine surpassed Marxism by subjecting it to the same method of dialectic analysis suggested by the author of the *Communist Manifesto* himself.

How did Haya blend Einstein into this curious philosophical potpourri? Easy: If the German physicist had put an end to the notion of the Newtonian universe (governed by immutable laws and predictions) by adding a fourth dimension to the perception of reality, then the element of uncertainty and inconsistency that was present in matter should also affect politics. But how can anyone talk about laws governing history, politics, or the economy when not even modern physics can avail itself of this rigid and mechanistic characteristic?

Beginning with his theoretical rupture with Marxism in the 1920s, Haya de la Torre had a *fortissimo* confrontation with Moscow, which made him the *bête noire* of Kremlin's most obedient leftist Marxists. In addition to his theoretical heresies, the Peruvian thinker and politician proposed other interpretations of international relations and economics that would serve as a foundation for all social-democratic thought, later called the Latin American democratic left.

Haya's most important proposition was the following: If imperialism was the final stage of capitalism in Europe, then, as the Space-Time-History analysis revealed, in Latin America it was the first. One had to go through the constructive phase of capitalism before thinking about destroying it. Latin America had to be developed with the assistance of imperialism and in the same way as the United States had been. This capitalistic phase would, however, be temporary and characterized by pure democratic forms of government. And it would be directed by five inflexible radical approaches presented by APRA in its 1924 Manifesto:

1. Act against all empires.
2. Politically unite Latin America.
3. Nationalize land and industry.
4. Maintain solidarity with all oppressed peoples and classes.
5. Inter-Americanize the Panama Canal.

The craze to inter-Americanize the Panama Canal—which occupied most of APRA's international agenda—was paired with other curious and rather moody political priorities such as immediately nationalizing gold and . . . vanadium. Haya never became president of Peru and upon his death was mercifully spared from seeing the disaster provoked by his disciple Alan García (the only Aprista president lineally descended from Pizarro). He was the most prolific of the political leaders of the Latin American democratic left, and APRA (his personal creation) was the only party that succeeded in having repercussions on and imitators in the entire continent. There were Apristas from Argentina to Mexico, with a special abundance of them in Central America and the Caribbean. Incredibly, they're still there.

Paul Groussac or Rodó could offer up flowery tributes to Latin American spiritualism. Haya could dream about nationalization and believe that the government had an important responsibility in developing the economy. Yet after the tangible and repeated failure of all these assertions in most of the world, only the most obstinate idiocy can continue repeating what reality, without the least bit of compassion, has discredited.

3

THE IDIOT'S BIBLE

*"In the past few years I have read few
things that have moved me so much."*
—Heinrich Böll, speech in Cologne (1976)

For the last quarter of the twentieth century, the Latin American idiot has relied on the significant advantage of having a type of sacred text at his disposal, a bible that contains almost all of the stupidity that circulates in the cultural atmosphere the Brazilians call "the festive left."

We are, of course, referring to *Open Veins of Latin America,* a book written by the Uruguayan Eduardo Galeano at the end of 1970, whose first Spanish edition appeared in 1971. Twenty-three years later—in October 1994—Spain's Siglo XXI published the sixty-seventh printing, an accomplishment that undeniably shows the incredible abundance of Latin American groups classifiable as idiots, as well as the extent of this phenomenon beyond the borders of this culture.

In fact, many of those sixty-seven printings are translations into other languages, and there is a good chance that the image of Latin America engraved into many impressionable heads of Latin Americanist youths educated in the United States, France, or Italy (not to even mention Russia or Cuba) has been created by this colorful work devoid of order, harmony, or common sense.

Why? What's in this book that causes thousands of people to buy it, many to read it, and a large percentage of them to regard it as a diagnosis and an analytical model of our situation? Very easy: Galeano (who as a person deserves our complete respect) uses lively, at times lyrical, and almost always effective prose to summarize, assimilate, and mix together André Gunder Frank, Ernest Mandel, Karl Marx, Paul Baran, Jorge Abelardo Ramos, Raúl Prebisch (prior to his repentance and *mea culpa*), Che Guevara, Fidel Castro, and other distinguished "thinkers" of crude intelligence and ridiculous reasoning. Therefore, his work has become the bible of the left. Everything is there, vehemently written, and if interpreted from a literal fundamentalist viewpoint (and if believed and acted upon) one should take up arms or—for the more pessimistic types—immediately get a rope and hang himself.

But, what does Mr. Galeano essentially say in those dreadful pages? Let's have a look at the introduction, dramatically subtitled "120 Million Children in the Eye of the Hurricane." Let's clarify, by the way, that all of the quotes that follow are from the aforementioned sixty-seventh edition, published in Spain in 1994 by Siglo XXI[1] for the use and enjoyment of the Iberian people (people who are, of course, poorly depicted in this work). A matter of *historical-masochism,* as Jiménez Losantos likes to say.

Latin America is the region of open veins. Everything, from the discovery until our times, has always been transmuted into European—or later United States—capital, and as such has accumulated in distant centers of power. (p. 12)

Although the introduction doesn't begin with this statement but rather with another one that we will quote later, it would be worth our while to examine this first because this hemophilic metaphor that gives the book its title is a solid clue that will lead us to the precise source of Mr. Galeano's analytical distortion: a case of historical-economic anthropomorphism. Galeano believes that Latin America is a listless body that fainted between the Pacific and the Atlantic and whose entrails and vital organs are its fertile mountains and mineral reserves, with Europe (first) and the United States (later) as a pair of bloodthirsty vampires. Naturally, from this lurid anthropomorphic premise it's not difficult to surmise the zoological fate that awaits us in the book: predatory American eagles fiercely in search of carrion, multinational octopuses hoarding our wealth, and imperialist rats conspiring in all manner of filth.

This ancient mythological vision—like Europa, the beautiful princess carried away on the back of a white bull; the Titans supporting the world; Romulus and

---

[1] *Translator's note*: The following quotes are from Cedric Belfrage's published translation of *Open Veins of Latin America*, published by Monthly Review Press, 1973. All page numbers correspond to this published English text.

Remus nursed by a peaceful she-wolf—really belongs to the world of poetry and fables and has nothing to do with the phenomenon of underdevelopment, although Galeano is not the first contemporary writer who has indulged in such poetic license. A noted American writer, who did much in the middle of the century to support and keep the Latin American idiots of that time alive and kicking, once wrote that Cuba—Castro's Cuba—was like a great phallus about to penetrate the United States' vulva. The vulva was, of course, the Gulf of Mexico, and there were certainly many who believed that in this statement (more Freudian reflection than obscenity) a brave anti-imperialist condemnation had been made. Something of this nature occurs in *Open Veins of Latin America*. The title's uncontrollable hemorrhaging begins by degrading the sobriety required by this subject. Let's see how this unfortunate literary spasm coagulates.

The division of labor among nations is that some specialize in winning and others in losing. (p. 11)

And so, with this forthright sentence, the book begins. For its author, as well as for the corsairs of the sixteenth and seventeenth centuries, wealth is a treasure chest sailing under a foreign flag and all you have to do is board the enemy's ship and whisk it away. The incredibly simple and fundamental concept of modern wealth being created only by negotiating good business dealings is so obvious that it never seems to cross his mind.

Sadly, there are many Latin Americans who share this view of zero-sum gain. They assume that what one has reflects what was stolen from somebody else. It doesn't matter that experience shows that it's more advantageous not to have a poor and despondent neighbor. After all, our volume of business, as well as international harmony, depends not only on our own economic health but on our neighbor's as well.

It's strange that Galeano did not study the U.S. situation with less ideological prejudice. Which neighbor does the United States have a better relationship with, the rich and stable Canada or Mexico? Which border does the United States have problems with, the one to the north or to the south? And if the evil American plan is to keep other countries specializing in "losing," then why did it join with Mexico and Canada in the North American Free Trade Agreement (NAFTA), whose stated goal is for all three nations to profit?

Any objective observer who puts himself in 1945, the year World War II ended and the United States was by far the most powerful nation in the world, can see how, although gradually increasing its global wealth, America's relative authority was diminishing, because thirty other countries were dizzily ascending the economic ladder. No one specializes in losing. Everyone (at least anyone who does his job well) specializes in winning. In 1945, of every dollar exported in the world fifty cents came from the United States; in 1995 it was only twenty cents. This does not mean that some leech has latched itself onto a vulnerable *gringo* artery and is bleeding it dry, especially since Americans are becoming more and more prosperous. Instead, there has been an increase in production and international business that has benefited all of us and has reduced (in a healthy manner) the relative importance of the United States.

But our region [Latin America] still works as a menial. It continues to exist at the service of others' needs, as a source and reserve of oil and iron, of copper and meat, of fruit and coffee, the raw materials and foods destined for rich countries which profit more from consuming them than Latin America does from producing them. (p. 11)

This delicious paragraph contains two foolish remarks that tickle the Latin American idiot's palate, even though it should be known that the first one— "they are stealing our natural wealth"—is much more popular than the second— rich countries "profit" more from consuming than Latin America does from selling. Since the second part of the statement will be repeated and explained later, for now we'll concentrate on the first one.

Let's suppose Mr. Galeano's gospel is adopted as the official Latin American policy. Mexico and Venezuela shut down their oil exports; Argentina stops selling its beef and wheat overseas; Chile jealously hoards its copper and Bolivia its tin; Colombia, Brazil, and Costa Rica refuse to market their coffee; and Ecuador and Honduras do the same with their bananas. What will happen? Not much will happen to the rest of the world because Latin America barely constitutes 8% of all international trade. But for the countries south of the Rio Grande the situation would become terrible. Millions of people would lose their jobs, the ability of these nations to import would disappear almost entirely, their health system would be on the verge of paralysis due to the lack of medicine, and a terrible famine would ensue due to the shortage of feed for livestock, fertilizers for cultivation, and spare parts for farm implements.

Actually, if Mr. Galeano and the idiots who share his analysis were consistent with the anthropomorphism they support, they could easily arrive at just the opposite conclusion. Since Latin America imports more than it exports, it's the rest of the world's circulatory system that is at the mercy of the bloody Latin American sting. Therefore, it would be possible to create an antidote book presenting passionate accusations against Latin Americans for stealing computers and planes from the *gringos*, televisions and automobiles from the Japanese, chemicals and machinery from the Germans, and so on ad infinitum. That book, however, would be just as incredibly boring as the one it's countering.

The taxes collected by the buyers are much higher than the prices received by the sellers. (p. 11)

If Galeano's previous reasoning is ludicrous, then this one could be included in the most exacting anthology of great economic absurdities. According to Galeano and the host of Latin American idiots that heed his theories, the rich countries "profit more consuming [Latin American products] than Latin America does producing them." How do they arrive at this marvelous conclusion? Easy: the rich countries tax the consumers, which apparently makes the nation wealthy.

Clearly, here we see two idiocies superimposed that—being anthropomorphic about it—create a third. On the one hand, Galeano is unable to understand that if Latin Americans do not export and get foreign exchange they're going to have a hard time importing anything. On the other hand, he doesn't realize that the taxes consumers pay for those products do not constitute the creation of wealth but rather a simple transfer of wealth from one's own pocket to the public treasury, where more than likely a good portion of the money will be misspent, as usually happens with government expenditures.

But where Galeano and his followers show a complete lack of the most basic understanding of economics is when they not only view taxes as a "wealth maker" for the state, but also are even unable to realize that these taxes do nothing but discourage imports. In other words, taxes clearly decrease the flow of blood from Latin America's veins, because, although the Latin American idiot is incapable of seeing it, our tragedy is not hemophilia (carried out by developed nations) but *hemophobia*. We don't have enough goods to sell overseas nor do we produce enough of them. Here Galeano cites Covey T. Oliver, coordinator of the Alliance for Progress in 1968, for the purpose of criticizing him:

> **To speak of fair prices is a "medieval" concept, for we are in the era of free trade. [Galeano then concludes that:] The more freedom is extended to business, the more prisons have to be built for those who suffer from those businesses. (p. 11)**

Here, then, is the theory of *fair prices* and the dread of the marketplace. For Galeano, economic transactions should not be subject to the free exchange of supply and demand; instead, goods and services should be assigned a *fair* value. In other words, prices should be determined by saintly officials devoted to these tasks. And I suppose that the model Galeano had in mind comes from the Soviet era, when the National Price Committee in Moscow relied on a series of overwhelmed bureaucrats—highly trained in prestigious universities—to set some 15 million prices every year. With complete accuracy, they determined the value of an onion in Vladivostok, a *sputnik* antenna up in space, and a gasket for a toilet installed in some village in the Ural mountains. This practice explains the chaos, which was very well predicted by Ludwig von Mises in his book *Socialism,* gloriously yet futilely published in 1926, that ensued from that experiment.

It's a shame that no one explained to Mr. Galeano or to the mass of idiots following his arguments that the market and its prices, regulated by supply and demand, are not a trick to rob anyone. It is a moderate system of indicators (the only system that exists) that came into being so that production processes could rely on an internal logic capable of rationally guiding those who carry out the delicate tasks of estimating costs, setting selling prices, earning profits, saving, investing, and perpetuating the ever cautiously and steadily increasing production cycle. Doesn't the Latin American idiot realize that Russia and the Eastern Bloc were impoverishing themselves as they became bogged down in the financial chaos created by the growing distortions in prices arbitrarily set by *fair* bureaucrats? And that each decision confused the production guide even more until the real cost of goods and services had little or no relation to the prices paid for them?

But let's go back to Galeano's basic reasoning scheme and let's agree (so that we get this straight) that Colombians should receive a *fair* price for their coffee, Chileans for their copper, Venezuelans for their oil, and Uruguayans for their wool. Shouldn't Americans also ask for a *fair* price for their penicillin and their planes? What is a *fair* price for a drill capable of striking oil or for "chips" that have cost hundreds of millions of dollars in research and development? And after having established a global agreement that all goods should have a *fair* price, all of a sudden a terrible blight comes and destroys the world's coffee supply, except for the coffee grown in Colombia, and a worldwide struggle ensues to get it. Should Colombia keep the *fair* price and ration its product among all of its clients without taking advantage of this opportunity? What did Cuba do in the 1970s, when 80% of its transactions were with the Eastern Bloc at a *fair* price (that is, at a price fixed by the Committee for Mutual Economic Aid [CAME]), but then saw how sugar prices suddenly jumped from ten to sixty-five cents a pound? Did it keep its sweet exports at a *fair* price, or did it take advantage of the shortage, charging what the market could bear?

To ask for fair prices is as infantile, or idiotic, as it is to complain about the economic freedom to produce and consume. The market with its winners and losers (and it is important that everyone understands this) is the only economic impartiality possible. Everything else, as the Argentines say, is just talk, pure babble from the ignorant left.

Our inquisitor-hangman systems function not only for the
dominating external markets; they also provide gushers of
profit from foreign loans and investments in the dominated
internal markets. (p. 11)

It's very likely that Mr. Galeano never bothered to think about where those loans came from. Maybe he doesn't know that they come from accumulated wealth, amassed in other countries by millions of people working incessantly, who earn more than they spend and, consequently, want their efforts to be rewarded with profits.

Why would a Fiat executive, or a shopkeeper in Berne, or a skilled worker at Mercedes Benz go and buy stock in General Motors or deposit his savings in an international bank? Could it be to make a poor Bolivian child happy—something that belongs to the respectable field of charity, but not investments—or does he do it to get a return on his capital? From which Paleo-Christian handbook did the Latin American idiot learn that earning profits from invested capital is something ethically reprehensible and economically injurious?

A more serious look at this matter will show that 90% of the world's investments are between developed countries because the "gusher" of profits that flows from the country receiving the investments to the country doing the investing is much more profitable, secure, and predictable among prosperous nations, which have reliable legal systems and societies hospitable to foreign money. Did Galeano and his acolytes notice that the poorer nations are those barely doing any business with the rest of the world and are places where almost no one wants to invest?

In the United States, for example, unions (those which don't believe in the hoax of open-vein systems) ask, beg, the Japanese to build their Toyotas and Hondas there and not in the Asian archipelago. France and Spain, to cite another case, fiercely fought over an amusement park that Disney wanted to set up in Europe, because that "vile penetration of culture" (as it would be called by Ariel Dorfman, that delirious writer who accused Donald Duck of being a tool of imperialism) would probably attract large numbers of tourists. The park, by the way, ended up in the neighborhood of Paris, to a certain suicidal satisfaction of those Spanish idiots from the confused peninsular left.

Production methods and class structure have been successively
determined from outside for each area by meshing it into the
universal gearbox of capitalism. . . . To each area has been
assigned a function, always for the benefit of the foreign
metropolis of the moment, and the endless chain of depen-
dencies has been endlessly extended. The chain has many more

than two links. In Latin America it also includes the oppression
of small countries by their larger neighbors and, within each
country's frontiers, the exploitation by big cities and ports of
their internal sources of food and labor. (p. 12)

There you have it. For Galeano, in accordance with his living gospel, economic relationships between humans function as a kind of dialectical and relentless *matriushka,* the Russian dolls where a smaller one is stored within another, and another, and another, until you end up with a tiny indefensible figurine barely an inch tall.

We should take pause at the beginning of that absurd sentence, because this is anthropomorphism's original sin. Galeano says that "production methods and class structure have been successively *determined* from outside." This word—*determined*—is in itself a conspiracy theory of history. Galeano was incapable of imagining that Latin America's integration into the world economy had not been determined by anyone, but rather that it just happened, as with the United States or Canada, purely by the nature of things and history, without anyone—whether person, country, or group of nations—planning it. Which nation or persons assigned Singapore, beginning in 1959, the role of being an Asian economic supermarket specializing in high-technology goods and services? Or—on the other hand—what cunning group of nations drove Nigeria and Venezuela, two countries blessed with immense natural resources, to their disastrous situations today? What strange and benevolent hand placed the Argentines among the most prosperous citizens on the planet for the first quarter of the twentieth century? Since Galeano likes economic determinisms, let's look at the United States and find out what tremendous power shifted the center of economic gravity from the Atlantic coast to the Pacific and is today moving this center noticeably southward. Is there also an invisible hand pulling imperialism's own strings?

Is it seriously possible to say that the exploitation of the colonies by voracious mother countries explains the underdevelopment of some at the expense of others after what was experienced in the last centuries? What is the current status of Spain or Portugal, two of the modern world's most tenacious imperial *patrias*? At the dawn of the twentieth century (which is closer to the colonial period than to today), weren't Buenos Aires and São Paulo wealthier than Madrid and Lisbon? Haven't Spain and Portugal fared much better without their colonies than with them? Wasn't Scandinavia better off not having any colonies than Russia and Turkey were with theirs? Can the wealth of the little country of Holland be explained by the islands it controlled in the Caribbean and in Asia? The small country of Switzerland has more wealth without ever having conquered a single inch of foreign land. In England's case, the Ruler of the Seven Seas in the eighteenth and nineteenth centuries, wasn't the British economic power established on the backs of *Gurkha* soldiers and Coolies, the Galeanos of this world ask? Of course not. Germany, which at the beginning of the twentieth century hardly had any colonies—and those that it did have took much more than they gave—right at the zenith of the Victorian era, had an economic power greater than the British.

It is true, however, that Latin America—as would befit a region essentially based on European culture—forms part of an intricate capitalist world that was affected by the United States depression in 1929, the discovery of penicillin, or the "tequila effect" of the Mexican debacle. Those circumstances affected everyone; only the Amazon or Congo bushmen can avoid them. What does Galeano think happened to the developed countries when in 1973 oil producers raised the price of crude several times?

Of course, Latin Americans form part (unfortunately not a very important part) of the world's capitalist machine. If the Latin American idiot would study how some previously destitute nations succeeded in placing themselves at the economic forefront, instead of complaining about something that is as inevitable as it is advantageous, he would see that no one stopped Japan, South Korea, or Taiwan from becoming economic empires. When Chile stepped forward, approaching "tiger" status, this distinction, far from closing the door to trade, prompted an invitation to join NAFTA and an incessant flow of investments into "the country with the crazy geography."

The rain that irrigates the centers of imperialist power drowns the vast suburbs of the system. In the same way, and symmetrically, the well-being of our dominating classes— dominating inwardly, dominated from outside—is the curse of our multitudes condemned to exist as beasts of burden. (p. 13)

Those who believe in an atrocity of this caliber are not capable of understanding that "classes" don't really exist. A society consists of millions of people whose access to available goods and services is not partitioned into rigid divisions but into almost imperceptible and shifting gradients that make it impossible to lay out the path of the supposedly ideal justice pursued by our tireless idiots.

Let's take the example of Uruguay, Mr. Galeano's homeland, one Latin American country whose wealth is less poorly distributed. In Uruguay, of course, there are still rich and poor people. Let's believe, naturally, that the rich Uruguayan man who has a mansion and a yacht at Punta del Este has fleeced his fellow citizens of the fortunes he now enjoys, since very few others can display such wealth. After having made this spiteful calculation, we go to the next level and see that only a small percentage of Uruguayans own their own home or even a car, from which we can deduce the same: the well-being of home owners or car owners rests on the discomfort of those lacking these goods. But how far can this chain of predator and prey go? To infinity: there are Uruguayans with air conditioning, washers, and telephones. Did they steal these middle-class objects from poorer Uruguayans? There are those whose only modern convenience is electric lighting, as opposed to a neighbor who lights his dwelling with kerosene, which would lead us to state that a bare-footed Uruguayan has been ambushed by a neighbor, almost as poor as he but who succeeded in placing a piece of leather between the soles of his feet and the stones in the street.

Did Mr. Galeano stop and think from whom he stole his relatively comfortable existence as a globe-trotting intellectual? If his pleasant and luxurious standard of living is better than his average compatriot's, Galeano's own logic should make him realize that he's depriving someone of those things he enjoys but doesn't deserve. Quite unbecoming behavior for an honorable revolutionary perpetually rebelling against the abuses of this most cruel world of ours.

The strength of the imperialist system as a whole rests on the necessary inequality of its parts, and this inequality assumes ever more dramatic dimensions. (p. 13)

This stupidity is spread under the pompous name of the *Theory of Dependency.* There were—in these lucubrations—two capitalisms: one marginal, poor, and exploited; the other central, rich, and exploiting. One feeding off the other. This is nonsense. It's likely that Mr. Galeano confused what he called the "necessary inequality of the parts" with what any other well-informed observer would call "comparative advantages," which determine what countries can and cannot successfully and competitively produce.

In truth nothing nor anyone—except in domestic cultural factors—has prevented Mexico from producing television and radio sets instead of Japan, which stripped the Americans of their nearly total control of this domain since the beginning in the 1950s. Nothing nor anyone is preventing the very educated Argentines from the extraordinarily profitable creation of software programs, an industry the United States has excelled in.

This is not—as Galeano believed—about predator nations taking advantage of their neighbors' weakness to loot them. Instead, they exploit their own competitive advantages as much as possible in order to offer the market the best goods and services at the best possible price. Spain, for example, "sells" its sunny countrysides, its beaches, its ancient Moorish architecture, its romance, its wonderful fishing sites, and its art museums. For many reasons—almost all of them of a cultural nature—Spaniards cannot produce precision machinery at competitive prices like the Germans or Swiss can, but experience, trial, and error has made them become one of Europe's best hosts. What's wrong with that?

By definition, almost every community now in existence can find its own survival niche, since if this were not the case the community would not exist. What country in the Americas—aside from Canada and the United States—has the highest standard of living and the highest income in the New World? Answer: the Bahamas. A few small islands with sand and palm trees placed by God in the Caribbean, inhabited by 200,000 dark-skinned people who receive a few million visitors every year. What did tiny Grenada live on before the revolutionaries wanted to have it emulate neighboring Cuba? Answer: tourism, a medical school, and nutmeg exports. If there is anything that shows the practical experience of the twentieth century, it's that there is not a single nation, whether small, fragile, distant, or bereft of natural resources, that cannot survive and prosper if it knows how to intelligently utilize its comparative advantages.

How do New Zealanders, situated at the antipodes, divided into two islands, with a population of barely three million bucolic survivors, have a European level of economic development? Because, instead of reading Galeano, they work on producing and selling the wool from some 60 million sheep, exporting fruit and flowers, and—for a few years now—offering travelers a good deal on ecological tourism.

If "imperialism" exploits inequalities instead of allowing everyone to benefit from mutual comparative advantages, why didn't those imperialist scoundrels stop Chile's producers from filling a niche in America's consumption of Chilean wine, asparagus, and other vegetables, and just close down their markets in order to crush them? If the international "market" is made up only of giants annihilating the weak, why are Israel, Andorra, Monaco, Liechtenstein, Taiwan, Singapore, Hong Kong, Luxembourg, Switzerland, Curaçao, the Cayman Islands, and Denmark among the world's richest (and smallest) nations? Moreover, within Latin America itself, why is Uruguay wealthier than Paraguay? Is it because Uruguay is preventing Paraguay from developing? Why is Costa Rica more prosperous than Nicaragua or Honduras? Is it because the Costa Ricans practice evil imperialism or because they do certain things better than their Central American neighbors?

The United States citizen's average income is seven times that of a Latin American and grows ten times faster. And averages are deceptive. . . . According to the United Nations, the amount

*shared by 6 million Latin Americans at the top of the social
pyramid is the same as that shared by 140 million at the
bottom. (p. 13)*

What Galeano is incapable of understanding—and let's assume his figures are
correct—is that the average United States citizen also creates seven times more
wealth than his southern neighbor, since—otherwise—he wouldn't be able
spend what he doesn't have. Consumption (dear idiot) is an outgrowth of production. And the reason that a poor Indian in the Andean Altiplano consumes
fifty times less than a foreman in Detroit is related to the goods or services that
each creates in their respective worlds. And, by the same rule, those alleged 6
million Latin Americans—among which our Uruguayan essayist is no doubt
included—amass the same amount as their 140 million fellow countrymen
largely because their income has been attained by producing just as much and
as well as what is produced in more developed areas.

Apart from this obvious example, there are other important details that Latin
American idiots tend to ignore. The first is that if the more developed nations
didn't import huge amounts of minerals, fuel, or food, the Third World's situation would be much more serious than it is, as poor exporters of sugar and
bananas found out when the European Union restricted their imports. Likewise,
if we Latin Americans want to continue enjoying stereo systems, good medical-
research equipment, or the latest treatments for heart disease, it is to our advantage that the developed countries don't suffer a crisis, since most of our comforts come from them.

Finally, it would be wise to caution Mr. Galeano and his followers of the
complete absurdity of comparing levels of consumption between countries
that do not have the same growth rate in production, much less in productivity. If a *campesino* in the mountains of Honduras currently lives without electric lighting or running water, just as inhabitants of California did in 1890, it's
no one's "fault" that Californians now live infinitely better than today's
campesinos, much less should any "blame" be inferred from statistical comparisons. If today Bolivia and Peru are backward in relation to England and
France (relatively more backward than they were in the past), it's because they
haven't had the knowledge, power, or desire to behave as productively or
socially as those countries barreling toward modernity and progress. How can
a farmer in Ecuador expect the same compensation for his work as an American farmer when the American's productivity is 100 times more? In the United
States, less than 3% of the population works in agriculture, feeds 260 million
persons, and produces a surplus, which is later exported. That's why *gringo*
farmers earn more.

The banal reasoning that Latin American poverty is due to overpriced production equipment is also not valid. It's a fallacy usually illustrated in the number of sacks of coffee or bunches of bananas needed to buy a tractor today in comparison with what was needed twenty years ago. The truth is that today it costs a modern farmer—whether American, French, or Dutch—much fewer hours of labor to buy that tractor because his productivity has increased dramatically. The input—measured in hours of labor—is much cheaper today than it was yesterday. That's the key.

In 1868—an example that has been recorded thousands of times—Japan was a medieval kingdom, a closed, isolated theocracy, not seen by Western eyes until Commodore Perry's visit in 1853, and a country that had not experienced the first or even the second industrial revolution. In 1905, however, Japan was already an economic power capable of defeating Russia in war and competing in the international market with various products.

The comparative consumption fallacy is a gross error by Galeano. The only valid way to accept comparing consumption levels would be to group countries that seriously want to advance and then have someone or something try to impede them from doing so, but this type of atrocity has never been seen in the contemporary world. Not even when Turkey tried to do it after the First World War, nor when Japan, South Korea, Taiwan, Singapore, or Indonesia proposed to do the same in the second half of the twentieth century. Today, the average Japanese or Singapore citizen certainly consumes infinitely more than his Latin American contemporary, but this only means that he consumes more because he produces more. Why the Latin American idiot's noggin can't comprehend this is a mystery. Could it be because his head is stuffed with the following monstrosities?

Latin America's population grows as does no other; it has more than tripled in half a century. One child dies of disease or hunger every minute, but in the year 2000 there will be 650 million Latin Americans. (p. 14)

This paragraph, which was completely mistaken in its demographic prediction (in the year 2000 the Latin American population will actually be 30% less than what Galeano claimed), is followed by a somber and quite accurate description of the region's dreadful levels of poverty, the squalor in the *favelas,* and the undeniable horrors of illiteracy, unemployment, and diseases. So far this picture is correct. No objection here. Who could doubt the existence of starving masses in Latin America? The problem arises when Galeano tries to discover the causes of this situation and writes:

Even industrialization—coming late and in dependent form and comfortably coexisting with the latifundia and the structures of inequality—helps to spread unemployment rather than to relieve it. . . . New factories are built in the privileged poles of development—São Paulo, Buenos Aires, Mexico City—but less and less labor is needed. (p. 14)

So, the solution to Latin America's problem cannot be industrialization, given that Galeano—just like the Luddites of the nineteenth century who tried to destroy the looms and power machinery under the assumption that these devices would eliminate their jobs—believes that industrialization is harmful.

It's interesting to speculate what would have happened to South Korea or Taiwan if Mr. Galeano, with these ideas in his head, had been named minister of the economy in those countries. After all, at the beginning of the 1950s, both Taiwan and South Korea (which just had gone through a horrible war) were two destitute countries with no other form of substantial production capability aside from agriculture—and even this was lacking. Both were submersed under the weight of poverty, illiteracy, and subhuman living conditions.

But where Galeano's reasoning—and I fear also the reasoning of the Latin American idiots to whom, with a certain sadness, this book is dedicated—reached a level of utmost paranoia and irrationality is on the subject of birth control. According to *Open Veins of Latin America*, the high rate of population growth in this part of the world is not alarming because:

Most Latin American countries have no real surplus of people; on the contrary, they have too few. Brazil has thirty-eight times fewer inhabitants per square mile than Belgium, Paraguay has forty-nine times fewer than England, Peru has thirty-two times fewer than Japan. (p. 16)

It's as if Galeano and his horde don't realize that the need to control the birth rate doesn't depend on the availability of land but on the amount of goods and services that a community generates and on its ability to absorb the population reasonably well. What good does it do for a poor woman living in the *favelas* of Rio or La Paz to know that the seventh child she is expecting—which she'll have difficulty feeding, much less educating—will live (if he indeed survives) in a country infinitely less populated than Holland?

If any actual injury could be inflicted on the poor wherever they are in this world, it would be to encourage them to have children irresponsibly. Galeano's scheme, however, becomes monstrously judgmental and damaging when he states that the real intentions of locally or internationally financed birth control programs are a universal offense:

*Its aim is to justify the very unequal income distribution
between countries and social classes, to convince the poor that
poverty is the result of the children they don't avoid having,
and to dam the rebellious advance of the masses. (p. 16)*

All this is because, and here comes one of the most incredibly stupid sentences in the entire book, very fairly winning its fame for being the Latin American idiot's bible:

*In Latin America it is more hygienic and effective to kill
guerrilleros in the womb than in the mountains or the streets.
(p. 16)*

The treacherous imperial powers, with Wall Street and the CIA in the lead, in cahoots with the corrupt and complicit bourgeoisie, accomplish this by distributing condoms in order to prevent the decisive revolutionary backlash. This is the final battle that Galeano sees for the future, and whose paradigm and model Castro embodies, since:

The bronze eagle of the **Maine**, *thrown down on the day the
Cuban Revolution triumphed, now lies abandoned, its wings
broken, in a doorway in the old town in Havana. Since that day
in Cuba, other countries have set off on different roads on the
experiment of change: perpetuation of the existing order of
things is perpetuation of the crime. (p. 18)*

I assume that, after this eloquent paragraph Galeano uses to practically culminate the prologue of his book and declare his love for the Cuban dictatorship, the reader can arrive at two interesting conclusions. First, within the sentence's fundamental irrationality, Galeano's discourse remains coherent. If there are any evil capitalist powers determined to pillage Latin America by purchasing our products or granting us cruel usurious credits and loans (in addition to the nefarious exploitative investments and Herod-like genocide on our unborn revolutionaries) it is only logical for us to get off this bus at any corner in this barbaric world and take the other road: the glorious Cuban path.

The problem—and here is the second conclusion—is that Cuba, after the fall of the Eastern Bloc, is showing desperate signs of wanting to open its own veins so that capitalism will suck out its blood, while it confronts its final crisis by following the *adjustments* given in the IMF's handbook. The island is, in fact, screaming for loans and foreign investments in order to create joint ventures from which it can strip its workers of 95% of their wages, using the cynical pretext of having to pay their foreign partners in dollars, and then pay the workers in useless and devaluated pesos that can be exchanged on the black market forty to one. This Cuba that Galeano gives us as an example is crying and pleading from every forum for the United States to lift its ban on trade, that cursed embargo, and to return and exploit the poor Cubans in its cruel traditional way. In the meantime, the island continues to have, based on large-scale abortions, the continent's lowest birth rate and highest suicide rate. This, despite being fourteen times larger than its Puerto Rican neighbor and proportionately much less populated, contradicting Galeano's handbook.

Galeano's Cuban paradise—from which anyone who can will escape aboard anything that floats or flies—has for some time now not exhibited its noble heroic combatants as its main attraction, but instead the sweaty and overworked buttocks of its poor Tropicana mulatto women, and the promise that there, on that poor island, you can buy any kind of sex with only a handful of dollars, and sometimes even with just a plate of food; less, much less, than what it costs to purchase Mr. Galeano's book at your friendly neighborhood bookstore.

4

WE'RE POOR:
IT'S THEIR FAULT

The underdevelopment of poor countries is historically the
result of the enrichment of others. Ultimately, our poverty is
due to exploitation in which we are victims of the world's rich
countries.

As this statement shows, which could be uttered by our idiot, the blame for what
happens to us is never our own. Somebody else—a business, a country, a person—is always responsible for our condition. We love being incompetent with a
clear conscience. We take morbid pleasure in believing that we are the victims
of some injustice. We exercise imaginary masochism and fantasize about suffering, not because poverty in Latin America is imaginary—it's quite real for the
shantytowns of Lima, Rio, and Oaxaca—but rather because we love to blame
some evil villain for our shortcomings. Mr. Smith, an executive of a lightbulb factory in Wisconsin, is a reprobate subjecting us to hunger, a highway robber
responsible for the miserable $1,000 annual per capita income in Honduras (yes,
even our macroeconomic data is conveniently tallied in dollars; how nice!). Mrs.
Wayne, a real-estate agent in Miami, who covets others' possessions, is capable
of the worst injustices, such as keeping 12 million Peruvians out of a formal job.
Mr. Butterfly, a computer-chip manufacturer in New York, lives a life of torment
thinking about the Hell that awaits him in the afterlife because he owes his mil-
lion-dollar enterprise to the Guadalupe-Hidalgo Treaty, which in 1848 stole
more than half of Mexico's territory and gave it to the United States.

If this onanism of suffering were original, it might actually be nice, one of many other elements in our political folklore. But it's imported from Europe, specifically from a line of thought that at the beginning of the twentieth century tried to justify why the Marxist revolutionary prediction concerning wealthy countries failed, arguing that capitalism would survive thanks to imperialism. This brilliant idea gained even more strength with the independence movement of the postwar era, when all of the colonies that were freed from their rulers believed it was necessary to despise the wealth of the rich in order to feel more independent. Respectable figures such as Pandit Nehru and Nasser, and later some distinguished thugs who took over certain African governments, expanded *urbi et orbe* the cult against the rich. Latin America—always so original—made this its personal mantra and incorporated it into the deepest crevices of academia, politics, communications, and the economy. We Latin Americans made contributions to the esoteric theories of dependency, and figures such as Raúl Prebisch and Henrique Cardoso gave them intellectual respectability.

For starters, poor Marx must be jumping up and down in his grave with these theories. He never supported such an idea. Rather, he praised colonialism as a way of accelerating the arrival of capitalism in underdeveloped countries, this being an indispensable step toward communism. Few men have so vigorously sung the modernizing glory of capitalism as Marx (even without seeing Napoleon on a CD-ROM or faxing a letter to his friend Engels). It would never have occurred to the intellectual father of the cult against the rich that Latin America's poverty was directly proportional to, and caused by, the wealth of the United States or Europe.

No one has christened this ideology as well as the Venezuelan Carlos Rangel: "Third worldism." And no one has better defined its mission than France's Jean-François Revel: "Third worldism's objective is to blame and, if possible, destroy developed societies, not to develop those lagging behind."

Simple logic should suffice to invalidate the statement that our poverty is the wealth of the rich, since it's obvious that if wealth is created and not something that already exists, one country's prosperity is not the result of another's wealth being stolen. If services (which constitute three-fourths of today's U.S. economy) do not use raw materials from Latin America or anywhere else, how, without using magic, could those services be the result of the plundering of our natural resources? If the United States' annual $6 trillion economy is eight times greater than the three major Latin American economies combined (the "giants" Brazil, Mexico, and Argentina), in order for the aforementioned premise to be true, it would have to be shown that at some time these three economies jointly, for example, produced eight times more than they do today, and, when added together, the giant three's production reached a number similar to $6 trillion. If we delve a little into the past, we'll see that $6 trillion is as strange a concept for our current or past economies as solitude is for the Chinese or Hell for the Eskimos.

One could argue that this is not a fair comparison since the United States did not exactly steal everything that it produces but rather it pocketed the necessary resources and then built its own wealth from them. But this argument would invalidate the entire premise that our poverty is due to the exploitation that made us victims, since the exploitation concept rests completely on the idea that wealth is not made but distributed. If it does not exist, it is created, and if it is created, no country's wealth is another's poverty. Even the worst colonial government from the Renaissance era until today has brought the victim country tools of knowledge or technology, providing them some development (at least economically if not politically or intellectually). What would Latin America's economy be today in comparison to wealthy countries if we had not had contact with "the white man's" economies? It's hard to believe that the combined production of Mexico, Brazil, and Argentina would be only eight times less than that of the United States. Peruvians will probably continue patting themselves on the back for the agricultural virtues of the terraced hillsides, a noteworthy invention of the pre-Columbian period but not exactly the forerunner of, for example, the steam or internal-combustion engine (to mention just two rather antiquated capitalist inventions).

Does this mean that there was no plundering during the colonial era or any imperialist injustices during the times of the republic? Yes, there was, but that has as much to do with our current state of underdevelopment as the relationship our intellectuals have with common sense. When our *criollos* confronted the royal Spanish armies (made up of Indians) and cut ties with the motherland, as a region we were much wealthier than the United States, and that was after the pillaging of the colonial era had ended. Furthermore, Spain squandered the gold it carried off on useless European wars instead of using it productively. Therefore, unless we want to go back to grade school, we cannot attribute Spain's current relative prosperity to its previous wealth. Some Peruvian accountant, with patriotic patience, has calculated in present-day numbers the sum of all the gold plundered in the colonial era (this calculation could not have come at a more opportune time than for the 1992 World Exposition in Seville). Spain and Portugal, colonial powers par excellence, are among the poorest countries in the European Union, while Germany, the continent's great driving force, was not a colonial power (not to mention the fact that Germany began its development at the beginning of the twentieth century and from then on has survived colonialist adventures such as Hitler's, which brought the country, economically speaking, many more problems than benefits). The colonialism practiced by the former USSR did not succeed in developing any country. The Cuban economy, deprived of suckling the Soviet teat for its subsidy of more than $5 billion a year, is now begging for outside currency, creating a mystical cult of spine-chilling dimensions to the Dollar God, headed by General Castro himself.

When people talk about the responsibility of colonialism and the exploitation of the weaker countries by the stronger, the reference is usually made to recent centuries. This is a convenient trap. By focusing only on the modern age, it is easy to ignore that colonialism is as old as humanity itself. As far as we know, no part of the world that conquered another, either in antiquity or during the Middle Ages, achieved development comparable to capitalism.

Among the countries to achieve development in recent times have been some that did not possess any important natural resources or conquer any other country. At the end of the Korean conflict, South Korea was left stripped of all industry, since this was all in North Korea. Singapore had no natural resources and lacked cultivable land. In a few decades both South Korea and Singapore (it's becoming quite boring always citing the tigers, but what else can we do?) achieved an economic boom that Latin American countries, much richer in raw materials, have not attained. The countries of the Commonwealth of Independent States (the former Soviet Union) have, on the other hand, all the natural resources in the world and are still suffocating from underdevelopment.

For the first thirty years of the twentieth century, Argentina was an economic world power, much more advanced than many European countries that today have surpassed it. In the decades since then, no one can claim, without embarrassing himself, that Argentina has been a victim of colonialism and significant exploitation. Latin America's recent history is full of virtuous revolutions, such as Mexico's, Bolivia's National Revolutionary Movement, Juan Velasco's revolution in Peru, and Fidel Castro's in Cuba. All rebelled against economic imperialism and selling out to the bourgeoisie. At the end of this process, none of the four countries was better off than before it began. It can be said that in Mexico's case there was relative improvement only when the Revolution, as pliable as putty, conveniently changed its principles and sold itself out to the bourgeoisie.

Since neither resources nor endless incomes are considered wealth, it would be of no use to divide the prosperity of the United States among all Latin Americans—because it would evaporate immediately. Simply transferring this wealth would not solve the basic problem, namely, how to create it. If Latin Americans were to retain the per capita income of the United States, keeping in mind that we have a little less than twice the number of inhabitants in the United States, each would receive around $10,000 annually. If we appropriated this income every year, at the end of five years our situation would not be much better than the current one since the money would not have created businesses or needed job opportunities. Of course the option to invest the money is ruled out since this would contradict the axiom that wealth is not made but stolen. We would not have left underdevelopment behind. In the meantime, our neighbors to the north would be faced with two options for that five-year period: praise the virtues of autophagia or—something more palatable—get to work and try to double the appropriated annual income, currently at $21,000, so the Americans would be able to again enjoy a similar income.

Multinational companies are plundering our wealth and creating a new type of colonialism.

One has to ask why world powers like the United States, Europe, and Japan would plunder our wealth by such strange means as internationalization instead of something more expeditious like sending in an army. It's a mystery why these thieves in search of others' fortunes spend so much money performing studies, building factories, transporting machinery, technology, and managers, promoting products, distributing goods, and employing workers, not to mention paying the customary bribes (an indispensable component of operating costs). What's even more bizarre is actually how in many of these situations profitable returns often cause these enemies of our prosperity to spend even more money to expand production. Why don't they just avoid all these costly charades and send in their military forces and carry off our cornucopia once and for all?

For one simple reason: a multinational corporation is not a government but a business, completely incapable of using physical force against any country. Even though in the past a confrontation with a United States international company in Latin America could have brought about military retaliation, that has not happened for decades. Companies come when they are allowed to come and go when they are forced to leave. The odd thing is that they keep coming to our countries despite the many times in the recent past that our governments have forced them to pack up their belongings and leave. With strange stubbornness foreign capital returns to the place where it has received the worst treatment. It enjoys a good beating. It's more masochistic than some of the Marquis de Sade's protagonists.

A multinational company is not a charity fund, of course. It does not give away money to the country it invests in, precisely because that is what it does—it *invests,* an activity that cannot be separated from the perfectly respectable goal of making a profit. If General Motors or Coca-Cola devoted itself to constructing the entire costly production line referred to earlier in this chapter, and didn't expect to get a cent of profit from it, respect for them would be lost ipso facto. If they dedicated themselves to philanthropy, they themselves would disappear in no time.

Rather, what these companies do is look for profits. The whole world operates on the expectation of making a profit. Our entire modern structure rests on this foundation. Even genetic engineering and biotechnology, which ultimately are nothing more than manipulative experiments on human and animal genes, in the long run can only yield their desired medical results if the companies that invest fortunes in scientific research believe they will be able to turn a profit. That's why today there exists something so controversial as the patent for human genes. Maybe someday genetic engineering will produce a Latin American intellectual capable of understanding that the quest for profit is healthy and ethical.

It is important for us—and within the intellectual reach of even the most mentally challenged patriot—that these businesses already established in our countries earn profits. Moreover, it would be good if they made billions and, if possible, trillions of dollars. These companies bring in money, technology, and employment, and any profits that they receive will come from being able to sell the goods and services that they produce. If these goods are sold within the country, the local market grows. If they are exported, the country has succeeded in securing a venue for its local products, which otherwise it would not have had. Therefore, our countries profit from a firm's decision to maintain as well as expand its investment in the nation where it has established its business. For any two-legged creature with the ability to reason, all of this should be easier to digest than lettuce.

Major automakers have, for example, announced that they would like for Brazil to be something like the second industrial automotive capital in the Western Hemisphere. What does this mean? It means they want to double their automobile production, which would require these multinational giants to invest a total of $12 billion. Volkswagen, the Satan of the steering wheel, exploiter of our people, devourer of our gold, will inject into that unfortunate country—oh, the horror of it all!—$2.5 billion in order to increase its production to one million vehicles. Ford, the bloodthirsty Moloch on whose altar we sacrifice our children, has announced another $2.5 billion investment. And so it goes. General Motors, a company that was without a doubt created to defile our honor and deprive us of our soul, hates us so much that it employs 100,000 Mexicans, Colombians, Chileans, Venezuelans, and Brazilians. The French company Carrefour, a true imperial Napoleon of foreign capital, inflicted 21,000 jobs on us in Argentina and Brazil, less than half the number mercilessly imposed on us by Volkswagen in Argentina, Brazil, and Mexico.

Until 1989, there was what we in Latin America called "capital flight." In the end, though, the money our own capitalists withdrew exceeded the amount of investment dollars that came to us from outside Latin America's borders. For that year specifically, the "flight" (what lunacy using such foul-sounding police terminology to talk about the economy) totaled around $28 billion. The situation five years later was just the opposite. In 1994, some $50 billion arrived in Latin America all wrapped up in a bow with a card attached reading "foreign capital." Therefore, the "plundering" is recent. Never in the postcolonial history of Latin America was there any such deluge of foreign capital. This, considering that 1994 experienced a decrease in foreign investment of around 30% compared with the previous year, due to the fickleness of Mexican policies, which resulted in even more investment reductions in 1995. Moreover, these investment ups and downs show that there is no guarantee that our markets will attract foreign money. Just like a flirtatious woman, money will make you beg.

A quick look at the 500 largest companies in Latin American shows—oh! oh!—that less than half of them are foreign. In 1993, only 151 of the 500 were foreign, which means that 349 of the largest companies in Latin America were—are—companies that our patriots call "national." In this era of openness to foreign capital, from general imperialism and sell-outs to the bourgeoisie, it seems that still not even half the companies handling the most money come from our enemies' shores; instead they come from our own. What does this mean? First of all, if someone is plundering our wealth, the primary plunderers are not foreign multinational companies. Second, when an economy is opened to foreign capital local investments also benefit, provided that there are some minimally attractive conditions. It doesn't matter whether the business is foreign or domestic; the general movement of the economy pushes the country forward into the area where firms, foreign and domestic, operate. Third, our problem is still—despite everything—how to get more foreign capital to come in instead of go out as it has been, leaving us for other areas (Asia, for example). If we could blame someone for economic imperialism, it's our own Latin American companies that are inundating the very same Latin American countries. A veritable avalanche of Latin American investments is moving through many countries between the Rio Grande and the Straits of Magellan. This is what allows the Chileans to manage private pension funds in Peru, for example, or Chile's Embotelladora Andina to buy the Coca-Cola bottling company in Rio de Janeiro, or Televisa to acquire a television station in Santiago. We cannot blame the developed countries anymore for monopolizing foreign investments; we ourselves have become compulsive foreign investors in Latin America.

Not long ago our problem was not foreign capital but rather the lack of it. Today, we should regret that there is not $100 or even $200 billion of foreign investment. Our problem isn't that 15% of all Japanese foreign investments are going to Latin America, but rather that only 15% and not 40 or 50% is headed our way. At the beginning of the 1990s, 15% of Spain's foreign capital investments came *to Latin America*. What should upset us is that our mother country didn't invest more.

Much of the foreign capital goes into the securities markets, but takes off as soon as a hair-raising crisis appears (such as the devaluation of the Mexican peso at the beginning of 1995, with its consequent "tequila effect" in countries such as Argentina, or the squabble between Peru and Ecuador that same year). This means that those dollars still do not have enough confidence in us; they are only dipping their toes in our waters. This being the case, how can anyone complain about any pillaging? The problem is that those investments do not stay. Aren't many of those dollars speculative, you may ask? Yes, but that's the nature of dollars. They make our economy breathe and even provide capital for our own companies. By the way, the macroeconomic effect of those dollars is no small matter; many times they compensate for our trade deficits, helping to avoid massive devaluation that would cause inflation to shoot up. And lastly, foreign investments spread confidence to other foreigners with well-lined pockets.

Foreign investments alone have not rescued any country from its misery; this will not be possible unless a strong national market, with domestic savings and investments within a free society, is developed. But in this world of frenzied global competition, foreign investments are a way of being pulled into the modern age. The progressives of this world would like to take us back to the autarkic communities of the Dark Ages. Progressivism is science fiction turned into politics: tourism to the past.

Our poverty is closely tied to the progressive deterioration of the terms of trade. It is extremely unfair that we have to sell our raw materials at low prices and buy industrial products and manufactured capital goods from rich countries at high prices. A new, more equitable economic order is needed.

It's also not fair that the sky is blue and that iguanas are ugly critters. The difference is that we can't do anything about these natural injustices. But for manmade ones we can, as long as an "I didn't do it" look isn't the response to every blunder committed by our leaders. It seems that, in Latin America, trade is a form of serfdom that we are subjected to by the great powers; this after almost two centuries of independence. We forget that toward the end of the nineteenth century—in 1880, for example—many decades after the Monroe Doctrine, Latin America's participation in world trade was similar to that of the United States. Until 1929, many years after any American military marauding took place in our lands and after the Platt Amendment was passed (a limitation on Cuban sovereignty imposed by the U.S. Congress in 1901), our countries' export quota was 10% of the world total, a number not the least bit inconsequential for nations enslaved by the emerging power from the North and by traditional powers from beyond the Atlantic. In those times, when our military and political vulnerability was much greater with respect to the great powers, our ability to export was, comparatively speaking, better than today's. The world needed our goods and, in the global commercial market, we meant something. The economic benefits we received from those sales were considerable because, since our products were highly valued in the eyes of the buyer, the demand—and consequently the prices—were respectable. How can we blame the rich countries that Latin American products ceased being as valuable as they were in the first half of the twentieth century? How is economic imperialism to blame that the products we offer on the world market are less appealing now since buyers' needs have changed?

Immediately after the war, when the international trade organization called GATT was born (now replaced by the World Trade Organization), the bulk of the world's trade was in raw materials (which we had a lot of) and manufactured goods (which for some reason we had no desire to produce). Today, this has changed drastically as the service industry has blown into our lives like a hurricane. Services now constitute a fourth of the entire world's trade and soon will be a third. In countries such as the United States, services already account for three-fourths of the economy, which makes any statement that America's prosperity is related to its trading terms with Latin America ridiculous. In a world where the service industry rules, our products become less attractive with each passing minute. Therefore, our lament shouldn't be that they buy from us low and sell to us high, but rather that, if we follow our lazy attitude of essentially exporting the things nature generously dropped in our laps, we will become completely dispensable as suppliers of goods on the international market. The threat, dear idiots, is not serfdom but insignificance.

We should be grateful that this transition from an industrial economy to a service economy has been relatively recent. We should be grateful that this has made it possible for our traditional products to still excite a few well-to-do palates for some decades, allowing us to play our small role in the world's growing postwar trade (trade has grown tenfold since the creation of GATT). Trade has been one of the factors responsible for the fact that Latin America's per capita income grew 162% between 1960 and 1982. If the service economy had made its phantasmagoric appearance a few decades earlier, these figures—which have certainly not solved our poverty problem—would probably have been much lower for our area of the Western Hemisphere. Surprisingly, the equivalent of $7 billion is generated annually in regions where raw materials and traditional commodities still dominate exports, as is the case in Central America. That figure is Lilliputian in comparison to exports from the small Asian giants with smaller geographic surfaces and fewer resources spewing forth from the earth. But the figures are high if you keep in mind how really insignificant those products, which make even this figure possible, are in the present-day economy. It's hardly serious to claim, on the threshold of the twenty-first century, to be somebody important in the world by waving a banana in one hand and a coffee bean in the other.

Except in very unusual cases where one trade partner aims the barrel of a gun at another, the poverty or wealth of our countries (concerning exports) has depended primarily on our ability to produce what others want to buy. Furthermore, in many cases we have "restricted" rich countries, barricading our economies inside veritable tariff fortresses. While their markets were semi-open, ours were closed. This allowed us in 1990 to have a trade surplus of $26 billion for the entire region—a huge chasm of export revenues over import costs. No one sent in the big guns to open our tariff-cemented walls, and evidently neither did they retaliate as is done today, for example, with Washington attacking Japan in revenge for its trade deficit. The powerful economies were not sufficiently open then, nor are they now. But in commercial trade there was no colonialist use of force; Latin America could block the influx of many exports from the rich countries and assure that its own exports brought in a few billion dollars, even in an international economy that relied less on raw materials.

Let's look for a moment at what happened in commercial trade between us and the despised United States. In 1991, when Latin American countries began to boldly open up their economies to imports—what the idiot calls "tariff disarmament"—our lives were filled with consumer goods from those powerful countries that previously caused us to lose so much sleep. It just so happens, however, that the United States also receives many of our products. As a result, in that year Latin America exported a total of $73 billion, while it imported a total of $70 billion. Where is the commercial imperialism? Where are the "unfair trading terms"? Commercially speaking, in the 1990s, Latin America profited from the U.S. market just as the United States has with the Latin American market. Half of Latin America's exports go to the United States. If the United States wanted to do without our exports, it could do so easily. But the effect for us would be devastating—since we haven't developed any domestic markets capable of sustaining the growth of those products which today have a venue through the export pipeline (albeit insufficient in comparison to the ideal or to other areas of the world). Each time an American regulation obstructs Latin American products from being imported (Colombian flowers, for example), we shriek like magpies. We complain about the trading terms, but when that trade is threatened we become hysterical. So what do we want? Do we want them to buy our products or not? It's true that since 1991 the United States has exported more to Latin America than to Japan. But it's because we want it to be that way, not because we have a gun pointed at our head. Finally, we are the beneficiaries of these imports. We acquire consumer goods at lower prices and in many cases of better quality. The United States is of course not the only powerful country that buys our products and, incidentally, slips dollars into our economies. In 1991, our exports to Spain increased 20% while our markets received only 4% of Spain's exports. Who is "exploiting" whom? If we didn't export those amounts to the United States and Spain, we would be much poorer than we already are.

A curious defect in our political experts and economists has prevented them from seeing that the solution to the diminishing importance of raw materials is to diversify the economy, to begin producing things more in tune with the reality that has made our traditional products as passé as the rationalizations of those who believe low prices are caused by a world conspiracy. Countries like Mexico are showing that diversification is feasible. In 1994, 58% of Mexican exports were metal products, machinery, industrial and automotive spare parts, and electronic equipment. The state-controlled oil company, Pemex, today contributes only 12% to Mexico's total exports, when in 1986 oil constituted 80%. Similarly who would dare say, without getting tongue-tied, that Mexico's problem is the sale of cheap raw materials and the purchase of expensive manufactured products?

Of the ten Latin American companies with the highest sales in 1993, only four—that is, less than half—sell raw materials. The others are in the automotive industry, business, telecommunications, and electricity. In 1994, the Latin American company leading in sales was not a business offering raw materials but telecommunications. Latin America's economy, although still very dependent on raw materials, *is* becoming diversified. As long as this continues, the problem will be overcome, a problem not caused by any conspiracy but by changes in the world reality, namely raw materials no longer being a seducer of markets.

Does this mean that we should toss our raw materials into the ocean? No, it means that we shouldn't rely on them—but let's profit from them as much as we can. Often incompetence has prevented us from making a sufficient profit from the use of those raw materials. How much oil and gold remain to be found? Probably a lot. If we hadn't waited so long to bring in investors willing to run the risk of development, we would have more oil to sell. Here then, one arrives at the conclusion that trading raw materials for manufactured products is just as unfair as our needing imperialist investors to extract the raw materials from the places where nature has buried them. Panama is eagerly exploring its subsoil for gold and copper. Today, mining constitutes 5% of its economy, and the authorities believe that it could reach 15% by the year 2005. Who is responsible for the mining industry comprising only 5% and not 15% of Panama's economy today? Our illustrious intellectuals and politicians would undoubtedly say that it's the multinationals' fault since they didn't offer their services earlier to come and find the gold and copper.

There are, however, Latin American raw materials that, in addition to being exploited, exploit the rich. Oil has been a plentiful and valuable commodity in some countries. Those countries form part of the international cartel called OPEC (Organization of Petroleum Exporting Countries), which one fine day in 1973 decided to increase its prices astronomically, bringing the powerful countries whose industries needed this source of energy to their knees. A country like Venezuela has so exploited the price of its petroleum resources that between the 1970s and 1990s it received the "meager" sum of $250 billion! What did it do with the money? What it did is much more responsible for the poverty in Venezuela than the prices the world has paid for the Saudi-Venezuelan oil those twenty years.

Another way of escaping the claws of imperialist civilization is for Latin American countries to do business with each other. In 1994, for example, almost a third of Argentina's exports ended up in Brazil, its partner in the common market Mercosur. A third of the pharmaceutical products bought in Brazil, a total of $5 billion (everyone knows that in Brazil the pharmacy is as popular as the church), are manufactured by Latin American companies. Some countries in the area have set in motion a vast project for an interconnecting natural gas pipeline, a network that will be worth billions of dollars when finished. Is anyone threatening to invade the territories south of the Rio Grande in any of this? Are Tokyo, Berlin, or Washington decreeing the selling price *manu militari*?

Unfortunately, Latin America is once again beginning to prevent the import of products from the infamous shores of prosperity. The process, slow but menacing, is dictated by the fallacious notion that a good part of our inability to rapidly create prosperous local economies is the voluminous influx of imports that causes trade imbalances. After its financial crisis in January 1995, Mexico immediately raised its tariffs. Argentina, affected by this shot of "tequila," did the same, and its government proposed that all Mercosur countries raise the tariffs on products coming from outside the borders of the member nations. Latin America continues to place many restraints on foreign trade—even on areas where tariffs have been lowered—by using open-ended or veiled regulations that increase the price of imports. (One shouldn't forget that the tariffs themselves, despite being lower than before, continue to penalize the consumer.) The psychosis created by the traumatic devaluation of the Mexican peso has

placed the trade deficit at the top of many Latin American countries' list of enemies. The only problem: the Mexican crisis was not caused by that deficit. It was
caused by a lack of political confidence (the result of the prevailing system) and
the capricious fixing of the Mexican peso at levels no longer justified by market
reality. A trade deficit in itself is not bad. It just means that there are more
imports than exports, and imports benefit consumers. Deficits can put pressure
on the money supply if there are no other resources for bringing in dollars to offset the effects of trade imbalances on the balance of payments. In which case,
to avoid greater problems, it's best to let the currency reflect the real price. To
equalize the trade balance, the solution is not to punish consumers but to export
more.

If any criticism can be made against rich countries, it's not that they are imposing unfair trading terms but that they are still not opening up their economies
enough. And they are even placing barriers to letting many of our products
enter. For example, it costs the twenty-four richest countries in the world $250
billion a year to protect their farmers from competition. Our political charlatans
should be ceaselessly denouncing this type of nonsense. Any damage done by
the rich to the poor, in the global economy, is because they don't dare let us compete in their markets on equal terms. The rest—trade stipulations based on the
price of outgoing raw materials and incoming manufactured products—belongs
to our idiots' idle fantasy and the ideological Paleolithic era in which they continue to exist.

There will be no more poverty when we put an end to the economic differences characterized by our societies.

The only thing that makes any sense in this axiom is that poverty and economic
differences exist in our countries. There is not a single society without economic
differences, especially in countries where they have adopted policies of equality
predicated by Marxists. We have very poor societies. But they are not the poorest in the world. Our per capita income is five times greater than that of southern Asia and six times greater than that of black Africa. Even so, half of our people are submerged beneath what in economic jargon is called (invoking
geometry to refer to the matters of the stomach) the "poverty line." It's also true
that there are economic disparities. In the streets of Lima or Rio de Janeiro it's
not difficult to cross from opulence to destitution within a few yards. Some Latin
American cities are veritable monuments to economic contrasts.
But here stop the neurons of him who uttered the memorable sentence preceding these lines. As for the rest, logic is overwhelming: there will be no poverty
when there are no economic differences. Does this mean that when everyone is

poor there won't be poverty? Every government having proposed abolishing poverty has through its "equalizing" methods succeeded—effectively, we might add—in reducing many of the disparities, not because everyone has become rich but because almost everyone has become poor. Not *everyone* has become poor of course—the elite ruling class managing these socialist policies has always become rich. In Latin America we are experts on this. Think of Nicaragua's Sandinista experience. What did the boys in olive green accomplish when they proposed to obliterate poverty by putting an end to differences? A 90% drop in the average wage. Wouldn't you know, though, that the authors of that heroic deed saved themselves from the classless society; they all helped themselves to grand properties and amassed enviable capital resources. Popular wit christened this pillaging with the ironic name "the piñata." In Peru, Alan García planned to do something similar. The result: while the capital resources of those governing grew in bank accounts in tax havens all over the world, the money belonging to the Peruvian people turned to dust. So for whoever had 100 *intis* in the bank when Alan García assumed power, barely 2 intis remained by the end of his term. In Bolivia, Hernando Siles Zuazo, although less predatory than the Sandinistas or García in Peru, turned the banking industry into a circus. In order to withdraw small sums of money from the bank you had to go to the financial institution with potato sacks, since it was impossible to carry in your hands or pockets all the bills needed for minor expenses. The list goes on, but this suffices to demonstrate that Latin America's recent history has specifically proved what a government can accomplish when it proposes to break the backs of the rich in order to straighten the backs of the poor.

For starters, in our countries it's the government, or more exactly the state, who is rich. The richer our governments, the greater their inability to create societies where wealth extends to many citizens. Incredible cases have been recorded, one being the wealth acquired by Venezuelan oil: $250 billion in twenty years. That is certainly wealth. No private Latin American enterprise has generated such a fortune in postcolonial history. What became of this wave of prosperity controlled by a government that said it was acting on behalf of the poor?

There are more such cases. The Cuba of "social justice," whose government proposed banishing poverty from the Caribbean island once and for all by expropriating from the rich to avenge the poor, received subsidies totaling $100 billion from one Soviet government after another over the course of three decades. In Cuba, though, the government has been the rich one. Have you seen the living conditions of the Cuban people improve thanks to the money the government received on their behalf? Revolutionary ineptitude has caused even the wealth of the governing rich to reach such low levels that only the most intimate circles of power can retain a monetary fortune. In Brazil, the largest company is not private but government-owned. How could it be any other way in the country where Getulio Vargas instilled the idea that government was the engine of wealth? Are the inhabitants of the barren Sertão backwoods or the starving children of the shantytowns in Rio aware of the money that Petrobrás generates for them? How much of the wealth represented by Brazil's 147 public companies is accessible to them? In revolutionary Mexico, which ended when Porfirio Díaz sold out to the bourgeoisie, the oil company, the leading business in the country, had a net worth of $35 billion and annual profits of nearly a billion dollars. Have the Mexicans in Chiapas seen one peso of that treasure?

The richest of them all, the government, dedicates its money to everything but the poor (except during election time). The money goes to pay political cronies, enlarge surreptitious bank accounts, finance inflation, and for stupid expenses like armaments. The Third World—a concept more suitable for Steven Spielberg than for the world's political and economic reality—spends on armaments four times the amount of foreign investments made in Latin America. A large percentage of these expenditures comes from our region's public coffers. Governments calling themselves defenders of the poor become rich and spend the money—whatever monies they don't steal—on things that never benefit the poor. A small portion is allocated for the poor in the form of subsidies and social programs but is soon eaten up by the inflation that results from government expenditures.

There are still insufficient examples of failed policies defending the poor in Latin America that would prevent socialist escapades from running rampant continentwide. Costa Rica, a country whose democracy sets an example for all Latin America, is seeing how in the mid-1990s its social-democratic government increased public spending by 18%. The result: inflation and economic stagnation. A policy weighted down by good intentions—to help the downtrodden—is accomplishing just the contrary: making the poor even poorer. As usual in a climate of this type, it's the rich who are best protected against an economic crisis fueled by the friendly government that calls itself a partner to the poor.

Experience teaches us that the best way to help the poor is to not try to defend them. No genetic defect is forcing our poor to be that way. Moreover, whenever Latin Americans have had the opportunity to create wealth in the few societies where they are permitted to do so, they have. For several countries—Mexico, the Dominican Republic, Peru, and El Salvador, to name just a few—an essential source of foreign currency is the money sent back home to the poor from relatives living abroad. Most of these relatives didn't go in search of work carrying personal checkbooks in their backpockets. In a short time they succeeded in making a living overseas, some with great success, others less successfully but with enough money to be able to help those they left behind. The most remarkable example of Latin Americans living successfully in exile is the Cubans. After several years of exile, the Cubans in the United States—some 2 million, including the second generation—produce $30 billion worth of goods and services per year, while the 10 million Cubans on the island produce only one-third that amount. Are there any biological defects in the Cubans on the island that prevent them from generating as much wealth as those elsewhere? Some cerebral defect? Unless some phrenologist can prove otherwise, there is no difference between the brains of those on or those off Cuba. There is simply a different institutional climate.

Enthusiasm is beginning to build concerning the activity of our stock markets and the improvement of our macroeconomic numbers. Latin America, however, is far from breaking free from its straightjacket of poverty because, among other reasons, it still doesn't invest or save enough. In 1993, investments in these unfortunate lands totaled some 18% of the GDP. In "developing" Asian countries—another gem in the secret language bureaucrats of international economy use—the figure is 30%. This was not the first time in the twentieth century's history that our economies have grown. It has happened before and yet poverty did not decrease significantly because of it. For example, we grew at a respectable rate of 4.5% between 1935 and 1953 and 5% between 1945 and 1955. None of this gave the poor access to wealth-creating ventures, or introduced free institutions that would defend property rights and the sanctity of contracts, or reduced the cost of doing business, facilitated competition, or eliminated monopolistic privileges—all indispensable factors in a market economy.

When our countries have an institutional climate that favors enterprise, attracts investment, and stimulates saving, and when success is not limited to those who swarm around the government like flies to receive monopolies (most privatization in Latin America is a monopolistic concession on payment of a bribe), then our poor will stop being poor. This doesn't mean that the rich will cease being rich. In a free society wealth is not measured in relative terms but in absolute ones, not collectively but individually. It wouldn't help anyone to distribute the net worth of the rich in each of our countries among the poor. The sum each would receive would be small and wouldn't guarantee future subsistence since the distribution would have completely wiped out the existing wealth. If we were to divide the estimated $12 billion net worth of Mexico's telecommunications company, Telmex, among the 90 million Mexicans, each would receive the monumental sum of . . . $133! It's more to the Mexicans' advantage for this business to continue employing 63,000 people and generating juicy profits of $3 billion a year, keeping the company operating and expanding.

The culture of envy believes that by taking away the yachts belonging to the Azcárragas (Mexico) and the Cisneros (Venezuela), or the jets owned by groups like Bunge y Born (Argentina), Bradesco (Brazil), and Luksic (Chile), Latin America would be a much fairer place. Maybe the fish in the sea where the Azcárragas and the Cisneros sail, or the clouds where Lázaro de Mello Brandao and Octavio Caraballo's planes fly, would appreciate a little less disruption by these "intruders." Maybe our idiots would sleep better, or pat themselves on the back, or their elated joy of revenge would get their adrenaline flowing. But there can be no doubt that Latin America's poverty would not be alleviated one bit. The philosophy of economic revanchism—what Von Mises called "the Fourier complex"—is due more to one's resentment of one's own condition than to the idea that justice is a kind of natural law of compassion relentlessly carried out against the "haves" in favor of the "have-nots." True, our rich, with few exceptions, are rather uncouth and ostentatious, common and arrogant. So what! Social justice is not a code of conduct, a British boarding school with a matron who slaps the wrist of anyone who misbehaves. It's a system, a sum of institutions arising from a culture of freedom. Until this culture exists among us, it will be a "members-only" club. To open the doors to this club we don't have to close it down but instead change the rules of the game.

The strange thing about capitalism is that the key to its success lies in the disparities, making it by far the best economic system. The best, which is to say, fairer, more equal. What incentive does a Cuban have to produce more if he knows he'll never be entitled to private ownership of the means of production, nor to reap the benefits of his efforts, and he'll forever be a sheep in an indistinguishable flock behind a despotic shepherd? If the incentive for this disparity disappears, the overall product and wealth in its entirety also disappear and what remains to be distributed is therefore even less.

The key to capitalism is that capital growth exceeds population growth. With time, what seemed like a luxury for the few becomes mass consumption. How many Dominicans considered poor today have a radio and television? For a poor person in the Middle Ages, comparable items were inconceivable luxuries. Sooner or later, capitalism makes commonplace those objects that were initially flaunted by the rich. This is no consolation to minimize the terrible effects of poverty. It's simply a demonstration that the most restrictive capitalism, enriching a few, also enriches others, although very slightly. The freest capitalism, one that abides under an equal rule of law for all, does the same thing but multiplied a hundredfold.

Free capitalism is one that does not accept the existence of oligarchies sheltered by power. Although the word "oligarchy" has a special place in the perfect Latin American idiot's dictionary, it's not an invention of his but rather an ancient term used by Greek philosophers. Yes, there are oligarchies in Latin America. They are no longer oligarchies of landowners and ranchers; instead they are industrial oligarchies and business groups that have prospered under protectionist power. To eliminate these oligarchies one doesn't have to eradicate their external manifestations—their money—but rather the system that made them possible. If these oligarchies, faced with coming of age, and being emancipated from state tutelage, continue to fatten their bank accounts then . . . long live the rich!

There is yet another explanation for our poverty: foreign debt is strangling Latin America's economies, and the great international banking industry is profiting from its usurious interest rates.

Foreign debt doesn't amount to a hill of beans. The best demonstration of this is that today anyone who has even the slightest understanding of the economy is not concerned about it, despite the fact that the region's total debt is greater now than in previous years, when the continent's political song and dance was limited to the tune of the $550 billion debt. Until recently, nothing titillated our politicians more or better induced Pavlovian reactions in our intellectuals' salivary glands than the foreign debt.

The debt is nothing more than the result of Latin American supplications to foreign governments and banks that began in the 1960s with a fervor that belies our traditional cult of "dignity" and continued throughout the 1970s. Latin America's total debt went from $29 billion in 1969 to $450 billion in 1991 as the region from Mexico to Patagonia turned into a zoo of white elephants that provided no returns to the people in whose name the grandiose public works were undertaken. The banks, burgeoning with dollars to be used wherever possible and whose existence was justified by the interest earned from the loans being issued, joyfully greased our machinery of public life. Can the banks be criticized for giving us the resources our imploring hands requested? Let's pretend that the international community had not given us the loans. What would we have been saying then? Instead of being a "usurious bank" it would have been a "racist," "stingy," or "voracious" bank. The banks only gave us what we asked for, not what the gun-toting imperialists made our governments accept. Looking back at it now, however, Latin America would no doubt have retained greater government control if the world had been less acquiescent to our insatiable begging. The largest Latin American debtor is not a private businessman but the government. There is not one Latin American country where the government doesn't owe at least half of the foreign debt.

Interest rates are high, you say? Interest rates are like elevators or ocean tides. Sometimes they go up, and sometimes they go down. If it's agreed that the debt will be subject to flexible interest rates, no one can shoot the banker when one day he raises the rates because the market set them there. At the beginning of the 1980s the United States raised its interest rates to fight inflation. Was the Reagan administration's decision to fight inflation a Machiavellian conspiracy craftily planned to make Latin America's debt seem more unwieldy than it already was? Proof of Latin America's magic realism is that there is a legion of people capable of believing this.

If the conspiracy were true, the imperialists got their just deserts. In 1982, a memo from Mexico was sent directly to Washington with a simple message: We cannot continue paying the debt. We all know what came afterward: a financial cataclysm. The vengeance of Latin America's history of suffering remained forever indelible in a brief paragraph on a piece of official paper. The consequences were not a medieval-style punishment for the borrower who confessed that he could not repay. Instead, there was an overall crisis in the world financial system. Another characteristic of the somniferous affair of Latin America's foreign debt is how countries can stop paying their debts whenever they wish without incurring any significant reprisals, except for difficulties in taking out new loans. (What nerve!) Thanks to Mexico's capricious decree, nine of the top ten American banks were on the verge of becoming insolvent, and no one retaliated against the catalyst of the crisis. Consequently, the debt became a double-edged sword. On the one hand, there was a threat to the Latin American economy since it owed money to the lenders. On the other hand, it kept the creditors hanging, their solvency partly relying on the myth that the debt will one day be repaid in full. The golden rule with debts is never to say that the loan will not be repaid, even though payments may already have stopped. The world of international finance is mind-boggling. The world banking industry is a fraternity of simpletons lending clients money so they can repay the previous debt that was borrowed to pay the debt prior to that one.

Accompanying Latin America's debt is the assurance of impunity. Each time arrears accumulate, especially now in times of economic growth, the banks are very tolerant. Between 1991 and 1992, $25 billion in arrears had accumulated. Did any bank or government say a word about it? Quite the contrary: while the arrears were accumulating the United States forgave more than 90% of the bilateral debt owed by Guyana, Honduras, and Nicaragua; 70% of that owed by Haiti and Bolivia; 25% of Jamaica's debt; and 4% of Chile's debt.

As for the trade debt, with a little bit of imagination—this premise being an optimistic one—and a playful nature, its structure can be molded like clay. The first country to figure this out was Bolivia, which in 1987, after having reduced its inflation, asked for money to buy out its entire trade debt at 11% of its value. So, without complaining or groaning, almost like magic, Bolivia reduced its total debt from $1.5 billion to $259 million. Then came Mexico, thanks to the Brady plan. In February 1990, it convinced the good-hearted commercial bankers to convert the debt to guaranteed negotiable bonds. Where was the trick? Easy, those bonds were 65% of the value of the debt instruments. It convinced another group of bankers to exchange its debt for guaranteed bonds with a 6.5% yield. With a single blow, using numbers instead of insults, Mexico slashed the debt it owed. Since then, most Latin American countries have "restructured" their debts—a nasty term simply meaning that the tyrants in the world banking industry forgave a huge percentage of these countries' debts in exchange for the remaining debt to be paid off on mutually convenient terms, which (in the context of minimally sensible economic policy) means easy. In 1994, for example, Brazil changed its payment timetable and structure to $52 billion, sweeping $4 billion of principal and $4 billion in interest under the rug. Recently Ecuador, the unfortunate victim of global racketeering, succeeded in reducing its debt principal by 45% through restructuring and simply exchanging smiles with its creditors. In the first quarter of 1995, Panama had nearly reached a similar agreement. Reducing one's debt with commercial banks is much easier than snatching the billfold from an unsuspecting tourist arriving at Lima's Jorge Chávez airport.

The debt is such an unimportant topic of discussion between the international community and Latin America that the debt instruments are being revalued on the secondary market. Plainly said, this simply means that the world thinks that a good macroeconomic situation in Latin America gives them reason to believe our countries will continue making future partial payments, since Latin America is solvent. Moreover, the current trend is that private companies, which offer stocks and bonds on the international stock markets, hold much of the new debt. The world is again accepting the myth that someday the debt will be paid off. And since we all know that the financial world is the land of hopes as much as reality, the key is not paying off the debt but rather believing that it will be paid off, believing in the simple fantasy that repayment is possible. The only thing missing in these trade-debt situations is sticking one's tongue out at the creditor. In government-to-government debts, one just needs to shake hands with a group of bureaucrats meeting under the aristocratic title of the *Club de Paris*, something already accomplished by many countries.

If Latin America's foreign debt were strangling the continent's economies, it would not be possible for many of these countries to have billion-dollar reserves as they have today. Nor, of course, could they attract the volatile migratory capital—"swallow" capital, as it's known in Spanish—that comes to Latin American stock markets to earn fabulous, fast-moving profits in national company stocks whose yields regurgitate such returns.

Without a doubt, paying the debt is a burden. For Bolivia it means allocating a little more than 20% of its export dollars to service its debt. For Brazil it's 26%. None of this is pleasant (remembering that these are inevitable consequences of our governments' irresponsibility), but the payments are spread out in installments in accordance with each country's ability to pay. Besides that, a normal relationship with the financial community allowed a country such as Mexico to receive an astronomical international aid package at the beginning of 1995 in order to rescue itself from its own incompetence and for Argentina to protect itself from the ensuing "tequila effect" with credits from the imperialists.

For years foreign debt was the great excuse, absolving Latin America's conscience of any blame. This excuse was so attractive that our politicians—for example, Fidel Castro and Alan García—swore in public that they would not pay the debt while secretly continuing to pay it. Alan García, the prince of demagogy, made famous the refrain "ten percent" (indicating he wouldn't pay more than 10% of the total amount of export sales). But in the end he paid more than his predecessor, Belaunde Terry, who never publicly objected to his obligations to the bank and still reduced the payments substantially. As for Fidel Castro, a champion veteran of anti-Western causes, he tried to start a debtor's club, a kind of insolvency union, to confront the powerful and refuse to pay. Shortly afterward it was discovered that he was one of the most punctual payers of his debt to the capitalist banks, at least until 1986 when he declared bankruptcy and stopped making payments altogether. Bankers should be told to find those specimens in a continent's political fauna that roar the loudest against usurious banks and foreign debt because those species will, without a doubt, be their most exemplary clients.

The International Monetary Fund's demands are plunging our people into poverty.

Funditis, like the Ebola virus, is a virus that causes hemorrhaging and diarrhea. The hemorrhaging and diarrhea caused by funditis, less degrading than those caused by the Ebola virus, are verbal. This particular virus attacks the brain. Its victims, who are found by the thousands throughout Latin America, discharge a torrent of words day and night, clamoring against the common enemy of Latin American nations and underdevelopment in general: the International Monetary Fund. They lose many hours of sleep, foam at the mouth, and blow smoke out their ears, obsessed by the creature that lives only to snatch away the last crust of bread from the lips of the emaciated child in the slums. Marches,

demonstrations, proclamations, coup d'etats, counter-coups. How many political lamentations have paid homage to hatred for the International Monetary
Fund! For the "progressives," this institution became in the 1980s what United
Fruit was a few decades earlier: the flagship of imperialism. Not only poverty but
also earthquakes, floods, and cyclones are all spawned by the Fundist's plans, a
perfect glacial conspiracy designed by its managing director. Is there anything
that the IMF is not capable of doing? Maybe precipitating a South American
defeat in the final round of the Soccer World Cup, but it's best not to test the
IMF.

What exactly is this monster that devours impoverished countries? Is it an
army? An extraterrestrial? A nightmare? Where does it get its power to inflict
hunger, sickness, and helplessness on Latin America's downtrodden? It's truly
quite sad to reveal what the International Monetary Fund really is. Far from the
fantastic mythology that has been woven around it, it's simply a financial institution created as part of the Bretton-Woods accord during the uncertainty
immediately following the Second World War when the world was pulling its
hair out trying to solve the problem of how to dig itself out of the economic hole
into which the misfortunes of war had put it. The agency was to function as a
conduit for funds that were paid in and then directed toward a specific destination according to monetary needs. Over time, the IMF began sending the bulk
of its funds to countries today known as "underdeveloped." Those funds did not
come from some philanthropic volunteer's imagination but from the economic
giants. Latin America became one of the areas where the IMF would try to ease
the financing problems faced by certain governments.

Were our governments obligated to accept the IMF? It was an impossible and
heroic task to stop the Monetary Fund's troops from entering our countries,
right? It was so impossible and so heroic that we didn't have to do a thing. All
we had to do was not ask for help and, if it was offered, slam the door right in its
face. In fact, many of our governments did just that. Others signed letters of
intent with this agency and then blew off the agreement.

Some governments have sought aid from the IMF contingent upon certain
macroeconomic policies—conditions which were actually negotiated with the
applicant country. These dynamics ("I will give you money, but I would like you
to take certain steps so that this aid has some meaning") are the result of a decision made by the donor countries. The IMF will help certain governments in
exchange for a certain rigor in administering public finance. No one has a pistol
pointed at his head, forcing him to accept the conditions. Nor does anyone have
the right to appropriate someone else's funds (this part is usually forgotten by
our patriots who bellow against the frigid—and rather devoid of sex appeal—
Mr. Camdessus, the managing director of the IMF). Our barking at the Fund is

simply because this institution doesn't give away dollars (which don't even belong to it in the first place).

In many cases, not accepting the IMF as a mediator has made the defiant country an enemy of the other financial institutions and of some major governments donating foreign aid. Is this unusual? Governments and banks, which are not forced by any natural or human law to provide social assistance, much less charity, prefer some type of guarantee, especially after the cataclysmic effects of the debt crisis at the beginning of the 1980s. Therefore, although it's always in the hands of the country to decide whether it wants a little *fundistic* push out of paralysis, it can suffer the consequences of not complying with the Fund's agreement insofar as it can find deafer ears at other financial organizations. Peru's Alan García did this (and he was not the only one).

Is the IMF the answer to Latin America's problems? Anyone who believes this deserves to have a privileged entry in the idiots' registry. This simple method of aiding government accounts in exchange for a little restriction on fiscal spending in order to contain inflation is not going to create vigorous societies where wealth flourishes like flowers in the spring. Furthermore, adopting certain fiscally disciplined measures without opening and deregulating stale economies is what has contributed greatly to liberalism's association with the IMF over these past years and, incidentally, has established the equation that states: the more IMF, the greater the poverty. Thanks to this, the history of the IMF is the story of how the most boring man—its managing director—has become the most hated man.

The IMF is neither the key to prosperity nor the ticket to success. To attribute these false characteristics to the Fund is one way of deepening the hatred for this agency, since no macroeconomic policy tied to the IMF's fiscal mathematics will ever suffice to solve the problem of poverty. These solutions are not found in the stiff, well-dressed IMF officer's briefcase; they were not yet even born when the reasons for our postcolonial failure manifested themselves. Only the institutions of the country in question can produce that miracle.

Our countries will never be free as long as the United States participates in our economies.

Peruvians call a tortuous relationship between a husband and wife amor serrano; the greater the abuse, the greater the love between them. The greatest sign of love is a slap, a karate kick, or a head bash. There is nothing more touching, sentimental, or exciting than a beating. Between Latin Americans and the United States there is *amor serrano*. As we saw previously, no one defined this relationship from the Latin American's point of view better than the Uruguayan

José Enrique Rodó: USA-mania. This refers to the maddening fascination for everything American, a fascination that is both healthy and envious, as much holy in essence as vile in form. We all have a *gringo* inside of us and we would all love to grab a *gringo* by the scruff of his neck. Throughout the twentieth century, we always defined Latin Americans in contrast to the United States. It's admiration rather than laughter that Fidel Castro provokes when, without allowing his beard to tremble, he denounces the bombardment of microbes from American laboratories destined for his country. The last bombardment, according to the General, provoked an epidemic of optical neuritis on the island. All of us have a Yankee spying on us from under the bed. Reclined on the psychiatrist's couch a star-spangled red, white, and blue flag emerges from our subconscious before any shame for our own past.

The worst Yankee offenses have, of course, been military. The only thing our patriots forget to add is that the United States' interventionist mistakes and defeats have probably been more significant than its victories. It was never able to overthrow Fidel Castro or the Sandinistas; it had to support Perón; and three years of criminal acts by Cedras, François, and Constant had to pass before its troops could finally land on Haiti, that veritable nuclear power in the hemisphere. And it was in Haiti where the Americans ran into danger when they faced a highly sophisticated and powerful resistance when attempting to place Aristide in the seat of power. The United States has also been accused of economic corruption. From American universities where our patriotic redeemers hold professorships or from research institutions financed by *gringo* foundations they pontificate: "We are an economic colony of the United States." They assure us that the submission inflicted on this hemisphere's Latinos by the Americans is the main reason for our inability to become part of civilization. We believe that we are the slaves and whores of the empire.

A quick look at this common truism unfortunately conjures up an incredible fantasy. For starters, half a century of anti-American sentiment has been very profitable for us. Hating the United States is the world's best business. The returns: economic and military assistance (the direct offspring of the *amor serrano* relationship) totaling $32.6 billion between 1946 and 1990. El Salvador, Honduras, Jamaica, Colombia, Peru, and Panama have each received billions of dollars. On loan? No, as a gift. For each rhetorical missile that has left our intellectual arsenals, one financial missile has been fired from the other side. No other country in history has so rewarded the intellectuals, politicians, and countries that hate it as has the United States. Politically speaking, anti-imperialism is the most profitable way of making love.

To what extent does the United States stick its nose into our business? To say "a lot" is what the *gringos* call "wishful thinking." The truth is that we have much less of an impact on Washington than we think. Both times in Latin America's postcolonial history when our countries were caught in the crossfire, our only importance was geopolitical, as part of the "influence zone." The first time was in the nineteenth century, around the time of our independence, when the United States fought European powers in order to establish its political sovereignty on these shores. Economic issues were not even discussed, since the United States was not in a position to do so. Until World War I, a century after the Monroe Doctrine, it was England who invested more than the United States in Latin America. The second time was of course during the Cold War, when communism established several beachheads on the continent. But not even then did the United States take an overwhelming economic interest in the countries south of its borders. Its priority was geopolitical, not economic. The numbers scream louder than the *criollo's* anti-American vocal cords. In the 1950s, American investments in our countries barely totaled $4 billion. In the 1970s, it was $11 billion, microscopic sums in today's world. In more recent times the only sure thing is that the United States has become quite disinterested in Latin America (and in all underdeveloped countries). In all these years only 5% of U.S. investments have gone to foreign markets and only 7% of its products have been exported. Seventy-five percent of its investments have gone to developed countries, not south of the Rio Grande. The Aristotelian enslavement that America's international companies have allegedly imposed on us does not make sense simply because until just yesterday, sales and investments in the United States have been ten times greater within its own territory than in the entire Third World combined.

These numbers will slowly change as the economic opening currently happening in traditionally uncivilized areas of the world begins to attract the corporate giants from other areas, in light of the lower costs and market growth in these countries. Latin America is gradually becoming one of those areas of interest. But this phenomenon is so recent—and cannot yet be categorized amid our continent's combined economic profits—that assessing the absence of freedom in our countries in terms of American economic colonialism is, politically speaking, one of the most painful displays of unrequited love.

How can our countries be important to the imperialist monsters when General Motors, Ford, Exxon, Wal-Mart, AT&T, Mobil, and IBM each have annual sales greater than any Latin American country except Brazil, Mexico, and Argentina? How are we to believe that we are vital to the strategic plans of economic imperialism when General Motors' sales are three times larger than Peru's total production? It's precisely because General Motors is obsessively oriented to the U.S. market that their sales fell sharply in 1994. If this company had its sales radius focused a little more on the benefits of imperialism, it would be less vulnerable to any shrinking of its sales in the United States.

In the mid-1990s the American presence in our economy, as well as the presence of other capital exporting countries, began to grow. This is significant. First, because money and technology from stronger countries are helping to boost our dormant markets. Second, because with the powerful nations competing for our markets, our consumers become the beneficiaries. Third, because finally our whiny anti-imperialists will be partially correct. Although economic imperialism was at one time in a position to function as a mini-state within Central American territory (the United Fruit Company and its military backing in Guatemala in 1954, for example), there are many more examples of our governments expropriating imperialists or expelling intruders who naively came to invest because the American military was ordered to support the dominant position of some international company in Latin America. It should also be stated that no expropriation of or prohibition directed against American investments was ever in itself a motive for the United States to send in the Marines. What better illustration is there than the Cuban revolution, which expropriated from dozens of American companies and citizens? And what about Fidel Castro's constant howls in favor of lifting the American trade embargo? Isn't this the best example of how economic imperialism is a fantasy? How can denouncing economic imperialism be compatible with continual pleas for the U.S. economy to stop *ignoring*—that being exactly what an embargo is—this Caribbean nation?

THE CURE THAT KILLS

The state represents the common good against private interests that only seek their own enrichment.

Wow, this sounds great! The perfect Latin American idiot propagates this idea in forums and from balconies, drawing immediate applause. And really, at first sight this seems like a plausible concept. It also allows the Latin American idiot to present himself as a man of progress. He makes an idea that is dear to the continent's populism his own: if poverty is the result of a wicked rape perpetrated by the rich, if the poor are getting poorer because the rich are getting richer, if the latter's prosperity is at the expense of misfortune for the former, then there's nothing more natural than for the state to administer justice by defending the interests of the immense majority of the destitute against the outrageous voracity of a few capitalists. By repeating the opening assertion, which vibrates like an undeniable truth in the feverish air of the public plazas, the perfect idiot eventually begins to believe it himself. If he said it and didn't believe it was true he'd be called a cynic or an opportunist, and not simply an idiot overwhelmingly refuted by concrete experience.

In fact, the history of the twentieth century negates this proposal. Instead of correcting inequalities, the state blindly intensifies them. The more it confiscates from society, the greater the inequalities, corruption, waste, political clientelism, exclusive privileges at the expense of the governed, high taxes extorted from its citizens, costly tariffs, terrible service, and as a result of all of this, distrust by the very citizens the institutions theoretically represent. This is the undeniable reality found in most of our countries.

If the idiot repeats an assumption already refuted by facts, it's only because he's bewitched by an ideological superstition. For him, the evils committed by the state are only temporary; they will be rectified when honest and efficient government officials are placed here and there. It isn't a structural problem. The state should do this or that, he will continually repeat, generously using that verb "should," which expresses only an assumption, a suspicion, or maybe even an idyllic utopia. The perfect idiot can't measure the distance that exists between "should" and "is," which is the same as between "is" and "seems." He depicts the state as a type of Robin Hood, but it isn't. Whatever it takes from the rich it keeps for itself, along with whatever it takes from the poor.

The state has several beneficiaries: an oligarchy of businessmen overprotected from competition who owe their fortunes to captive markets, tariff barriers, licenses granted by bureaucrats, and laws favoring licensees; an oligarchy of political power brokers for whom the state fills the same role as a cow's udder for a calf; a unionist oligarchy tied to government-run businesses, generally monopolies, that concede them one-sided, disastrous collective bargaining agreements; and, of course, a network of bureaucrats raised under the shadow of this corrupt welfare state.

Only a purely ideological elaboration could allow the perfect idiot to present Octavio Paz's philanthropic ogre as Robin Hood. He accomplishes this by raising theoretical constructions without subjecting them to tests. The idiot is a total utopian. He is not discouraged by refutations inflicted by reality, since utopia is a resistant bacteria. An example of this: socialism. For a century or more, socialism was the heir of the future due to purely ideological assertions. It was said that the winds of history were in its favor. Capitalism seemed to be sentenced to an unavoidable death. But reality was another matter. Capitalist economies many times showed their ability to recuperate, and socialist economies their flagrant tendency toward stagnation and recession. Despite this evidence, however, socialism continued reaping cultural and ideological victories and capitalism, insults. How many intellectuals, in order not to be judged reactionaries or ignorant of the historical process, joined this movement! They only admitted the failure of communism when they saw it reduced to nothingness in the former Soviet Union and its satellites. Jean François Revel gives an explanation for this strange phenomenon: its success is in "its ability to project mental constructions on reality that can resist evidence for long periods of time, to remain blind to the catastrophes that they themselves caused and which ended only when it disappeared under the convergence of objective bankruptcy and subjective profiteering." The subjective, represented by theoretical dogma, tends to outlive the objective for a long time.

Today, even the Latin American idiot himself knows that no country is prosperous if it doesn't develop its markets. Even Eastern European countries are encouraging investments and private business, and countries still considered communist, such as China and Cuba, are twisting the old Marxist dogma to justify market practices.

We Latin Americans have yet a more personal example of reality's rejection of our perfect idiot's ideological and rhetorical speculations: the depletion and failure of the ECLA (Economic Commission for Latin America) model based on the theory of dependency. According to this theory, typical of what a Third Worldist might say, rich countries would like to arrange things in such a way as to keep us underdeveloped, accentuating the dependent nature of our economies and subjecting us to unfair "terms of trade." From such a fable arose an economic policy called "inward development," or "import substitution," which, to the joy of our idiot, required the government to be highly interventionist and regulatory.

In Latin America, tariff barriers, import and export licenses, price and exchange rate controls, subsidies, all types of red tape, paperwork, and regulations contributed to the growth of the state, increasing its functions and authority in a suffocating and tentacular manner. What was the result? Did it truly pave the road for us to development and modernity? Quite the contrary. Instead of stimulating production and favoring the creation of wealth, the bureaucracy discouraged it. Giving some government official absolute power over business resulted in unlawful influence-peddling, and in the end—whether to get special privileges (typical for mercantilism, the source of ill-gotten wealth) or to obviate a labyrinth of restrictions—corruption flourished. The protagonist of this model isn't the market or the law of fair competition but the state, since everything converges in the vital centers where the bureaucrat, not the businessman, is the one who makes the decisions.

The intervening and regulatory state, the supposed rectifier of economic and social inequalities, is also the father of a luxuriant and parasitic bureaucracy that is to blame for government-owned companies being costly, mammoth, and profoundly inefficient. These companies are corroded by political clientelism and infested with corruption. Through increased prices, tariffs and taxes, and a nonstop supply of terrible service, they extort from society, creating fiscal deficit and thereby also inflation and impoverishment. Such is the reality that the perfect idiot refuses to see. That's why the solution he proposes—more government, more regulations, more controls, more interventionism—is actually the fundamental cause of our problems. This is equivalent to a quack doctor giving a hypertensive patient medicine that increases his blood pressure.

Certainly the idiot has himself understood (although a bit late) that the ECLA model is not applicable to our times, which are characterized by regional economic integration and economic globalization. It's a law of the times, a law that gives the market the role that the ECLA gave to the government. Overwhelmed by this reality, the Latin American idiot every now and then says he accepts it, although reluctantly, with reservations and restrictions. (He talks about gradual openings and social market economies to appease his ideological atonement.) But he refuses to eradicate his old superstition of the beneficent welfare state, and he still raises his fist on balconies and in forums protesting against neoliberalism—identified by him as savage capitalism (could his incredibly deplorable model of capitalism be a civilized one?), advancing instead his governmental dogma as a factor of social justice.

Incredible but true. When we call him an idiot, a perfect idiot, it's because he still believes he is a man of progress, distributing slanderous epithets (right-wing, extremist) to those who dare question his dinosaur, the welfare state.

Let's hear another of his assertions:

Neoliberal policy, called free business or free market, is profoundly reactionary. It is supported by the right and is the same as letting a fox loose in a henhouse. The left asserts that only the state, by vigorously intervening in the economy, can get development to yield social benefits that favor the people.

The left, the right: continentwide our idiots are always speculating about these two words. When the elixir that they sell us (the extreme, interventionist, regulatory government) turns out to be ineffective, as their last resort they use an attractively labeled bottle. What is certain is that the word "left" awakens "beautiful vibes" in certain sectors of our society, especially among the intellectuals and academia. This is understandable. Forty or fifty years ago, the left was an expression of a reformist movement. *Grosso modo,* the left was seen as taking the side of the poor against the right, who were only interested in preserving an old anachronistic order supported by the rich, the landowners, the military, and obscurantist sectors of the clergy. Ever since then the label "the right" has had a negative connotation for us. In the mind of the people, this is the ideological attire of a reactionary who drinks whiskey at the club, while seated on his lofty surname. The left, on the other hand, connotes an image of rebellion, red flags flapping in the breeze, of people oppressed since the times of their ancestors, finally rising up against unfair privileges.

It's simply a subliminal phenomenon, a cheap game of illusions, because none of this applies today. The left, fanatical nationalism, populism, and even the tropical version of social-democracy, not to mention the revolutionary option, have made a catastrophic journey throughout the Latin American continent. They have left many countries in ruin: Peron's Argentina, Allende's Chile, Alan García's Peru, Castro's Cuba.

What is pejoratively and intentionally christened as the "right," or the "new right," or better yet "liberal," has absolutely nothing to do with the recalcitrant conservatism of times past. Quite the contrary. It represents an alternative for change, perhaps the only one that Latin America has after the failure of government control, nationalism, populism, and armed revolutionary adventures. It's an alternative free of ideological prejudices that is not based only on theoretical premises but also on a simple reading of reality. We have limited ourselves to figuring out how and why countries that thirty years ago were underdeveloped and poorer than us have now ceased being poor—the famous Asian tigers, for example. This path, the only one that has created prosperity for the developed countries, combines a culture and social behavior based on practicing diligence and savings, acquiring advanced technologies with a competitive free trade policy, eliminating public and private monopolies, opening to international markets, attracting foreign investment, and above all respecting laws and liberty. Our principal idea is exactly this: that freedom is the foundation of prosperity and that the state should cede to society what it has arbitrarily confiscated so that society can become a producer of goods and a promoter of services.

As we have reached the end of the twentieth century, the notions of left and right (originating during the French Revolution) have lost their initial characterizations. They are probably anachronisms in a world that no longer questions democracy or the market economy. That's why Fukuyama is already talking about the end of that part of history. The differences between the left and right can exist in the arena of developed countries, within liberalism. The contrast between the two, however, would be on how to best combine assistance and effectiveness and not on which economic system to choose, since the confrontation between socialism and capitalism ended with the virtual disappearance and collapse of the former. Today there is only one option for a viable society: democratic capitalism.

Our perfect idiot doesn't want to admit this kind of proof. In a *désespoir de cause,* he resorts to the old dichotomy of the left against the right, trusting that a purely semantic or emotional factor can tilt the scale in his favor. His is the old scholastic stratagem of vilifying anyone who questions his dogma. Neoliberalism is an anathema the idiot is trying to lodge into the public conscience through frenzied repetition, as was done in the Middle Ages with heresies.

The Latin American idiot has not yet realized that today his political think-ing, christened by himself as vanguard, is behind the times. Maybe it always has been. The model he proposes is ultimately the same mercantilist or pat-rimonial model (as Octavio Paz called it) that the Spanish Crown bequeathed to us, coming to the Americas on Columbus's caravels. Carlos Rangel in *The Latin Americans: Their Love-Hate Relationship with the United States* writes, "The monopoly, the privileges, the restrictions to the free activity of individ-uals in economics and other areas are traditions deeply anchored in societies of Spanish origin." Rangel reminds us that according to this Spanish mercan-tilist spirit, which in the Middle Ages was the absolute model, individual eco-nomic activity was almost a sin. The theocracy and authority of the Spain that colonized us, committed to the Counter-Reformation, always stifled individ-ual initiative with all kinds of regulations. The wealth among us didn't come, as was the case with the early New England colonies, from effort, hard work, savings, or rigorous ethics, but rather from pillaging sanctified by govern-mental recognition and sinecures. Since those days, the guardian state has, among us, been the dispenser of privileges.

That state, so beloved by our perfect idiot, is, naturally, a child of the past, an heir of habits and methods that have always provoked schemes, influence-ped-dling, corruption, and fraud. "Faced with this situation," Rangel wrote, "the spontaneous reaction from a government head, heir of the Spanish mercantilist tradition, will always be one of intensifying control, multiplying restrictions and increasing taxes."

As an offspring of scholasticism and neoscholasticism, in the heart of the per-fect idiot there beats the religious and medieval idea that censors wealth, view-ing it as an illegal appropriation and reprehensible expression of greed. His con-demnation of the business world isn't much different from what was done to prosperous businessmen by St. Bernardino in the fourteenth century or later by St. Ignatius of Loyola. "In the attack against rapid development, branded as sav-age capitalism," writes Colombian economist Hernán Echavarría Olózaga about our social-democrats, "one can detect the influence of medieval scholasticism's sermons against greed and competition. Both the attacks and the sermons have the same origin and the same lineage, which we observe are in the spirit of oppo-sition to the industrial revolution and against modernism."

Unconsciously inheriting scholasticism, our perfect idiot also inherited Marx-ism, which, according to Octavio Paz, among Latin Americans consists much more of belief and religious faith than of a supposedly scientific method of ana-lyzing the historical process. In the Latin American idiot you will easily find an echo of Proudhon's comment that "property is robbery," as well as Marx's the-sis on man's exploitation of man. There, in the subsurface of his feeble political training (a mixture of Marxist Vulgate and populism), has remained the idea that a businessman is an exploiter, getting rich off the labor of others.

Of course, more recent references help to substantiate the economic theses that the perfect idiot makes his own. Take Keynes, for example. He gives the idiot his ideas of a mixed economy, of governmental planning and intervention, and of monetary issuance as a way of reactivating demand and making up for the shortage of resources. Our perfect idiot believes that this is also a means not only of development but of what he defines, with grandiloquent pomposity, as social investment. He's a friend of the great money-printing machine. And he considers the policies dedicated to assuring sound money as reactionary, neoliberal, and contrary to popular interests.

With all of these theories, coupled with those of Sir William Beveridge on the welfare state (no doubt also misinterpreted), our perfect idiot has in fact generated catastrophic policies in many countries on this continent. The monetary turmoil, caused by the intrepid Keynesian thesis, has created inflation, institutional disorder, a real decrease in income, and, as a result, the impoverishment of wage earners. Social investment, conceived as an authoritarian division of wealth on a microeconomic level or as a government program financed by monetary issuance, is what induces social depression. In this case, the fox in the henhouse is not the businessman but the state, which is plucking the chickens mercilessly.

Once again reality, and that alone, inflicts a convincing (although at times late in coming) rebuttal of the ideological utopia. On a continentwide scale, Cuba and Chile illustrate two concepts of diametrically opposed development: one state-controlled, centralist, and planned; the other, liberal. The first one leads toward widespread poverty and the second toward overcoming the dead weight of underdevelopment and even poverty itself. It should be acknowledged that Castro has provided the most consistent diagnosis of our troubles, which has then been noised abroad by the perfect Latin American idiot. If poverty, as the idiot suggests, is the product of plundering, if the notorious increases in wealth are nothing more than labor being exploited by capital, everything will be corrected by socializing the means of production and eliminating private property. If multinationals exploit poor countries by carrying off their wealth, then the wealth should be expropriated. If the *campesino* is a victim of a villainous exploitation by large landowners and agricultural businesses, the land must be collectivized. And here we see how Cuba, using these approaches that Castro himself is now finally although pathetically attempting to correct, has ended up where it is.

Chile took the other path, applying the liberal model of opening itself to international markets; privatizing businesses and entities that were previously government monopolies; eliminating subsidies, procedures, and regulations; and allowing free entrance of foreign investments. In the last few years, this country has recorded an uninterrupted GDP growth at an average rate of 6% (10% in 1992 alone) with visible economic and social results: unemployment in 1996 was less than 4.7%, and the labor force had grown to 4,860,000 persons in 1994. From 1992 to 1996 incomes rose in real terms by 17% with no decrease in commercial profits. Its foreign investments beat the rest of the continent's records (a little less than $5 billion in 1993), a contribution that by itself represents one fourth of the world's total investments, which—also another record—represented 27% of the gross domestic product in 1993. Savings in Chile constitute 21.5% of this GDP. As a result, according to the French newspaper *Le Monde,* Chile is almost the only country in Latin America where poverty has decreased instead of increased since the beginning of the 1980s.

Such are the facts, supported by numbers. Naturally these are convincing to those who study them objectively, but not for the perfect idiot, who, clinging to his ideological superstitions, opposes them using all types of excuses. In Chile, he will tell us, there are still disparities, there are extremely rich and extremely poor people, and poverty still affects 26% of the population. This is true. However, the dynamics of liberal economics have succeeded in decreasing the percentage of poor people from 44% to this 26% level in only five years, and all indications show that it will continue to decrease. At any rate, Chile's poverty is not attributable to the liberal model. It was inherited from the previous regulatory governmental model that the perfect idiot likes so much.

According to him, Cuba's poverty is attributed to the "blockade" imposed by the United States. This blockade is nothing more than the prohibition of American companies from doing business with Cuba, and this argument is just an excuse, since the catastrophic situation on the island is a direct result of applying the same system there that failed in the former USSR and in the East.

However, the perfect Latin American idiot distances himself from that model by proclaiming himself a nationalist or a social-democrat and speaks of a social market economy in order to oppose the proposed liberal one, christened by him as savage capitalism. If we let him extensively expound his thesis, he will talk about a mixed economy, about the need to control trade and imports, about reestablishing subsidies, about allowing governments freer monetary management to finance social investment projects, and everything else that makes up his ideological hardware store. Hence, his most beloved model is Alan García's in Peru. God help us!

It is a strange defender of the poor who will speak copiously on their behalf and then, when he has the reins of power in his hands, increases poverty even more, just as Mr. García did with his disastrous policies. When everything crumbles down around him, the perfect idiot is left with subliminal emotions tied to the terms left and right. Labels from the past. He's from the left and we're from the right. He is a progressivist, a populist, a renovator, and—why not, since it's such a lovely word?—a revolutionary. We are the reprehensible friends of the rich. This rhetoric energizes and sustains him, even though the train of the new era has left him standing at the station. He continues to believe that he's a vanguard repeating the fifty-year-old thesis that brought the continent to a bottleneck. But what does that matter? Our idiot still believes that he's in fashion, like those little old ladies who throw themselves on the dance floor when they hear a tango, that supple, passionate dance of their youth, forgetting about their gout and rheumatism. Nothing can be done; he's incurable. If you don't believe this, let's hear again what he has to say:

Social security, public services, and businesses that have a strategic value for the country must become monopolies of the state and not be left in the hands of private capitalists.

Yet another dogma, also refuted by concrete experience. A useful idiot—you must have already noticed—always tries to place this debate on the purely theoretical field by supporting himself on his idealized vision of the state and his demonized vision of a private businessman. Once again, ideology provides him an intellectual and a practical excuse for not seeing the overall catastrophic reality of businesses and services administered by the state in Latin America.

For example, it would be worthwhile to ask a Colombian what happened with the government-run railroads. Why did the state itself bring about its ruin, as it did with the seaports company Puertos de Colombia or the Institute of Territorial Credit, which was in charge of housing programs, or with the government-run electric company that left the country in the dark for months in 1992 due to the wild rationing produced by incompetence, waste, clientelism, and scandalous corruption? Or ask the Colombian, subjected to endless waiting lines, all types of obstacles, and bad medical services, what he thinks about the Social Security Institute? And how does he explain the fact that with a billion-dollar budget and an army of 33,000 bureaucrats this institute serves only 23% of the population?

Things similar to what the Colombian thinks about all of these government public service agencies could also be said by Peruvians, Argentines, Mexicans, Brazilians, Venezuelans, Dominicans, and all Central Americans, not to mention the most unfortunate of all, the Cubans, who suffer from colossal government inefficiency on that unfortunate island. What made Argentine President Menem privatize the government-run telephone company? Anyone who lives in Buenos Aires could tell us. And it certainly wasn't a privatizing frenzy but an unavoidable necessity that persuaded Mexican President Salinas de Gortari—despite being heir to the PRI party's tradition of state control—to privatize banks, Mexico's telecommunications company Telmex, the airline Compañía Mexicana de Aviación, the National Credit Associations, sixteen sugar mills, plus another hundred or so companies. The autonomous institutions created in Venezuela are related to the spectacular growth of bureaucracy and the incredible amount of public spending that has brought that country one of its most serious crises in its history. Never has so much wealth been so irresponsibly squandered in the name of the supreme state, to the detriment of the standard of living of the middle and lower classes.

Reality also shows us the other side of the coin. In Chile, the vast majority considers the creation of a private pension and health care system a great benefit for employees and workers. Twelve years after this liberal reform was started, the investment funds, which belong to the workers and are managed by the private economy and not the government, have reached $25 billion. Each Chilean worker has his own personal log where he records the money he has accumulated. Only a perfect idiot would think of returning to a government-run pension system that would consume all of this money (as fast as a can you burn a newspaper, as Hernán Echavarría Olózaga says) in bureaucracy and create a jungle of obstacles and middlemen to pay out the pensions, if indeed, after all its inefficiencies, there were pensions left to pay.

Despite this same factual evidence, the stupidity of our perfect idiot has no limits. In several Latin American countries, where a project similar to Chile's was presented, the idiot stood up on the parliamentary bench to yell, all the veins in his neck swollen with anger, that the workers' money was not going to go into capitalist pockets. Never has his ignorance of macroeconomics been so astonishing, nor his demagogy more base, since in reality those he was defending were not the workers but the unions of the government-controlled social security system. Once again the political power brokers, bureaucrats, and unionists from government businesses join in common cause against the true interest of a country's wage earners.

How does one explain to this swarm of perfect idiots that without accumulating capital there is no development, and without development unemployment and poverty will continue to reign among us? How can they expect countries like Brazil, Colombia, Panama, Mexico, and Peru, where more than 30% of the households live below the absolute poverty line, to acquire equipment, goods, and services (and consequently employment) with an irresponsible and spendthrift state? How can he not understand that a country's true capital, productive capital represented by machinery, equipment, factories, and means of transportation, is created only by the private businessman and not the bureaucrat?

How does one explain to the populist politician, to the irredentist ECLA supporter, to the professor or student impregnated up to his ears with Marxist Vulgate, to the priest of liberation theology hypnotized by the medieval idea that the rich are the enemy of the poor, or to the raving guerrilla dedicated to freeing us from who-knows-what through acts of terrorism and violence, that their ideology has nothing, nothing new, to offer our poor countries?

Who is going to remove the cobwebs from our perfect idiot's head when he continues insisting that it was his government formula, and not the liberal model, that produced the economic miracles of Japan, Korea, Taiwan, and Singapore?

The Asian economies reached their high levels of prosperity thanks to the planning and intervention of the state that the neoliberals are so opposed to.

This statement either shows bad faith or gross ignorance. "Dear friend," one would like to kindly say to the perfect idiot, "there is a fundamental difference between a state that intervenes to destroy a market, preventing the laws of free competition from playing out and replacing it with authoritarian-imposed monopolies, and a state that puts itself at the service of production and the market, as was the case in Chile, Hong Kong, Japan, Korea, Taiwan, and Singapore. If the state comes onto the field—to use a soccer term—it's not so it can shoot, score, or block goals, but to respect the basic rules of competition, like a referee does with a whistle." There is no government intervention or planning among those countries. The famous Japanese Ministry of Economy, MITI, is supported by private investments, technological developments, and a highly competitive market.

Naturally, the judicial framework and guarantee of order and security required for productive activity are the state's obligations. We liberals have never questioned its essential functions, such as administering justice, maintaining the basic legal order, and protecting citizens. Among us Latin Americans, though, the state carries out these functions in such an inept way because it is embroiled in jobs that are better handled by the private sector. At the heart of this debate is the conception of the role of government. There can on the one hand be an economy where the state plays an important role as in Korea, Taiwan, or Singapore by placing itself at the economy's service and respecting its laws, and on the other a "state economy" where the government attempts to impose its own laws and usurp economic freedom, always with deplorable results.

The government can't just brush aside the social problems.

Of course not. There, at least on this tiny matter, we don't disagree and there is nothing stupid in expressing this idea. We liberals believe that the state should aid the helpless, the marginalized, or those who for some reason or another are unable to take care of themselves and who would be crushed if exposed to the strictest laws of the market. Our disagreement with the perfect Latin American idiot is the way in which this common goal is accomplished.

The liberal Chilean José Piñera Echeñique maintains that our continent is not poor but impoverished because of the mercantilist or patrimonial capitalism that sprouted in our countries. This system, plagued with privileges, monopolies, and perks, has been an inexhaustible source of inefficient and corrupt economies—a flagrant cause of underdevelopment, discrimination, and injustices whose principal victims have been the poorest in our societies. This system, says Jean François Revel, is characterized "by rejecting the market and all freedom of trade and prices; by an unreal monetary policy, separated from the international world; by colossal investments squandered on megalomaniacal or unproductive industrial complexes; by disastrous military expenses; by banks being sterilized through nationalization, preventing credit from functioning according to economic criteria; by a customs protectionism that suppresses competition with the outside and involves a degradation of quality in local products; by a revenue economy, a plethora of parasitic employees that has ultimately made the return to a market system impossible without unleashing endemic unemployment; by the impoverishment of the population, accompanied by the enrichment of the political and bureaucratic class through corruption."

Alan García's Peru and the Sandinistas' Nicaragua—not to mention Cuba— illustrate very well the catastrophes this system brings about. Always speaking on behalf of the people, the Sandinistas, in ten years, succeeded in reducing the consumption of basic commodities by 70% and the buying power of workers by 92%. The numbers—always the numbers, the best expression of reality—are overwhelming against such a political philosophy.

Liberals consider it fundamental for the population to have access to essential public services: education, health, drinking water, nutrition, and social security. However—and here lies our primary difference—we don't accept the belief that the state should be the provider of such programs. The state should take advantage of competition in the private sector to directly provide basic services. Privatization is not, in this case, an end but a tool for expanding the coverage, quality, and efficiency of a social policy. Privatization, in other words, should replace public monopolies with competing commercial lenders, thereby giving the individual the complete freedom of choice.

In short, and hopefully this will help to eliminate the perfect idiot's prejudices against the liberal model, we believe that the government's role, diametrically opposed to the one the idiot defends, should focus on essential tasks: defend national sovereignty, preserve public order, administer justice, and, of course, protect the poorest sectors of the population. To do this, the government must distance itself from activities it tends to perform badly and stop being the banking government, the industrial government, and the commercial government that has done nothing more than hurt the productive structure of our countries.

6

"LET'S CREATE TWO, THREE,
ONE HUNDRED VIETNAMS"

*Only a revolution can change society and take us out
of poverty.*

It would help to remind the interventionist-crazed Latin American idiot that
there exist such things as earthquakes, cataclysms, tidal waves, heart attacks,
aneurysms, airplane crashes, and many other things beyond human control that
are capable of causing a change in society. Cosmic phenomena, natural catastrophes, personal tragedies, and thousands of other casualties in disguise have,
throughout the millennia and centuries, brought about more change than all
revolutions combined since Cromwell's partisans pared off Charles I's "crown"
to Ayatollah Khomeini's displacement of the Shah of Iran. But let's not be so nit-
picky with the idiot. Let's suppose that on verbalizing this prodigious phrase he
wanted to expressly exclude all forms of change that were not strictly controlled
by man. Okay, we can't deny that a revolution can change a society. But adher-
ing to the logic that says *only* a revolution can change a society is worthy of a
bunk at a psychiatric hospital. There are societies governed by strong-arm
regimes that can only be removed from power by violence. There are others
where it's unnecessary to blow the adversary's brains out. However, he who
defends violence is not appealing to logic but to arbitrariness. He wants, pas-
sionately desires, violence. But let's continue to indulge him. Let's say that revolutions are not only a way of seizing power but also a way of exercising it. This
exercising of power requires the use of revolutionary force—as much to

preserve power against real and potential enemies as to perpetrate the economic plunder necessary to end the old order. Let's say that the old order is obsolete and immoral, despicable and evil. It has to be changed and, if it resists, force will have to be used. But only if the outcome of this transformation is a change for the greater good would the idiot be justified in his emphatic assertion that a revolution is the only valid instrument of change.

There's a slight problem, though. Except for the British revolution of 1688 and the American revolution at the end of the eighteenth century, there's not a single case of a revolution that has achieved anything good. Moreover, no revolution has produced more benefits than problems (except for the British and the American ones, which go against the idiot's ideological compass, and possibly even the French revolution, which promoted some healthy principles in the midst of its innumerable atrocities). Like the revolution of an advancing wheel or a disc in motion, the revolutionary process, regardless of its speed, is a perpetual return to the past, a constant retreat to the original injustices. Latin American revolutions have produced dictatorships in every situation, from the Mexican to the Nicaraguan, from the MNR (Movimiento Nacional Revolucionario) government in Bolivia or Allende's in Chile. Yet, despite the latter two calling themselves revolutions, they were not true revolutions because a revolution implies a violent seizure of power and the abolition of the ruling system. In both of these cases, with all the arbitrariness and plunders that took place, and with all the economic calamities that were produced, it's not possible to strictly call them revolutions. Elsewhere the experience has been similar: All African and Asian revolutions engendered monsters. The Pol Pot and Mao exploits in Asia, or Mengistu's and the Angolan Popular Liberation Movement in Africa, to give just four examples, killed the supposed beneficiaries of these revolutions out of hate, fear, and hunger. Mao, the Great Helmsman, drove 60 million Chinese to their death with his collectivization of land. For them, the "Great Leap Forward" was a leap into the grave, not exactly trimmed with a hundred flowers. Haile Mariam Mengistu annihilated 1.2 million Ethiopians by concealing and thus accelerating a famine that could have been averted. Instead, he condemned his compatriots to hunger in order to torment the West with a guilty conscience and ask them for economic assistance. Angolan revolutionaries, after having eliminated any chance of free elections, needed the help of 50,000 Cuban soldiers and 5,000 Soviet advisors to keep the Liberation Movement of Angola in power with blood and fire.

In Latin America the revolutionary's backpack, which was believed to be loaded with goodness, has been invariably full of ashes. Whether they succeeded in taking power (like Castro and the Sandinistas) or not (like Peru's Shining Path and Colombia's Revolutionary Armed Forces), revolutionaries have been unable to learn from a century of totalitarianism. Persevering in mistakes and obstinately idolizing failures, they are blind to the lessons of the former USSR and central Europe and all the "liberation movements" (what a title) emerging in the underdeveloped world after the Second World War. They have made us believe that a different, original, "autochthonous" form of revolutionary socialism is possible, while a bevy of European and North American mentors, tourists from other revolutions, reporters from faraway catastrophes, impoverished heirs of the old renaissance utopianism tied to Columbus's caravels, all ceaselessly breathe life into their exploits. As shown in Régis Débray's masterpiece *Revolution in the Revolution?*, they make us believe that these revolutions are so unique that even the nature of the revolution has itself been transformed.

What revolution ever ended poverty? Did it in Mexico? It certainly didn't in Oaxaca, Chiapas, and Guerrero. Half of the Mexican people now live in poverty and most of those who don't owe their situation to those pro-imperialist, pro-capitalist and pro-bourgeoisie betrayals by the recent Mexican governments of the ideologist (this word is incredibly generous) of the Mexican revolution. The Mexican revolution has been so successful and so dedicated to endorsing revolutions taking place south of its borders (beginning with the closest one, the Guatemalan National Revolutionary Union in Guatemala) that a domestic revolution exploded right in its own face with ski masks and all, led by the perfect Latin American revolutionary: a middle-class intellectual, Subcomandante Marcos, a fan of the fax machine. The irony of all of this is tragic. Marcos's Zapatistas use the name of the hero of the 1910 Mexican revolution, Emiliano Zapata, a precursor in many ways to the PRI. From the 1910 revolution was born a political system, which in 1929 called itself the National Revolutionary Party (PNR) and shortly thereafter changed its name to the Institutional Revolutionary Party (PRI). Just as tragic is the fact that President Salinas's government greatly subsidized Mexico's poverty by placing Luis Donaldo Colosio in charge of the charity budget, giving him $3 billion to assuage the government's guilty conscience. A good portion of this money remained in the bureaucratic chain, and the little that was doled out was nothing compared with the PRI's political corruption and provincial tyranny. Chiapas received $200 million in 1993, and the the Zapatista crisis blew up in 1994.

Revolutions have been so successful in the countryside that wars have continued to erupt, despite the fact that for the past twenty years the National Bank of Rural Credit has awarded the *campesinos* $24 billion. (Actually only 20% of it was paid out since the rest went to irrigate—not the land but the bureaucrats' pockets.) In fact the Chiapas revolution has placed itself in confrontation with a government whose Constitution has since 1917 been, despite various amendments, essentially socialist and corporatist.

Was hunger eradicated in Nicaragua? If so, the stomachs of the unemployed and the underemployed—two-thirds of the population—were growling with joy when the Sandinistas lost the 1990 elections. What happened to the $3 billion that the sovereign Sandinista regime received every year from the former USSR? The accounting wizardry of the revolutionaries in administering that treasure was such that, at the end of Ortega's government, Nicaraguans had a per capita income of $380, ten times less than, uh, . . . could it be France's, Germany's, or England's income? No, Trinidad and Tobago. This figure can only be an estimate, since its 33,000% inflation doesn't allow for very orthodox accounting. What happened to the money that Ortega asked Sweden for in 1988 with the fish story that his country, as tropical and humid as they come, was experiencing a severe "drought"?

Did General Juan Velasco perchance succeed in banishing poverty and hunger from Peru? Maybe that's why 60% of the *campesinos* in whose name the revolutionary government expropriated land and carried out agrarian reform had, throughout the 1980s, divided that very same land into private parcels. The revolutionary impetus that the military regime gave Peru made it jump from the eighth-place position it occupied in Latin America at the beginning of the 1970s to . . . the *fourteenth* position in the 1980s! The military revolution and later Alan García's pseudorevolution took Peru's agricultural production, which in the 1960s was the second highest on the continent, to a very anti-imperialist second-to-last place. Undoubtedly the semi-revolutionary Paz Estenssoro achieved great things in the 1950s as the head of the MNR. This is probably why, decades later, when he returned to the government, this man who had nationalized the tin industry started the capitalist counterrevolution in his country, later continued by Paz Zamora, and currently carried out by Sánchez de Losada. It's true that Paz Estenssoro was revolutionary in something: he was ahead of Latin America (except in Chile) with his pro-capitalist measures, beginning in the 1980s, when this seemed impossible.

Could it be that Cuba has banished hunger? This is probably the reason why the mono-crop country not long ago began to import . . . sugar! It seems that Cuba has nothing in abundance and has a per capita income four times less than the Lilliputian Trinidad and Tobago (please note here the Cuban superiority to the aforementioned Nicaraguan situation, but this is not difficult to understand given that before 1959 Cuba was among the economic leaders of the continent). It should also be added that the geographical area of Trinidad and Tobago is forty times less than Cuba's.

If hunger could be abolished by decree, the Latin American revolution, a fanatical cultivator of decrees, devoted to regulations and red tape, would have already accomplished it. But it seems that it hasn't; hunger cannot be abolished by decree. It has to be abolished with prosperity, and no revolution has succeeded in bringing prosperity to Latin America. It has only brought corruption (the revolution has degenerated into a *rob*olution), dictatorships, and privileges for the governing caste at the expense of that majority of the population submerged in poverty. Our revolutions haven't produced anything but moral, political, economic, and cultural poverty. All the inventiveness paraded in guerrilla hotbeds and all the courage deployed in the mountains change into monotony, conformity, complacency, and at the same time cowardice, once in power. Latin American revolutionaries have only demonstrated the ability to capture and preserve power (and to do so they are capable of the most acrobatic ideological somersaults, the sweetest betrayals of their own creed, and the most Florentine opportunism). An enemy of class-based society, the revolutionary caste is an oligarchy. An enemy of military authoritarianism, the revolutionary caste depends on the use of force to remain in power. An adversary of imperialism, its existence would not have been possible without foreign subsidy. Yet it has not displayed too many hang-ups when it receives assistance not only from its ideological partners but also, thanks to a combination of entreaty and blackmail, dollars from the rich (no one is more protected in Cuba than the foreign tourist or capitalist). If the road to paradise runs through revolution, then the road is endless.

Dependent countries in Latin America should fight internally against oligarchies and capitalism and externally against imperialism by armed national liberation movements.

With a good sense of the remote possibility of winning any elections, the revolutionary carries out his objective exclusively by means of armed battles. Although he at times announces his goal as attacking the city from the countryside, he is actually just taking a detour, choosing the longest route: going from the city up into the mountains to later return to the city. You see, the revolutionary invariably comes from a middle-class urban setting. He isn't a child of the swamps and the forest, but of concrete and sidewalks. This strange creature has so much free time, so many hours to waste, that he has the luxury of taking a casual stroll through the mountains, sometimes for years, to end up (if he achieves his goal) living in the city—either in the suburbs or in the capital—where in reality his entire objective, namely power, is concentrated. In addition to being a loafer, the revolutionary is obstinately violent, even when the situation doesn't call for it. Armed conflict is the *sine qua non* for graduating as a revolutionary. Violence is history's midwife. You have to kill and face the risk of dying in order to pass the class with honors. The ceremony of blood and the orgy of homicide are the moving forces in the revolutionary movement, making homicide an objective in itself and the revolution the core of his ideological creed. The revolutionary must also suffer a little. If before seizing power he spends some time in prison, like Fidel Castro, and has said that history will absolve him, he'll earn many points (it doesn't matter that Fidel's brief stay, only nineteen months, was a bed of fragrant roses during which time Martha Frayde and Naty Revuelta brought him Swiss bonbons and English marmalade). The revolutionary earns a multitude of points if he serves a long jail time, like the Nicaraguan Tomás Borge during Somoza's regime, and if he has also been tortured. If in addition to suffering the revolutionary meets his death along the way, like Che Guevara, or the Peruvian MIR (Movement of the Revolutionary Left) fighters in the 1970s (like de la Puente and Lobatón), or the Peruvian poet Javier Heraud and his ELN (National Liberation Army), he will be immediately canonized at the height of revolutionary heroism, without having to go through the business of accumulating more secular honors in his pursuit of eternal glory. It must be added, of course, that canonization can also be attained if, instead of falling to fascist bullets, one falls prey to friendly fire (like Roque Dalton, the Salvadoran who was killed by his own revolutionary companions).

Many times the target of this violence is not the oligarchy or imperialism but the poor. How many of the big industrialists, businessmen, bankers, or insurers who kissed Alberto Fujimori's feet in Peru by the thousands after his coup d'etat in April 1992 have been killed since then by the Shining Path? Not one. The victims granted the privilege of being on the receiving end of revolutionary fire in Peru are the *campesinos* in the highlands and the rain forests, rural immigrants in the city, and, at times, the downtrodden middle class of the barrios in Lima. Not only that, the revolutionary's aim is off: his hand suffers a curious trembling when the target he's shooting at is imperialism. His attacks on embassies, for example, tend to only cause material damage, and if anyone dies from an explosion it's more than likely that it'll be either some local guard or an unfortunate resident of the area, completely unrelated to the imperialist motivations of an embassy that has probably denied the revolutionary a visa on more than one occasion. Colombia's Revolutionary Armed Forces and especially the National Liberation Army have a strange obsession with oil pipelines such as Caño-Limón-Coveñas. Could it be that this ties into Colombian guerrillas' anti-imperialist strategy? It appears, however, that these guerrillas have linked themselves intravenously with drug trafficking, an imperialist trade par excellence, whose economic aid serves as the oxygen for their lungs. In the 1980s, for example, yucca and banana plantations in the jungles of Caquetá, controlled by guerrillas, coexisted with coca plantations. In Lower Caguán, revolutionaries established a system where the *campesinos* would set their tables by the doors of the hotels and sell their product to drug dealers, who then paid a tribute to the revolution. The guerrillas allow lime, gray cement, urea, and red gasoline into their territories in order to produce cocaine. The Vichada zone, for example, with 100,000 square kilometers (38,610 square miles) of rain forest, is packed with coca thanks to the government established by the guerrillas, who turned the place into a bank for revolutionaries. This is just one of ten areas used by the guerrillas for similar purposes. Isn't drug trafficking, which involves an export product for rich countries whose demand controls our production and many of whose dollars are usually laundered primarily outside Colombian drug-trafficking countries, a much faster form of imperialism than exporting oil, a product whose exploitation, by the way, greatly benefits the country in question since there is a need for energy? That doesn't matter; the Latin American idiot doesn't see any contradictions. The narcotization of the revolutionary cause is good if it fills the revolutionary's pockets. Imperialism is good if it finances anti-imperialism. The annual $60 million that the Peruvian guerrillas have for many years received from the hands of drug traffickers are revolutionary dollars. Latin America's revolutionary cartridge belts are full of cocaine. The revolution has shifted from red to white. *Viva* the white revolution!

Neither is the idiot's slumber greatly disturbed that revolutions tend to generate the longest-lasting oligarchies and the cruelest imperialism. Those poor Sandinistas, victims of the imperialism that in 1990 threw them out of power through the ballot boxes, went home with millions of dollars of property seized from what the people's imagination has dubbed "the piñata." The *comandantes*, who have for the past few decades been less confident about their future, have safeguarded it with splendid mansions expropriated from their vile capitalist owners. Daniel Ortega, for example, who left behind a national debt of $11 billion, is still entrenched in a small palace worth more than a million dollars, which in Nicaragua is the equivalent to a European mansion worth several million. That doesn't matter; the revolutionary also needs to secure his future because otherwise, what would happen to the revolution? The revolutionary needs space to think and to feel at home, because if the revolutionary heart isn't happy, what would happen to the revolution? Now really, you can't condemn Ortega that on his visit to New York he protected his revolutionary eyes from the harsh rays of the sun with a fantastic pair of Ray-Bans. Without Daniel Ortega's shrewd vision, what would have become of the Nicaraguan revolution?

Imperialism is bad if others do it. If the revolutionary does it, it isn't imperialism—it's *liberationism*, like the one admirably practiced by the Cuban soldiers sent to fight in Africa to bring a little justice to the sub-Saharan Ovimbundus and Kongos, the Ethiopian Oromos and Amharas. The fact that General Ochoa, hero of the African wars, was executed on returning to Cuba is not a contradiction. It was the greatest expression of revolutionary gratitude, an award for excellence that a member of the revolution can receive at the hands of his government. Just because the Nicaraguans supported their Salvadoran buddies of the Farabundo Martí National Liberation Front (FMLN) with weapons and money doesn't mean that they were practicing Central American imperialism; they were practicing solidarity, continental fraternity. Even though the Guatemalan guerrillas of the Guatemalan National Revolutionary Unity (URNG) support Subcomandante Marcos in Chiapas—or (put another way) the Mexican revolution has transformed southern Mexico into a guerrilla sanctuary for the same Guatemalan URNG—it isn't imperialism against a neighbor; it's a postmodern revolution, a revolution without borders.

Friends, capitalism must be stopped. To do this you must learn how to use the tools. And who better to instruct us than Comandante Joaquín Villalobos, the star of the Salvadoran revolution turned wealthy businessman in San Salvador? Who would dare deny this revolutionary the moral authority to direct the future Latin American revolution the next time he draws his gun against capitalism, since he knows better than anyone else what capital gain is, having profited from it on the backs of his employees? Could anyone deny Fidel Castro the glory of his revolutionary victories after he confronted the capitalist monster from within, thanks to the many decades of economic apartheid, in which Havana's comforts and luxuries have been reserved for dollar-toting tourists and for himself? Is there anyone better qualified and ready to take on the dollar than he who has the texture, the shades, and the dimensions of that green bill studied down to a science that even Alan Greenspan would envy? To stamp out the rich, one has to live like them; otherwise, you can't know what you're fighting. Mansions, yachts, private beaches, wildlife preserves, planes, and love affairs are all indispensable elements of revolutionary sacrifice, a demanding test that places the enemy in the path, to try and to bourgeoisify the revolutionary. The revolutionary should suffer these extreme hardships for as long as possible, because revolutionary glory is proportional to the amount of time that he can resist the pain of bourgeoisie sensuousness.

In dependent countries it isn't necessary to wait until the conditions for class consciousness ripen; this process can be accelerated by revolutionary vanguards.

The idiot is—probably without knowing it—an admirer of the Platonic model of government: power for the educated aristocracy. The revolution he advocates isn't carried out by the people but by their ideological lawyers, the "revolutionary vanguard." This revolution represents the introduction of tribal magic to

Marxist science, a simple arranging of principles and ideological guides to give the confused and backward masses of the Third World access to the prerogatives of modern people. Instead of waiting for the masses to become aware of their plight, a complicated matter in countries with quite elementary levels of education, the leader of the clan can interpret the laws of history for them, decree on their behalf that the opportune time has come, and wham!, the march to a classless society has begun so it won't be late for its rendezvous with history (whereas modern countries, farther away from the revolution, will show up a bit tardy).

Once in control, intellectual arrogance mutates into an arrogance of power—in other words, authoritarianism. It's in the revolutionary's attitude of acting in the interests of the rest, given that his "vanguard" status places him on a more sophisticated level of understanding reality, where you will find amassed the truth of the revolution. The revolutionary in his entirety is the expropriation of individual sovereignty and the transfer of this sovereignty to a superior vanguard hierarchy. It doesn't matter that Marxism's central thesis states that socialism is the natural outcome of the capitalist process once feudalism disappears; all you have to do is jump ahead a few centuries to get there faster. Also, aren't our countries today more urban than rural thanks to the unstoppable development of the underground economy that erupted with country-to-city migrations and the rise of enormous marginalized districts and inner-city poverty belts? Doesn't all of this show that we are already leaving behind feudalism and jumping on the train to modernity?

Revolutionary conditions in Latin America are so objective that every revolution has experienced a distancing of the masses from the vanguard. To say nothing of Cuba: two million Cuban exiles are the result of three and a half decades of a revolution that forbids its inhabitants to leave. What would happen if they were allowed to leave? We got a glimpse of this in August 1994, when Castro's government, challenging the United States' open-arms policy with respect to Cuba's "boat people," began to relax the prohibition. Tens of thousands of people took to the sea in anything that would float, more willing to confront the selachians in the Caribbean than follow the vanguard dictates in Havana.

Was the Sandinista vanguard more successful in enlightening the masses about the virtues of the revolution? Not much, judging by its electoral defeat in February 1990 by an older lady who had a leg cast and walked with the aid of a cane, in addition to her having no access whatsoever to any means of communication. Perhaps the FMLN in El Salvador had more success opening the people's eyes? It doesn't look like it, judging by the elusiveness of the popular support for this party during the last elections, when the FMLN even changed its name hoping for better luck. It didn't even prevent ARENA (the National Republican Alliance) from winning—the party that the FMLN has opposed for so many years and whose old ties to the death squadrons made it the perfect enemy—or from Armando Calderón Sol replacing FMLN sympathizer Alfredo Cristiani as head of El Salvador's government. Were the vanguards of the Shining Path and the Tupac Amaru Revolutionary Movement in Peru better able to accomplish their objectives? They were, insofar as the dictatorship (that was established relatively easily in Peru in 1992 thanks to the discredit the other institutions suffered due to many years of conflict) has been backed—at least for a while—by the majority of the population. Maybe it's unfair to focus on the Shining Path. Why don't we talk about the Peruvian Communist Party, which since 1979 has participated in Peru's democratic process? This party has done such a good job of enlightening the masses that it has been unable to meet the 5% of the vote minimum needed in order to continue legally existing as a party. In Chile, the Manuel Rodríguez Patriotic Front was so successful in convincing the masses that the time had come that the dictator Augusto Pinochet received more than 40% of the votes after sixteen years in government; his principal contender, the Christian Democracy, an antirevolutionary party if ever there was one, got even more. The Chilean Socialist Party, a bit skeptical of its own ability in advancing the course of history, has been content to stay within the capitalist stage of development and leave the future of socialism to other generations since it has been co-governing with the Christian Democracy for some years now.

Will this information help enlighten the idiot? Not much. The masses are alienated by capitalism. They don't know what to do. The vanguard should continue its path. Another significant characteristic of the revolutionary is, of course, his refusal to read reality, his perseverance in magical analysis—which he calls scientific—about what is happening around him. He tries to fit the whole wide world into the narrow apertures of a few laws that even he doesn't respect since in order to apply them to Latin America he has had to twist them considerably. The idiot believes—at least says he believes—that, unlike fruit, conditions don't need to ripen. He's right. Revolutions should be carried out before the conditions are ripe because they, in fact, never will ripen: they're already a rotten piece of fruit.

The Andes should be turned into Latin America's Sierra Maestra.

What's idiotic is not so much insisting that Latin American policy should be *Cubanized* but believing that this 1960s rhetoric has died south of the Rio Grande. In several Andean countries there are still active guerrilla movements, filling those societies with blood and fear. And in almost every country, including those like Venezuela or Bolivia that have no Marxist terrorist groups, there is still a deep-rooted culture of political violence and a true Castroist sentiment that wants to see the revolutionary floods unleashed on the majestic Andean countryside, from the Antilles to the Antarctic. Even those countries which have renounced violence continue to cling to revolutionary ideas because they do not perceive it as a mechanism but rather as an entire map for society, or more exactly, for power. No leftist leader's little revolutionary heart has stopped beating, and this is obvious every time some new issue obliges the politicians of the various countries to take a stand.

The Andean idiot draws inspiration from the Antilles despite—if we take into account the stereotypes—there not being anything further from the tropical joviality than Andean melancholy. No big deal; we can unite the tropical atmosphere and the highland isolation because what is important is exporting the revolution. Why go to Cuba for revolutionary inspiration when the Andean world, older than the island, with a richer pre-Hispanic past and a postcolonial history almost two centuries old, has more than enough authority to make its own original contribution to the revolutionary cause? For one simple reason: because the Cuban revolution succeeded and continues to exist. It doesn't matter that it's wounded and suffering, that its fabric is a tangle of frayed edges; after all is said and done the label that hangs on the collar still says "Cuban revolution," just like it did in 1959. For the Peruvians, Colombians, and Venezuelans unable to lay their bourgeoisie governments to rest, it's natural for the Sierra Maestra to continue to be their point of reference. It's a source of emotional and political survival, the only trophy, albeit dented as it is, that they can show after decades of trying to be something more than a handful of impoverished *desperados* scattered throughout the national geography (in Venezuela's case these bandits have been missing since the time of Rómulo Betancourt and his Ministry of the Interior, Carlos Andrés Pérez, in the 1960s). But there's one little problem: the Sierra Maestra doesn't have the least bit of interest in emigrating to the Andes. Fidel Castro is only obsessed with shackling himself to Latin America's democratic presidents, for example at the Latin American Summits or for inaugurations. And when he doesn't make it onto the guest list, as happened at the Summit of the Americas in Miami 1994, he throws a tantrum. His ministers travel all over Latin America, not to encourage the highland revolutionaries and change the world but to go begging for commercial trade agreements from Latin American countries whose poverty the Cuban officials are the first to expose, a typical strategy of comparative exoneration each time they need to conceal their own defects. The Sierra Maestra is so forgotten that Fidel Castro has—say it isn't so!—changed his military olive green for the tropical *guayabera* shirt. Could there be a clearer illustration of Castro snubbing the Andes than his wearing a *guayabera* at the summit meeting of the heads of state? Could there have been a more resounding slap in the face of the revolutionaries, in the icy heights of the cordillera, than this tropical burn? Given Castro's obvious betrayal to internationalist principles and his timid position that everyone must choose his own path, the conclusion is simple: the love for the Cuban revolution is an unrequited love.

The Sierra Maestra, in the southeastern part of Cuba, was a mere accident of geography, far from the mythological scenario where those bearded men besieged Fulgencio Batista's regime until they ran him out of the country. The historical as well as the mythological significance of the Sierra Maestra (with the Cuban fiasco as proof) is being reduced to a geographical one where only in the glory-day fantasies of our contemporary revolutionaries does it still hold a place of importance. It's not fair to blame only our revolutionaries that this out-dated mythology continues to pervade factions of Latin American idiots. There's no doubt that Che Guevara's efforts to create "two, three, one hundred Vietnams" powerfully contributed to its continuation, despite the fact that his foray in the rugged Bolivian landscape ended in failure when he discovered that he had much less in common with the indigenous *campesinos,* whose priorities and customs were far from his violent form of guerrilla warfare. Havana's dialogues in favor of an international and a Latin American revolution were wearing thin as it betrayed a few of these folks here and there—depending on its tactical priorities of the time—and some of the ones betrayed included those it trained and armed. But we mustn't forget that it was an incessant and powerful dialogue that, and this is the most important point, was backed by the glamour of a revolution that seemed to be living proof that universal subversion was possible. What happened is that our revolutionaries, after years and years of failed attempts to take over power in the Andes, were left somewhat behind. If they saw Fidel wobbling around like an old man with rheumatism or like an Egyptian mummy escaped from a sarcophagus, descending the steps of his plane that takes him to bourgeoisie paradises (which today are his jet's only destinations), maybe Sierra Maestra would evaporate from their heads. But they haven't seen it. In general, they don't see much of anything.

The revolutionary still believes in Latin America as a single unit. In this regard, at least, he is a benign idiot. The only thing that remains salvageable from his revolutionary rhetoric is the transnational aspirations and his contempt for borders. This call for integration isn't bad, bearing in mind that the Andes, despite the time that has passed, continue to be a world where there are still terrifying border disputes, such as the recent conflict between Ecuador and Peru, or the one that every so often threatens to erupt between Colombia and Venezuela. It's interesting that an internationalist spirit still thrives (regardless of how convoluted it may be) in a region where the project for integration—the Andean Pact, whose treaty was signed in 1959—is making the slowest and most awkwardly moving progress of all of the Western Hemisphere's agreements, far behind the North American Free Trade Agreement or even South America's Mercosur. But this internationalism is skewed toward weapons and violence, when what is important in today's world are information networks and multinationals that manufacture their products everywhere and sell them all over the world, so it's now impossible to know where the goods being sold come from. Instead of yelling "Let's make the Andes Latin America's Internet," the idiot yells "Let's make the Andes Latin America's Sierra Maestra." Maybe they have something in common. Maybe the fate of our revolutionaries is to remain forever confined to the Internet as a type of computer game for children, a world of technological fiction where it would be possible to export images of revolutions and where the Sierra Maestra would again have some significance, although this form is less revolutionary than it was fifty or sixty years ago. If our revolutionaries succeed in logging themselves onto the Net from some Andean telephone jack, they will be able to live out their dreams in those computer monitors and no one will be able to accuse them, in their continental aspirations, of living in the past. Fidel Castro would undoubtedly have dropped his chin whiskers if, thirty years ago, he'd have known that the fate of the Sierra Maestra would be transformed into a bunch of action figures on a CD-ROM.

Violence is history's great midwife.

The idiot is metaphorical. He loves images, comparisons, hyperboles. He embellishes each of his political strokes of genius in order to give them a little more credibility. It's interesting to note that the enemies of democracy, from politicians to commentators, are in general much more bombastic in their rhetoric and language than those boring supporters of democracy, all of whom belong to the "Logic League." Many more grandiloquent and exciting formulas have been invented to set forth their totalitarian or semitotalitarian theses than for those explaining the absence of great ideological reformations, which generally implies a bid for democracy. Thus Latin American democracies have appeared very inept in dealing with the left. As a result, only right-wing authoritarians such as Roberto D'Aubuisson Sr. in El Salvador have been capable of fiercely confronting leftist rhetoric. Latin America's democracies have not known how to create an exciting, colorful, and crusade-like discourse, despite there being sufficient need for it in a democratic cause. One of its greatest challenges has been to convince the people to have faith in the system, even when they may have been greatly deceived by certain governments elected within the democratic framework.

Yes, the idiot does speak beautifully. Generally, though, his speech is superficial since his ideas are few and not very sophisticated, a simple handful of ideologically stereotyped mandates, which with a certain linguistic embellishment appear to create magic. Let's not forget how Marx, in his *Communist Manifesto,* utilized explosive images to accompany his prophecies and how the first Soviet revolutionaries, like Lenin and Trotsky, were consummate devotees of hyperbole. Our idiot has adopted this grandiloquent tradition, only in that, as in the case of Marx's notion of violence as history's midwife, he generally doesn't show much originality; he simply imitates old revolutionary adages.

For the revolutionary, history comes out from between the legs of its mother, pulled through by a midwife called "violence." It doesn't matter that this history is born without legs, is blind in one eye, or hunchbacked, breathing or not. What matters is who brought it into the world. What is actually born is of lesser importance. Many times revolutionary violence makes history. But that history is of cruelty and failures, not of humanity and success. The violence in El Salvador throughout the 1980s has certainly been historical. Those 75,000 deaths, though, caused by the FMLN and the dirty war of the death squads inspired by leaders like D'Aubuisson Sr., constitute neither glorious history nor fruitful sacrifice. The FMLN gave birth to a senseless trail of blood when its members didn't achieve power (or even electoral respectability in the March 1994 elections) and has now become part of the mediocre bourgeoisie machine. In Guatemala, the URNG certainly made history when it caused 100,000 deaths in more than thirty years of war. This, however, is not the history that they would like to have written, as isolated and semi-destroyed as they are, approaching a time of peace that will finally put them not in power but in bourgeoisie society. Did the savage Abimael Guzmán ever think, after subjecting the American continent to the bloodiest and most efficient Maoist mobilization of the 1980s and the beginning of the 1990s, that the history that was born from between his legs would be of his own capture and surrender, outfitted in a straightjacket, writing letters of remorse to a shogun disciple like Fujimori? So much for the midwife who delivered revolutionary history.

A new society will create a new kind of man.

Anyone who possesses a little decency, or who isn't a scoundrel, can't deny that the new man proposed by Che Guevara does indeed exist. Of course he exists. He's a Cuban with optical neurosis and an emaciated catlike body, floating on a drifting raft. He's a Peruvian who, after Alan García's vitamin injections of socialism, sees himself shrink two inches. He's a Mexican with his back wet from the Rio Grande, so patriotically running to Texas in pursuit of the land that the *gringos* snatched away from Mexico in the middle of the 1800s (after a brief period of independence, which is now impossible to separate from that beautiful film starring Clark Gable and Ava Gardner). Latin America's revolution and socialism have produced a new man. The idiot is right. The revolution is a laboratory of original specimens. No Latin American regime has succeeded in creating such a creature.

The revolution has an unmistakable Adam-like purpose. Its recruits believe that it is possible to stop history and make it start over again. If it can begin again, why not create a new kind of human being? What they forgot to tell us is whether this different and original human would be better or worse than the previous one. Would he burn more or less calories, have a longer or shorter life expectancy, have more or less job opportunities, be better or worse off?

The new society has interesting characteristics. At the moment, it's a deicide; it wants to do away with its creator. Not one revolution—whether successful or failed in its intent to seize power—has been embraced by the new man it has created. It's also a fervent worshipper of the almighty dollar. Not one revolution has ended its desperate search for dollars because it is unable to survive economically and is therefore condemned to a life of dependency and vulnerability. The new society is also a fugitive society; everyone wants to escape. They escape however and to wherever possible, as was seen when those 30,000 Cuban boat people preferred to cram themselves into the Guantánamo Naval Base, living in animal-like conditions, instead of remaining in Cuba after Bill Clinton and Janet Reno closed the doors to the U.S. Mecca. This is another characteristic of the new man; he is rabidly pro-Yankee. The Sandinistas spent years bellowing against the American embargo, imploring the enemy to do business with them— in other words to stop ignoring them as an economic intermediary. Fidel Castro is afflicted with that type of USA-mania that Rodó talks about in *Ariel:* all he wants is money from the United States. The new society is also a drug addict; it loves the cocaine business, whether in Castro's tolerant Cuban airports as Partner-to-the-Medellín-Cartel or in the thicket of the upper Huallaga river in Peru. The new man is every mother-in-law's dream: sickly, pro-Yankee, deicidal, a fugitive, and a drug addict.

It just so happens that the idiot is also solemn. He has no sense of humor. The revolution is one of the most serious achievements in Latin America's postcolonial history. He doesn't laugh or smile. The revolutionary (and his traveling companions) take themselves very seriously and shun even the slightest gesture of joviality, as if it were a sign of weakness that the enemy would take advantage of to defeat them.

Despite the characteristics that the revolution has attributed to the new man, the specimen raised by the revolution is essentially no different from any other. The forces that drive him are the same: freedom and progress. The revolution has destroyed societies and taken away their life's dreams, subjecting them to nihilism, but it hasn't succeeded in changing human nature. The new man who emigrates and establishes himself in another society begins to function within that society, despite having little experience and having been brainwashed by propaganda. He has the same chance as anyone else who tries to earn a living—by working—within a society that gives the individual some degree of sovereignty over himself. A new society which is suddenly stripped of its revolutionary leadership would not necessarily organize itself on a foundation of liberty and democracy. The absence of a libertarian culture would probably cause a new form of authoritarianism to resurrect itself. But if this same man is transported to a freer environment, as is invariably seen in all Latin American migrations, he's able to adapt immediately to the new system since what he essentially requires is to satisfy certain physical as well as spiritual needs that are no different from those of other humans. What the new man has lost by living outside a democratic culture he has retained in human nature.

In armed conflicts, everything that opposes the revolution should be considered a military target.

The idiot has bureaucratic complexes. This can be seen in his speech, weighed down with terms such as "process" and euphemisms that attempt to conceal the most menacing decisions and policies with the most normal and even the most neutral forms of discourse. So, when someone is killed, a "military objective" has been carried out. When a mayor of some poverty-stricken town in the Peruvian hilly countryside has his throat cut, as was systematically done by the Shining Path ever since it began its bloody crusade against the Peruvians in 1980, this is a "just execution." A curious observation: the revolutionary's metaphorical speech parallels the most tedious, calculated, *officialese* that exists, which should not be surprising since the armed struggles of these semiwarlike organizations greatly resemble those of the enemy that the revolutionary is supposedly combating, the military. An eternal enemy of the soldier, the revolutionary is indebted to him for everything in his revolutionary terminology. The Latin American idiot has learned from the military how to confine the borders of human existence to a chessboard, the most monotonous geometry of identical squares, a faithful likeness of a rigid and repetitive mentality, where life is limited to a handful of simple formulas.

The *campesino* whose cows they steal, the relative of a murdered policeman,

the businessman whose factory is left without electricity after the power trans-
mission pylon has been blown up, the daughter of the "justly executed" mayor
have no right to get angry about their own personal tragedies. If, after losing
some relatives or seeing their businesses ruined, they feel the slightest moral
perturbation about the virtuous revolutionary cause that annihilated their loved
ones or the product of years of work, there is no doubt that the revolutionary
should cut their heads off. The revolution demands masochism. You must enjoy
tragedy, and the more personal it is, the more exhilarating it is. You have to drink
champagne—or whatever is on hand—each time you slice a child's throat, and
fill the sky with fireworks each time you steal someone's livestock. In revolutions,
gratification is mandatory, happiness is a decree. To express reservations about
revolutionary policies—or revolutionary actions, if power has yet to be taken—
you are committing an offense of *lese-revolution*, the most serious of crimes. The
extreme action in armed struggles foreshadows what is to come once power has
been acquired: the obliteration of all forms of discontent with the revolution.
The revolution advocates a society of acquiescent men. The idiot fills his lungs,
and his throat hurls the most philosophical revolutionary sentence: Long live the
zombies! This, of course, has a dark side: violence. Peru, for example, has witnessed how the armed conflict declared by the Shining Path revolutionaries in
1980, with the blessings of European and American idiots (the species, as you
see, is transatlantic), already totals 30,000 deaths. Not all of this is the work of
the Shining Path. Much of it is the result of counterrebellions, the threat that
follows every uprising like a shadow. There is also material destruction, that
other form of death for a society. For example, in Peru this damage has totaled
some $30 billion over fifteen years, a figure considerably higher than the coun-
try's foreign debt and all foreign investments made in Peru since 1980. The revolutionary's glory would be to reduce the entire country to a pile of ashes. This
would allow him to begin anew, to play the role of Adam, which his ideology so
demands from him.

This is how the idiot expresses his deep social resentments, his ancestral and
familial frustrations, his racial rancor, and other types of frustration that dictate
his conduct when he preaches his politics. The revolution is, for a good number
of Latin American idiots, an expression of revenge (although it's not always clear
against what or whom). It's the perfect way to channel all the psychological
forces from the circumstances confronting his immediate surroundings. These
circumstances and surroundings can be a declining middle class, an intellectual
class with little opportunity to succeed, a group of parasites living off some subsidy, the borderline between the life of a *campesino* and a provincial city dweller,
a proletariat with aspirations of rising to the next level, or a university. Destroying, killing, and injuring are all ways of feeling alive and fulfilling oneself. There

are of course times when the idiot daydreams and even becomes excited. Some
of the idiots are even caring people. But the majority are probably individuals
tormented by deep envy that gives them free rein to defend the *tabula rasa.*

Let's create two, three . . . one hundred Vietnams.

Poor Che Guevara didn't suspect how ironic this sentence would sound in the
1990s. To transform Latin America into a Vietnam would mean to rapidly convert to capitalism. That is what Hanoi finally had to do in 1994 to lift the U.S.
trade embargo. Under a dictatorship that is progressively becoming less communist and more military, the regime has opened the country's floodgates to
Western capitalism. The devastation done by Coca-Cola is much more significant than that caused previously by the Vietcong communist insurrection supported by North Vietnam's army. No one made Vietnam carry out these policies.
Ever since 1973, when the United States accepted its cease-fire and Saigon
began to fall (its collapse happened a couple of years later), Vietnam has been
free to do as it wishes, without any foreign pressure except from its communist
neighbor, China. Moreover, Vietnam is itself the one that has taken other countries hostage, as displayed in its takeover of Cambodia. This invasion had the
virtue of ending the Pol Pot regime, but it certainly wasn't perpetrated in the
name of peace, civilization, and democracy. Propelled by the present and its own
failures, Vietnam is sailing all by itself toward capitalism (following the trend of
a Lee Kuang Yew authoritarian-style capitalism). No one else but the selfsame
Communist Party that led the government back in the days when the Latin
American idiots ceaselessly chanted "let's create two, three, one hundred Vietnam" is taking the country in this direction. This means one of two things: either
the idiot's subconscious concealed his closet capitalist tendency or the idiot was
supinely unable to anticipate the future, convinced that the success of socialism
would make this a universal reality, even in Latin America.

This "Vietnam slogan" has been, in fact, just another anti-Yankee sentiment.
But Vietnam, some decades later, has proved Washington right and removed Ho
Chi Minh's heirs. Few exclamations such as the one that introduces this chapter express Latin American's great failure so well. Many idiots couldn't even
locate Southeast Asia on a map, but the anti-American obsession turned Hanoi
into the Mecca of our Latin American aspirations. A severe punishment, a historical humiliation had to be inflicted, it didn't matter how, on our neighbor to
the north in order to avenge . . . what? Its military interventions, which lasted
for many years, in Nicaragua, the Dominican Republic, Guatemala, Mexico,
Haiti, Honduras, Cuba, and, indirectly, El Salvador, right? No. Rather, its success and status as the leading world power.

7

CUBA: AN OLD LOVE IS NEITHER FORGOTTEN NOR ABANDONED

"Only those who can swim will save themselves."
—spoken by Cataneo, a vocalist in the Trío Taicuba,
on the morning of January 8, 1959, when Fidel Castro arrived in Havana;
since then Cataneo has been known as "El Profeta" (The Prophet)

The Latin American idiot has had his most intimate and longest-lasting love affair with the Cuban revolution. It's an old love that has been neither forgotten nor abandoned. A historical and profound love that began long ago, in 1959, to be exact, when a deluge of bearded men, with Fidel Castro riding its crest, descended on Havana from the Cuban mountains.

That spectacle had a great impressional impact. They were the first beards and long tresses seen in the twentieth century; the Beatles and the hippies came later. It was also the first time that a revolution had overturned a dictatorial regime without any military backing. Until that time there prevailed the belief that revolutions were always possible with the help of the military, sometimes without, but never against the military. Fidel Castro showed that that assertion was false.

Nevertheless, we must start by pointing out that 99% of Latin Americans, including even the Cubans, were a bit ignorant in their judgment of the historical process that loomed over the island, which began on January 1, 1959. Who, back then, was not a Castro supporter? How could you not sympathize with that jubilant group of fighters who were going to bring justice and progress to José Martí's country? How could one not quiver with excitement on seeing the boys who had succeeded in toppling a military dictator backed by his army and Washington?

But from that simple act, evenly tinged with good intentions and imprudence, there immediately began to appear innumerable falsehoods that would later evolve into clichés, methodically disseminated by the Latin American idiot just so he would have an alibi for encouraging and justifying his adherence to a clearly unacceptable dictatorship. It's worth examining individually the fallacies that were most often repeated throughout these exhausting years of "shame and idiocy" (as Borges later said about the first Perón era, it being another fast-moving Latin American delusion). So, let's begin dismantling this arduous rhetorical structure.

Before the revolution, Cuba was a backward and corrupt country, which Castroism saved from its misery. It was the poverty and social inequality of the Cuban people that instigated the revolution.

There is no doubt that politically the Cubans suffered from that corrupt dictatorship, repudiated by most of the population. After almost twelve years of democratic governments based on the Constitution of 1940, on March 10, 1952, General Fulgencio Batista staged a military coup and overthrew the legitimate president, Carlos Prío Socarrás, fairly elected in the ballot boxes.

The government emerging from that criminal act, overwhelmingly rejected by the Cubans, lasted, as everyone knows, seven years, until the wee hours of January 1, 1959. The revolution that overthrew Batista wasn't supposed to establish a communist regime, but rather return to the country the liberties that were violated seven years earlier. This was in every organization's documents and manifestos—including Castro's—that contributed to ending the dictatorship. Except for the almost insignificant Communist Party—called the People's Socialist Party in Cuba—every political group proposed to restore democracy, as defined by the conventional terms of the West.

What is certain is that in the 1950s Cuba's situation was, economically speaking, much more promising than that of most Latin American countries. Between 1902 and 1928, and later between 1940 and 1958, the country had enjoyed long periods of economic expansion and was ranked along with Argentina, Chile, Uruguay, and Puerto Rico as one of the most developed countries in Latin America. Ginsburg's *Atlas of World Economics,* published at the end of the

1950s, ranked Cuba twenty-second among the 122 nations studied. According to economist H. T. Oshima of Stanford University, Cuba's per capita income in 1953 was similar to Italy's, even though individual opportunities appeared to be much more rewarding on the Caribbean island than on the European peninsula. How to prove this? A clear example: in 1959, when the revolution broke out, there were some 12,000 applications at the Cuban embassy in Rome from Italians desiring to go to Cuba. We don't know, however, of any Cubans who wanted to make the opposite trip. This information should really be taken seriously since there's no better way to measure the level of hope or belief for success in a society than through migration. If 12,000 Italian workers and farmers wanted to go to Cuba and settle on the island—just as thousands of Spain's Asturians, Galicians, and Canary Island inhabitants wanted to do—it was because this country that they selected as their destination had very high development opportunities. Today, on the other hand, there are millions of Cubans who would like to move to Italy, permanently.

Socially speaking, the picture was also positive. Eighty percent of the population was literate—an incredibly high percentage for that time—and the health indexes were those of a developed nation. In 1953—according to Ginsburg's *Atlas*—countries such as Holland, France, the United Kingdom, and Finland had proportionately fewer doctors and dentists than Cuba, circumstances that to a great extent explain the high longevity of Cubans at that time and the very low average of infant deaths at birth and the first month of life.

One final and disturbing piece of information, which alone is capable of explaining many things: based on 1994 prices and values, Cubans had a per capita import capacity that was 66% higher in 1958 than it is today. This, in a country with an open economy that now imports 50% of all the food it consumes, either shows the infinite ineptitude of Castro's regime in producing goods and services or the great dynamism of the pre-Castro Cuban society.

Cuba was the Caribbean brothel, especially for Americans. The island was controlled by Chicago and Las Vegas gangsters.

Cuba was not a den of iniquity. That's false. There were dozens of casinos in Havana, in which there was certainly the uncomfortable presence of the American Mafia. But that was of minimum significance to the Cuban society, which could have easily eradicated it, as had been done, for example, by the neighboring island of Puerto Rico. True, there were gangsters present (in fewer numbers than usually portrayed) because this business isn't one that tends to attract Dominican priests. But all that was needed was some legal action from a decent government to send them running.

Prostitution was another myth. The country had an incredibly low level of venereal disease, a statistic that shows that Cuba wasn't anyone's whorehouse. However, Havana being a large city and an old active seaport, it had a red-light district similar to those that can be found in Barcelona or Naples. American tourism tended to be of a family type, while prostitution was practiced essentially by and for Cubans, as in most medium or large Latin American cities.

Curiously, as news correspondents and travelers have recited over and over again, today is when Cuba has become a great brothel for foreigners who participate, as in Thailand, in sexual tourism, taking advantage of the country's never-ending economic poverty. This is easy to correct. Before the revolution, the Cuban peso and the dollar were equivalent in value and freely interchangeable, which didn't necessitate having the prostitutes favor the foreign customer, an issue that should calm those who harbor some expression of genital nationalism. If during some time in its tragic history Cuba has been a bordello for foreigners, that fateful circumstance must be chalked up to Castroism. Previously, it simply wasn't the case.

Despite all the inconveniences, the revolution has given Cubans a special sense of personal dignity.

It's hard to believe that Cubans today enjoy a higher degree of personal dignity. It's difficult to think that those who in their own country can't enter hotels or cabarets unless they can pay in dollar can feel dignified and proud of their government. It's also strange that a person who isn't allowed to read the books he wants, defend the ideas that he believes, or simply voice what he's thinking possesses any level of dignity. If dignity is defined as that feeling of rewarding inner peace that one enjoys when he's living in accordance with his own ideals, it's probable that in the Americas there isn't anyone more without dignity than those poor Cubans, obliged by their government to repeat slogans they don't believe, applaud leaders they detest, earn salaries in a worthless currency, and live day after day what on the island is called a *dual morality*, or a *yagruma moral* (the yagruma being a plant noted for producing leaves that have two completely different faces).

The revolution was necessary because the United States controlled the country's economy.

Strictly speaking, this is another myth, one deeply rooted in the Latin American idiot's conscience. The presence of U.S. capital on the island was confined to the sugar and mining industries, communications, and finance, and in all of these areas the trend was toward greater control by domestic businessmen during those last decades. In 1935, of the 161 sugar factories only 50 belonged to Cubans. In 1958, 121 were already controlled by them. That same year barely 14% of the capital (with signs of gradual reduction) was in American hands. In 1939, Cuban banks only managed 23% of the private deposits. In 1958, this had increased to 61%.

What characterized the Cuban economy, contrary to what the unrelenting Latin American idiot says, was that Cuban businessmen were very competent and energetic, something that had been very easily proven when they went into exile. Interestingly, the 40,000 companies created by Cubans in the United States today have a value several times greater than the sum of all U.S. investments made in Cuba before 1959. And one single company, Bacardi, paid the Puerto Rican government more in taxes in 1994 than the entire value of the Cuban nickel production at international prices for that same year ($150 million).

The United States is to blame for the revolution choosing the road to communism and Moscow's support because from the very beginning it opposed Castro.

In this case, the Latin American idiot is only slightly incorrect. What's true is that the United States distanced itself from Batista several months before his fall, declared an embargo on the sale of arms, and asked the dictator to find a political solution to the civil war that was tearing the country apart.

It's also likely that Batista's decision to hastily escape to the Dominican Republic on the night of December 31, 1958, was due to his perception that "the Americans had switched horses." In any case, what is for sure is that in 1959 the United States sent Ambassador Philip Bonsal to Havana with the express purpose of establishing the best relations possible with the new revolutionary government.

It couldn't be done. And it couldn't be done because, as Fidel Castro clearly explained many years later in front of Spain's television cameras, since his student days he was an avowed Marxist-Leninist. If he didn't mention it during the armed struggle, it was because he didn't want to frighten the Cubans. Castro, in a nutshell, deliberately wanted to ally himself with Moscow and from the beginning wanted to establish communism in Cuba (Tad Szulc describes it very well in his book *Fidel Castro: A Critical Portrait*). The *gringos* reacted to Castro's communism; they didn't cause it. That is the historical truth.

But if you don't want to accept Castro's own testimony, then you have to at least recognize what is happening in our time: the Communist Bloc in Europe no longer exists, there certainly isn't a military threat to Cuba by the United

States, and Castro stubbornly continues to repeat again and again the slogan "socialism or death," refusing to change the foundation of his system. Clearly, if there has ever been a confirmed communist to the death, this gentleman is Fidel Castro. How can anyone still say that in 1959 the United States pushed Castro into communism, if today the entire world, with Marxism no longer being even a viable option, cannot *push him* out of communism?

The U.S. blockade against Cuba is a crime that explains the economic disasters of the regime and the poverty of the Cuban people.

First of all, there is no blockade. Yes, the United States prohibits its companies from doing business with Cuba and American citizens from spending their dollars on the island. In political jargon this prohibition is called an "embargo," and it originated when Cuba confiscated American property at the beginning of the 1960s. At that time, property was confiscated without compensation and the American government reacted, first by renouncing the purchase of Cuban sugar and later by forbidding its companies to do business there. Later, other less significant restrictions were added, like refusing to allow any boat that had been docked at a Cuban port to anchor at a U.S. port for six months.

However, the accursed *embargo*—that prohibition against buying from or selling to the Cuban government—has a very limited effect. Anyone who has visited a *diplotienda*—an establishment in Cuba where purchases are made in dollars—can prove that there is no lack of American products, from Coca-Cola to IBMs, because it's very easy for exporters in Canada, Panama, or Venezuela to buy this merchandise locally and then export it to Cuba. However, there is virtually no product that Cuba needs that it can't buy from Japan, Europe, Korea, China, or Latin America. And any good quality and good priced Cuban product—sugar, nickel, shrimp, or other trifling things—can find an overseas market. The problem is simply that Cuba produces very little because its government is extremely inefficient and therefore the country lacks products to sell or foreign currency to buy them.

It's also not true that U.S. pressure has prevented Cuba from having access to credit in order to do business with other nations. If Cuba owes Western countries $10 billion, it's because at some time it was given credit. Argentina and Spain, for example, extended more than one billion dollars worth of credit to Cuba, which they have not been able to recover. France and Japan lost another good sum of money in the effort.

In short, Cuba hasn't paid its foreign debt since 1986 (three years before the Soviet Bloc disappeared, when it was still receiving an enormous subsidy of more than $5 billion a year). Obviously, if the island doesn't have any resources, insists on a legendarily fruitless production system, doesn't pay its debts, and accuses the moneylenders of extortion, all the while trying to coordinate debtors so that none of them fulfills his obligations—an undertaking that Castro dedicated a lot of time and resources to in the 1980s—it's natural that new credits or loans are not being extended to Cuba.

The U.S. embargo is responsible for Castro not changing his way of governing. If the United States maintains relations with Vietnam, why continue the embargo against Cuba?

Naturally, the embargo contained a political dimension in the U.S. response to Cuba's confiscations in the 1960s. In the middle of the Cold War, Cuba became a base for Soviet aircraft carriers anchored ninety miles from the United States, sponsored every subversive organization on the planet, and sent its military forces to African wars. It was to be expected that the United States would respond with some hostile measures or try to increase the cost to the Soviets for maintaining such a useful and dangerous peon in the heart of the Americas.

This phase has passed (something that Castro still laments), but the embargo remains in place. Why? The embargo has not been removed because the Cuban- American community (two million people if we include exiles and their descendants) doesn't it want it to be lifted, and neither the Democrats nor the Republicans are, as of yet, ready to sacrifice the Cuban-American vote. The Cuban problem has stopped being a U.S. foreign policy conflict and now become a domestic situation, something similar to what happened with Israel and the Jewish-American population. The embargo is simply a policy *that is*. It has existed since the time of Eisenhower and Kennedy, and leaders in the White House and at the Capitol view modifying that strategy riskier than keeping it.

However, even though the Latin American idiot may not want to admit it, Castro himself has the ability to lift the embargo. The 1992 Torricelli Bill, which regulates these sanctions, leaves the door open to a progressive dismantling of the embargo in exchange for measures leading toward economic liberalization and political openness. If Castro yielded to democracy, as South Africa did, the embargo would be over.

If there is hunger in Cuba it's essentially due to U.S. pressures.

Before 1959, according to the aforementioned book by Ginsburg, the caloric intake in Cuba exceeded by 10% the minimum limits indicated by the Food and

Agriculture Organization (FAO): 2,500 calories a day per person. That's to be expected. Cuba has good land, 80% of its territory is cultivable, rain is abundant, and agricultural productivity had increased so much that, before the revolution, the number of Cubans working in industry, commerce, or services, when compared with the percentage that worked the land, was much higher than in Eastern Europe.

What's surprising is that, even with these natural conditions and an educated population, starvation in Cuba affects thousands of people, causing malnutrition and leaving people blind, disabled, or with permanent pain in their extremities. In addition to the inherent inefficiency of the communist system in producing goods and services, in Cuba's case one has to consider the fact that Castro's government could have allowed itself the luxury of being even more inefficient given the astounding chunk of Soviet subsidy, an amount so large that historian Irina Zorina, of the Russian Academy of Science, has quantified it at more than $100 billion. In other words, this subsidy was four times greater than what the Marshall Plan provided for all of Europe, and three times greater than the amount given by Washington to the Alliance for Progress for all of Latin America. And this monstrous sum was dumped on a society that consisted of 6.5 million inhabitants in 1959 and which thirty-three years later just barely totaled 11 million.

Naturally, when this subsidy disappeared in 1992, it caused a violent contraction of Cuba's economy. The island lost 50% of its production capacity and had to cease operations in 80% of its industries. Here, in this combination of the system's inefficiency and the end of the subsidy is where you'll find the economic bankruptcy of Castroism. To blame the U.S. embargo for that economic disaster is to be dishonest and ignorant of the proof that supports the more obvious reality.

The Cuban revolution could be accused of being inefficient or cruel, but it has solved two of Latin America's most pressing problems, education and public health, while transforming the island into an athletic powerhouse.

This verse, this *mantra,* is one of the most recited by the Latin American idiot. Let's analyze it.

There is no denying that the Cuban government has made a serious effort to increase education, health, and sports. In other words, it has made an effort to offer its society three services, of which at least two—education and health—are important. However, any educated person knows that services must be paid for with either one's own labor or someone else's. And since Cuba produced very little, these services were paid by someone else's labor, which came to the island in the form of a subsidy. Of course, once the colossal foreign assistance ended, both the schools and the hospitals became entirely unaffordable.

Today Cuba has schools with no books, no pencils, no paper, and where many times students and teachers can't even show up because of the lack of transportation. It has buildings on the brink of collapsing from lack of maintenance, and in them, by the way, a sectarian or dogmatic indoctrination is imparted, very far from anything that resembles a good education.

Even more could be said about the hospitals: empty eggshell-like edifices with no anesthesia, no sutures, and at times not even aspirin, where the sick have to bring their own sheets because the hospital either doesn't have sheets or doesn't have detergent with which to wash those it does have.

It's important for the Latin American idiot, this hardheaded being to whom with a certain affection this book is being addressed, to realize that what seems to be a revolutionary accomplishment is nothing more than an absurd and arbitrary allocation of resources. Cuba, for example, has one doctor for every 220 people. Denmark has one doctor for every 450. Does this mean that a Danish revolution must be incited in order to double the number of its doctors, or could it be that Cuba has irresponsibly spent hundreds of millions of dollars educating totally unnecessary doctors if a rational way of organizing hospital services were implemented?

Any government that haphazardly allocates its society's resources in a single direction can achieve a deceptive and incredibly limited accomplishment, but this will always be at the expense of other sectors that would necessarily be left on the fringes of the development efforts.

It's obvious that every healthy society must employ its resources proportionately in order to avoid terrible distortions. If Paraguay, for example, concentrated all of its efforts on becoming a space power, it's possible that by the end of fifteen years it would have succeeded in launching an elated gentleman from Asuncion into orbit. But in doing so it would have foolishly impoverished the rest of the nation. Some experts have given such feats—typical of the Cuban revolution—the name "Pharaohisms."

But if it's absurd to judge what happens in Cuba by its educational or public health system, it's even crazier to base that judgment on its "athletic power." It's true that Cuba wins more gold medals than France in the Olympics. But the only thing this reveals is that the poor Caribbean island uses its meager resources in the stupidest way anyone could think of. How much did it cost for Cuba's basketball team to defeat the Italians? How much money was used to give Castro the satisfaction that *his* athletes—like someone who owns a stable of horses—won the competitions? Let's go back to the same argument: all of a society's economic means should move at the same level so that its results have at least some coherence. The pride that one feels when athletes win is perfectly understandable, but when this is artificially promoted we are not witnessing a feat but a folly—an absolutely crazy allocation of resources.

One last and perhaps the most important reflection: "democratic" East Germany *won* more medals than the "federal" West Germany. Does this mean that the communist model surpassed the Western one? Of course not. It's outrageous to judge a political model or system on some arbitrarily selected category. Racists in South Africa justified their dictatorship alleging that blacks in their country were the best fed and best educated on the black continent. In Spain, Franco asked that his regime be judged according to certain favorable statistical data. Something similar to this is what the Latin American idiot is doing in relation to Cuba.

Say what you will, Cuba is better off than Haiti and other Third World communities.

Of course Cuba is "better off than Haiti" or Bangladesh, but Cuba should be compared to countries that had the same level of development and progress in the 1950s, such as Argentina, Uruguay, Chile, Puerto Rico, Costa Rica, or Spain. Thirty-six years after the start of the revolution, Cuba is infinitely worse off than any of these countries, and the reasonable thing to do is to judge the island by the group of countries it accompanied before commencing the revolution and not by the most backward country in the hemisphere.

An interesting comparison to make would be with Puerto Rico, given that Puerto Rico also received (and receives) billions of dollars in U.S. subsidies. But while the Russian subsidies contributed to creating a fatal dependency in Cuba, incredibly setting the country back in real terms, in Puerto Rico just the opposite happened. In 1995, Cuba, with 11 million inhabitants, exported $1.6 billion, while Puerto Rico, with only 3.5 million inhabitants, exported more than $20 billion. And while Cuba suffers from a sugar economy that today produces the same as it did 65 years ago, Puerto Rico has ceased being a sugar-dependent economy and become a highly industrialized society where more than 3,000 American companies with a high level of technological development have established themselves. In 1959, when the revolution began, both countries had approximately the same per capita income. Thirty-seven years later, the Puerto Ricans have ten times the per capita income of the Cubans.

Another similar country would be Costa Rica. When the Cuban revolution began, Cuba had a level of economic development quite a bit higher than that of Costa Rica, with a notably better social welfare index. Now, the Costa Ricans, without any revolutions, without any executions, without any exiles, have succeeded in educating their entire population, and their public health system covers practically the entire country; with only three million inhabitants they export 20% more than Cuba.

The Americans aren't leaving Castro any escape. They're the ones responsible for the Cuban government's decision not to change its political model.

It isn't the Americans who aren't leaving Castro an escape: it's Castro who doesn't want to leave the governmental palace. It's that old leader who isn't ready to accept the changes that would let his society choose other leaders or other governing models. The road to political change is quite simple: declare amnesty, allow the establishing of noncommunist political parties, and begin to lay down the rules of the game for a multiparty electoral contest. This is similar to what happened in Portugal, Spain, Hungary, Czechoslovakia, Poland, and some half dozen other countries that did away with dictatorships. Castro, however, would have to accept the possibility of losing power and becoming the opposition. If he doesn't want to take this route, it's not the Americans' fault but his own fondness for the throne. What is certain is that, for years, the most respected opposition both inside and outside the country has shown itself ready to participate in a peaceful change. It is Castro, not the United States, who is rejecting that change.

In the final analysis, Castro hasn't fallen because he is a charismatic leader who is loved by his people.

How many people inside Cuba support Castro and how many of them reject him is something that can only be determined when there are multiple options and Cubans can vote without fear.

However, it's reasonable to believe that the level of support for Castro is much lower than our Latin American idiot would like. Why would a hungry society love Castro when he pays them with worthless money, has forced them for fifteen years to fight in African wars, and today torments them with all manner of hardship? To think that the Cubans support a regime that generates this miserable lifestyle is to believe that the political attitude of these people is different from the rest of the planet.

If in the rest of the world inflation, high rates of unemployment, or shortages of certain basic products are enough to swing electoral support from the ruling party to the opposition, then to assume that the Cubans support their government, despite living a type of daily hell, is to claim—and we insist—that the human beings born on that island behave differently than the rest of humanity they belong to.

On the other hand, the spectacle (in 1980) of 10,000 people crowded into an embassy to leave Cuba, or the 30,000 rafts hurled into the sea in August 1994, are signs that speak sufficiently well for themselves to show Latin American idiots that the people inherently reject the government that they endure. It couldn't be any other way after four decades of insanity, oppression, and dictatorship.

8

RIFLES AND CASSOCKS

Liberation theology focuses on the conflicts of the economic, social, and political processes that pit the oppressed people against the oppressive class. When the Church rejects class warfare, it becomes part of the dominating system.

This quasi-bellicose declaration is so blunt that it disarms you. The Church as a soldier of class struggle? The earthly representatives of the universal God taking one side over the other? God's agents of peace howling in favor of war? Who are these strange ministers of Marx? They are the successors of a movement that surfaced after a bishops' meeting in Rome—the famous Second Vatican Council—where they had the very decorous mission of modernizing the Church and bringing back a certain unity to Christianity, shattered some thousand years ago. If poor John XXIII and Paul VI had known what was going to emerge from that ecclesiastic Babel with the passing of time and a little twisting of the matter, they surely would have become devout Hare Krishnas. Some bishops and theologians became overly excited about the marvelous idea that the Church should be devoted to service and not to power—what is called a "sign of the times" theology, an *engagé* Church—and believed that the time had come to embrace a cassock-clad socialism. Several orders heard the call, but among them there immediately stood out the Jesuits, the order founded by the judicious soldier from Spain's Basque province of Guipuzcoa, who in 1521, after being wounded in battle, decided that the priesthood was a more sensible calling than the military. During the time of the Second Council the order began to be dominated by progressives, inspired by the theologian Karl Rahner, who had become a kind of "star" at that gathering and who through his disciple, Johannes Baptist Metz, taught that theology could not be separated from politics.

So far, great! The emissaries of Christ want to descend from heaven to earth, stick their noses into Man's mire, and give a helping hand in this world where many of the destitute can die of hunger while waiting for salvation. It's silly to refute liberation theology with the argument that religion shouldn't mix with politics. Religion has every right to become involved in politics, as does any individual, organization, or institution. No one can be denied the right to add to the headache of how to organize a decent society. Even though just the thought of mixing spiritual life with the political conjures up shadows of inquisitorial obscurantism and sectarian governments, we wouldn't be able to deny, without exceeding the necessary level of idiocy, that a priest has the same right as any layman to believe that a certain way of organizing society is more beneficial than another and to promote it through sermons and education.

The problem is something else: the nature of this commitment. There are two serious matters in the case of liberation theology, a term coined by the Peruvian Gustavo Gutiérrez in 1971 (*A Theology of Liberation: History, Politics and Salvation*) and whose fundamental principles remain the driving force for numerous theologians in Latin America, even though Gutiérrez himself has revised some of them over the years. First, this commitment on earth is through socialism and its instrument, the revolution. Second, focusing on a kind of fundamentalist Marxist reading, liberation theology gives the most trivial battle carried out on behalf of socialism the exclusive and enlightened appearance as the path to salvation. We'll talk about this latter one—socialism as a trampoline to heaven—later; the former—socialism as a slide toward earth—will be addressed now.

Liberation theology is bringing the Church down from its lofty elitism to an earthly reality, descending with Mao's "little red gospel" tucked under one arm. The brilliant observation that this Church, which wants to return to earth, makes is that down here the primary concern is class struggle: a dispossessed majority exploited by a privileged minority, a microcosm of a greater injustice: rich countries against poor countries. This observation came during the 1970s when the revolution was at its peak. It is, however, also an observation made in the 1990s by priests who are helping guerrillas in Colombia, priests in Mexico who are backing Marcos in protest against NAFTA, and priests who are condemning the Satan that is driving children into hunger in Brazil's *favelas,* as well as priests who are criticizing the peace talks between the URNG and the Central American Government of Guatemala. These priests want chaos. For better or for worse, Hegel's dialectic and Marx's application must be pushed through the eye of the contemporary Latin American needle. What the "trendy lefty" theology calls "conflictual"—a really irritating word—is nothing more than a Marxist reading of reality (the division of society between oppressors and oppressed). And, of course, it automatically prescribes dispossessing the former as a condition for liberating the latter. The term "liberation" is in itself conflicting. It urges the existence of an enemy that has to be fought in order to emancipate the downtrodden. Moreover, the Church cannot even opt for Swiss-like neutrality. It must meddle in every issue. If it refrains, it's part of the dominating caste. If it chooses to liberate the unfortunate by some means other than socialism, it's still an agent of the dominating system. Liberation theology, just like any communist regime, wants to place the individual in the predicament of being either a servant or a dissident.

Ever since the Church abandoned the catacombs many centuries ago to become the religion of the Roman state, it has been a participant in power. Even when the Roman state returned to its secular status, the Church retained its power, and its spiritual role was never separated from its social role of being close to the government. In Latin America, where power has indeed been unjust and exploitative, this taints the history of the Catholic Church. Liberation theology starts from an indisputable principle: the Church should reform itself not only because it has been elitist but also because its passivity has taken away from victims an instrument that would have been tremendously powerful in warding off injustice. Up to here, who wouldn't drop to their knees before the apostles of liberation? If, however, Latin American churches would besiege the dictatorships of our postcolonial history and the economic privileges granted by corrupt governments to their mercantilist parasites shielded by exclusive legislation with the same tone that Rome uses to vilify condoms, perhaps we, the authors of this book, would take up astronomy. If the Catholic Church had more democratic sanctuaries like the Vicarage of Solidarity in Chile during Pinochet's reign or what Cardinal Miguel Ovando y Bravo personifies in Nicaragua, the expansion of the Protestant Church, for example, would be less in Latin America. What is surprising is that liberation theology proposes, while confronted with all of this, the biggest, most sophisticated, cruelest of all systems of privileges: socialism (whether the revolutionary or peace-loving strain). Sandinista priests presided over a society in which the privileged governing leadership was in celestial contrast to the general poverty of the country. Nicaragua's per capita income—a little less than $400 a year—implies that if the average Nicaraguan wants to buy a Bible he will have to do it at the expense of other products, like food, and thus would have to fast for more days than he usually would have to if he hadn't purchased the Holy Scriptures. No society that has replaced capitalist exploitation with socialism has eradicated privileges; it has always just expanded and aggravated them. The Mercedes Benzes that Fidel Castro's government places at Father Betto's disposal when he visits the island differ in only one way from the cars that the wealthy Venezuelan Cisneros family use: Mercedes are denied to the average Cuban merely by the nature of the system. In other words, they are prohibited. While in Venezuela there are no such impediments preventing the pedestrian Venezuelan from one day—when those in power stop interfering so much—getting a good deal and buying himself a Mercedes.

Liberation theologians are parishioners of Napoleon's congregation, the head pig on Orwell's farm; for them, some are more equal than others. The religious class struggle essentially contradicts the universal nature of the divine heart. How can the same God who loves tycoons like the Forbeses and the Rockefellers, the Azcárragas and the Marinhos, envenom those who want to send these gentlemen to the most fiery of hells? Are they trying to tell us that the God of fraternity is, actually, fratricidal? Is the God of justice also the God of envy? The apostles of liberation theology believe that since class warfare already exists in history it must be adopted if we are not to ignore reality. The priests, however, haven't bothered to read a couple of fundamental sociological statistics. The first one states that in Latin America urbanization is not synonymous with industrialization. For the last thirty years, the *campesinos* who have emigrated to the city have transformed Latin America's capitals into a cluster of chaotic metropolises surrounded by poverty belts filled not by workers but by "casuals"—that is, small entrepreneurs. If all immigrants were workers, we would be an industrial paradise. Another fact that would have been able to take the red out of our infamous priests' eyes: the bulk of Latin America's workers are not unionized. In countries like Peru, an oasis for class struggles, only one out of ten went to the trouble of forming a union. The idea that class struggle is historical and therefore obliges the Church to adopt it is, well, ungodly. But reality is merciless toward the priests.

The Church should demonstrate those elements of the revolutionary process that are truly humanizing.

Within the revolution, the tonsured clergy has been assigned its role in the flowchart of power takeovers by the socialist vanguard, which is in charge of the New Man's paradise. The clergy is to determine and emphasize the humanizing aspects of their heroic deeds, because heaven forbid that the revolutionaries should lose their perspective on those key aspects that morally justify revolutionary action. The idea is twofold: First, make a distinction between the role of the clergy and that of the other revolutionary functions, thus giving a halo of holiness to their exploits, because without this visionary contribution the revolution runs the risk of becoming dehumanized. Second, feign moderation and balance in such a way that these "humanizing elements" suggest that there could be other, less-humanizing aspects that have until now obscured the positive side. With jesuitical skill, liberation theologians sell the revolution to the nonrevolutionary by assuring him that from the hand of the clergy—the ultimate interpreter of the revolution content—he will find humanity in the revolution.

Revolutionary priests look at the Church's past and condemn it. They do, however, take a few grams of virtue from certain periods of its history that, when combined, make the perfect recipe. The early Christians' idea of theology was too spiritual, an attachment to the Hereafter that separated them from the Herenow. The inspiration they received from their readings of the Greek classics was too literal, and although they loved the transcendental world as much as these revolutionary priests do, they differed in that they didn't keep in mind the worldly context. Those early Christians were right, though, that theology and the saintly life were one and the same, something that the Church of the socialist future wants to rescue. In the fourteenth century there befell what "progressive" priests believe to be the great catastrophe: theology was separated from spirituality, and their functions were then fulfilled by different people. A bad thing. This separation took away the critical, historical spirit from religious thought. Scholasticism then ruined it completely. The Church became revelation and explanation instead of reflection. By turning its back on reflection, it did the same thing to action and compromise. Only two thinkers escaped from the retrospective flames of this historical overhaul: St. Augustine, who made a "true analysis of the times," blending theology and spirituality yet keeping transcendentalism anchored to the earth; and, especially, St. Thomas, who in the twelfth century introduced reason to theology, transforming it into a science without losing the transcendental foundation. Thus the Liberation Church, by condemning the Church's sometimes too saintly, sometimes too scholastic past (and which forgot the anthropological aspect of Christian revelation), reclaims a theology that is a science and a spirituality that incarnates the previously overthrown fusion of religion and politics in worldly matters. Now, they're ready for the attack! For liberation theologians, matters of God were considered a social science. A social science that lets the cassock wander in and out of the mysteries of the revolution and imparts to humanity the revelation of the profoundly humanizing truth of the "reds"; a truth that in the 1960s and 1970s filled the mountaintops with the anointed and justified the exaltation of so many simians with military stripes; a truth whose guardians, even today, circle about the Golgotha highlands in many of our countries.

When a priest wants to leave the sacristy and jump into the pond to caress the human clay, he doesn't want to do it to learn, but rather to teach. In the words of Paulo Freire, a Brazilian icon to liberation theologians, he wants to "enlighten." Abandoned is the overriding concern for the traditional Church that used to cram scholasticism's truth down the throats of the infidels like a mother forcing soup on a child who is not hungry. Now the revolutionary spoon must be imposed on the infidels for their own good even if it chokes them. The revolution must be revealed to them; the truth that they ignore must be explained. No, their thoughts and desires are not to be listened to nor should they be shown how to reflect. They must be "enlightened." The revolution is humanity and it's unforgivable that they, mere humans that they are, ignore it.

Continuing with his biased research of the odd displays of virtue from the official Church, the progressive priest finds that John XXIII and Paul VI had in their time already spoken of a "liberation from poverty." No matter that these men were too timid to modernize the Church; they provided the guidelines and those must be followed to the end. The liberation theologian needs to find, in that condemnable ecclesiastic past, some institutional legitimacy. After sniffing around in the holy archives, he finds the Papal benediction. Today's mission is to rescue the spirit of Vatican II and free it from insecurity and timidity. If their situation had been different, the modern John and Paul would also have been cutting away the undergrowth that would "deliver" the Sierra Maestra, camping out and waiting for the final attack on the icy peaks of the Andes.

Never mind that the ecclesiastic hierarchy has denounced the theology of revolution in every language and that the Pope has issued two harsh statements (one in 1984, the other in 1986) against this strange ideological alchemy which they consider theological science. Nor does it matter that Pope John Paul, during his visit to Managua, publicly reprimanded the ex–Minister of Culture Ernesto Cardenal, a Sandinista. Let us forgive those popes who know not what they do.

The priest who reveals revolutionary scholasticism also has the duty to "liberate" the poor from the satanic enemy. Here, a fruit cocktail must be removed from the theological refrigerator. One ounce of Hegel—the idea of the conscience as a factor in liberty; another ounce of Freud—that human behavior is conditioned by the unconscious that represses our psyche; and one final ounce of Marcuse—the social repression of the collective unconscious that must be rescued by restoring its social conscience. This dialectic–psychosocial fruit cocktail—or minestrone soup, whichever you prefer—becomes a liberationist commitment. The people must be liberated from the repression that prevents them from realizing that they're being exploited. The revolution, that humanizing task of salvation, is the truth that will set them free.

A revolution, not reform, is the choice of our cassocked idiot. The experiments of the religious political parties in the past and present centuries ended poorly. For Latin America, in the modern age, this was quite serious. First, the Christian Democratic party in Chile governed against the poor and later burdened the government with the ever so appropriately named "Salvador" Allende and his Popular Unity party. Later, El Salvador's Napoleón Duarte sold out to the *gringos* and, in exchange for $4 billion of economic and military aid throughout the 1980s, governed against the people and its vanguard, the FMLN. No more religious or Christian Democratic parties! To get to heaven, use the revolutionary shortcut!

The priests from the Universidad Centroamericana who were assassinated were not Marxist guerrilla sympathizers. All they did was commune with different sectors of society.

Central America attracts revolutionary priests like jam does flies. No place fascinates them as much, no corner of the world whets their appetite as do El Salvador, Nicaragua, and Guatemala, arenas of great ideological and military outbreaks, where communist guerrillas tried to drive out governments protected by armed forces and military castes, who couldn't care less about what others would say. Their work in the 1960s was persevering, just like ants, and they were bolstered by numerous foreign priests, among them Spaniards, who emigrated to those centers of Christian revival to disseminate their apocalyptic predictions of the arrival of liberation while confronting scenes of undeniable poverty, violence, and despair. In El Salvador this began at the end of the 1960s in the Universidad Centroamericana, where progressive priests shocked the archbishop by trying to carry out Paulo Freire's idea of teaching and preaching "enlightenment." Numerous testimonies prove that this was so well managed and well organized that it seemed that an invisible hand—the Lord's?—was pulling the strings. The ecclesiastic initiatives coincided with the political designs of Latin American communism so much that even the arch-materialist Cuban regime, the enemy of all "creditable" spirituality, accepted using the Church as a vehicle of revolutionary propagation ever since the communist party's first congress assumed power. Priests were setting themselves up in one-horse towns abandoned by the nations' capitals in Central America and other areas, from Mexico to Peru, boring through stone until they created their niche which only by the end of the 1980s would attract public attention and sound the alarm at the continents' Bishops' conferences.

Liberation theology's tactic has always been the same: denounce the false democracy and its military machine—clearly a popular appeal in areas where military brutality had been commonplace—and condemn hunger—another recurring Latin American characteristic—without ever mentioning the destruction carried out by the guerrillas or the plundering and poverty that the *campesinos* and laborers suffered in those "liberated" territories. The ideological sermon was accompanied by an overwhelmingly evangelical one, specifically directed at a sector with little education and a great thirst for consolation and faith, but which left them stunned with the ideological drivel and evangelic-political sophistry. The lethargic and conformist attitudes of the Catholic hierarchy, which for many years allowed the liberation priests to act as they wished without a great deal of true resistance, were the best allies to the cassocked communists, assembling themselves under the raucous name—Homeric epithet included—the "people's Church."

In the specific case of El Salvador, Monsignor Freddy Delgado, who was secretary of the Bishops' conference, was one of the few exceptions within the Catholic hierarchy. From the outset, he saw the danger it entailed and denounced it. His testimony, compiled in 1988 in a terrifying document, tells all about the Universidad Centroamericana and its rector, the famous Father Ellacuría, who orchestrated the revolutionary capture of the educational center and challenged the status quo by showing understanding, tolerance, and affinity for the establishment's armed enemies (the FMLN). At one time, the Salvadoran guerrilla Juan Ignacio Oterao once related how the Jesuits served as intermediaries for the guerrillas by purchasing arms overseas through their bank accounts, devastating proof that some had sold out their vow of poverty to the devil. The same happened in Nicaragua, where Christianity, communism, and the Sandinista movement began to confuse their dominions until Monsignor Obando y Bravo incorporated the cardinalate into his country's political theology and destroyed the other less sophisticated, less spiritual version. Only by the end of the 1980s, when communism fell like a house of cards, did the priests, who were after all heirs to the only institution humanly capable of surviving two thousand years, start pulling some strategic strings and initiating "dialogues." Their position, of course, wasn't about asking the guerrillas to merge with civilian life, as eventually did happen thanks to President Alfredo Cristiani's efforts, but rather to assure that the government and the guerrilla movement were on equal footing, a tie that would put the communists in a position of shared power. The "dialogue" that finally disarmed the guerrillas and left the constitutional government firmly in place—Cristiani's dialogue—was not what Ellacuría and his followers had in mind. His final negotiation efforts were the last link in the strategic chain, the untiring task of undermining democracy that drove the Archbishop Luis Chávez crazy.

The insincerity of those calls for a dialogue was seen a few years later by the attitude of the Guatemalan Bishops' conference concerning the negotiations in Guatemala between Ramiro de León Carpio's government and the URNG. In August 1995, in a book with the pious title *Urge la verdadera paz* ("Urging True

Peace"), the Guatemalan Diocese explained that true peace wouldn't come with a cease-fire between the guerrillas and the military; peace would only appear when there was justice for all. No one could argue, however, without deserving a place in Hell, that peace would end hunger or even exploitation. But to speak like this at a time when the country (exhausted by three and a half decades of civil war) was celebrating a negotiated peace that for the first time seemed possible could only confuse the issue, taking away the true and immediate meaning of peace, diluting the gravity of the conflict that cost 100,000 lives in a murky swimming pool of sociology without a single drop of chlorine. The same effort of "equidistance" has been made in Chiapas by the famous Samuel Ruiz, the bishop of San Cristóbal who lives for Zapatista revolutionaries, not because they are considered the solution to the corrupt and socializing PRI, but because they preach the Marxist revolution—with some postmodern amenities like the fax and the Internet.

The atrocious murder of Ellacuría and his followers at the Universidad Centroamericana, the act of a death squad against one of the most powerful symbols of the de facto popular front, contributed in giving these priests the prestige of martyrs, making it very difficult to criticize their revolutionary escapades without appearing to condone the repugnant methodological homicide carried out by their executioners. The international press, human rights organizations, and "progressive" governments, not to mention conservative democratic governments paralyzed by socialist exorcisms, were quick to condemn the deaths caused by the Central American authorities. There have not, however, been any such condemnations of innumerable other deaths, including the killing of Francisco Peccorini, a philosophy professor from the University of California and relentless scourge to revolutionary priests, who was shot down by the FMLN in 1989 when he entered a radio station in San Salvador to debate against one of his favorite subjects, namely the "people's Church."

Father Ellacuría is the thinker who succeeded in attaining a higher union of Marxism and Christianity.

On November 16, 1989, a paramilitary commando entered one of the dormitories at the Universidad Centroamericana and machine-gunned to death six Jesuits and two cleaning ladies, unveiling all over the world a political litany that had little to do with the death of Ellacuría, Montes, and the others but a lot to do with propaganda. At the same time that they were being massacred, a group of armed orangutans had sent to the heaven of political holiness —via express— Basque priests of Salvadoran nationalization, who had for a long time been introducing, along with clouds of incense and missal sheets, the revolutionary thesis.

This story goes way back. While Jon Sobrino, Ellacuría's principal collaborator, concentrated on the theological factor, the rector Ellacuría, with the *Communist Manifesto* securely concealed under his skullcap, was in charge of the ideological sermon scarcely disguised behind the veil of spirituality. The political battle at this Central American University of "José Simeón Cañas" (Universidad Centroamericana), clearly won by the liberation theologians, had been so severe that the opposing groups slept in separate residence halls. Everyone in El Salvador knew that this center of indoctrination provided ecclesiastical dignity for the movement's ideological fuel and shelter against the "artificial" and "bourgeois" Salvadoran democracy. The battle in the Church for the revolutionary cause had already been won, clearly indicated by the death of Archbishop Oscar Arnulfo Romero, the man who reaped the most tearful lamentations from everywhere and even earned a rhythmic and contagious salsa-like obituary from Rubén Blades when in 1977 Romero succumbed to paramilitary bullets in his country. Child of the fantastic propaganda machine of the left, which—let's not forget—in the 1970s seemed to be a juggernaut capable of ending the free Western world from within, the myth of Father Romero exalted the supremacy of the "people's Church" in El Salvador. It was an ungodly lie that Romero was never a revolutionary or a partisan of liberation theology. Rather, it is said that he was a frightened man cornered by revolutionary nuns and priests who put him, in a fit of hysteria, into his office—bed and all—each time there was some administrative dispute. And because of his acrobatic attacks on the Curia, they succeeded in isolating the possible sources of support that the archbishop had hoped to find in this very traditional sector. The Pope had called him to Rome to give him a good yank on the ears for his weakness, but he returned ready to fight, daring to attack even the Marxist penetration of the Church. His death, one of the most counterproductive barbarities committed by the anti-communists, allowed the revolutionary church to pay him homage in martyrdom. Since then, Fathers Ernesto Cardenal, Miguel d'Escoto, and other relics of the Sandinista sanctuary have transformed his hesitancy and timidity into a self-sacrificing intrepidity for the socialist church.

Just like other myths—such as the one about the guerrilla priest Manuel Pérez in Colombia—Romero's and Ellacuría's myths expressed not only the predicament of the Church in Latin America but also the enormous entanglement of bad conscience, complexes, reversed racism, hunger for adventure, and revolutionary tourism by the European and American intelligentsia. Hispanic-Salvadoran Jesuits were frequently Spain's movie stars, where they were offered ecstatic hospitality by parishioners of foreign revolutions (i.e., "progressive journalists"). International milk and honey nourished the revolutionary priests' domestic forces well into the beginning of the 1990s until, crushed by the weight of the dust from the Berlin Wall, they began reducing the extent of their impact to the confines imposed on them by the success of democracy and the ideological revision of many of the figures from the left. Ellacuría himself had begun to shift from revolutionary activism to an apparent call for "equidistance" to a "dialogue" between the guerrillas and the government, an unmistakable Leninist tactic in moments of full retreat, but one that managed to hold off the liberationist tide a little longer. The fact that Guatemalan priests are now speaking reservedly and almost contemptuously about the negotiations between the Guatemalan government and the URNG shouldn't seem strange. In El Salvador, the dialogue signified the definitive defeat of the FMLN, later confirmed by the voters at the polls shortly after the end of the war, and there isn't any reason to believe that it'll be any different in Guatemala.

This perfect union of Marxism and Christianity personified in Father Ellacuría, the poet Cardenal, Bishop Ruiz, and so many others in Latin America sought, and still seeks, to revitalize and modernize the Church, only slightly rubbing its eyes and awaking from its slumber. What it did accomplish, after the events of Central and Eastern Europe, was to take the Church by the hand to that area of disrepute shared today by so many of our official Latin American institutions. In the case of the Church, the loss of popular and institutional respect has allowed other denominations to advance, a kind of "informal" challenge to the enormous Catholic institution from below, a mirror of what has happened at the economic level with so many Latin Americans working on the fringes of the government and its laws. Evangelical sects and Protestantism have been growing in countries like Guatemala and Peru while the official Church keeps losing strength. Proof of this can be seen in how the recent support of Peru's government for vasectomies has not brought about its downfall (some believed that the genital coup would achieve what the efforts of the democratic resistance couldn't for so many years). How much of this was caused by the supposed saviors of the Catholic Church and the liberation theologians is something that needs to be studied. But Ellacuría's contribution, just like those of his peers, of authoring a book full of humble intentions and missions, *Conversión de la Iglesia al Reino de Dios* ("Converting the Church to the Kingdom of God"), is probably not insignificant.

Where you find iniquitous social inequalities, there you will also find the rejection of the Lord.

If the average socialist uses "blame" as the axis of his world vision (someone is always responsible for the social ills), the liberation theologian carries this practice to celestial heights. So, behind every barefoot street urchin in the social sewers of Rio's shantytowns, behind every sandal-clad Indian who lugs a sack of Peruvian potatoes on his shoulders, behind every malnourished Haitian suffering from a swollen belly in the human clay of Cité Soleil, there lurks a devil. Thanks to liberationist theological sociology, Satan has been transformed into an economic system. Evil has become manifest in, naturally, capitalism. Every Latin America capitalist wears the imprint of a satanic pitchfork on his back. The obsession with assigning capitalism (which is nothing more than society's way of spontaneously organizing itself) moral—no, immoral—qualities leads one to the perfectly logical conclusion that capitalism, according to liberation theology, is Beelzebub himself!

Let's forget for a second this curious biblical metaphor that progressive theologians apply to reality (regardless of how much their intent isn't metaphorical but literal). This in itself is serious, because when God and the Devil are invoked to judge politics the likely outcome is a bonfire. Let's, however, allow the eternal fires to burn in one corner and we'll go to the other: the capitalist sin. It's believed that one man's poverty is another man's wealth, just like when the master kept his slave in a semi-animalistic state in order to live at his expense. Our burgeoning yet imperfect Latin American capitalism specifically owes a good part of its humble vigor to the ending of slavery. There has been a great deal of study carried out on the economic limitations that slavery put on capitalism and on how the origin of capitalism, with its activity, mobility, and technological voracity, assured the other's demise. That doesn't matter to the social priests. Poverty is the child of evil, of a scheme of exploiters, it's from a world in which wealth is a zero-sum equation with the victims at one end and today's masters of noose and axe at the other. This "thinking"—the word is exaggerated—is attractive. A poverty scandal requires a guilty party, and the only way to quell the convulsion produced by poverty is to direct this injustice-driven hatred against someone.

What is certain, however, is that capitalism is not an evil plot, nor is the capitalist's wealth built from the bones of the destitute, nor can poverty be blamed on those who aren't poor. First, capitalism is a term that simply describes a climate of freedom in which all members of a community voluntarily pursue their own economic objectives. Second, this process necessarily involves differences among people; each individual has his own personal goals, and the means of achieving them will vary accordingly. Third, there is no other alternative. In other words, there is no system that assigns each person an equivalent amount of wealth. If there is any system that fails to achieve this egalitarian objective, it's socialism, a true assembly of devils that wherever it has gone it has amassed a formidable amount of goods and left its victims thinner and more naked than any Christ painted by El Greco.

Of course, if economic systems could be endowed with morality, the villain wouldn't be capitalism but socialism, along with all of its Latin American derivatives, of which there are many: nationalization, mercantilism, nationalism, and others. What the "progressive priests" call capitalism has, in fact, been their own caricature. They exalt the powerful by attributing to them capitalist virtues when they have in fact been anticapitalist and parasitic, capable of buying laws and legislators, enjoying success without competition, and receiving protection under the generous auspices of the state. On hearing that capitalism is condemned to Hades, God, who usually doesn't sentence the unborn to Hell, must be frowning.

One may ask how the Church can separate men into the good and the bad if God's mercy is universal and if everyone, whether rich or poor, has the right to salvation. Liberation theologians love. They love the rich so much that to spare them from the burning fate of Hell, they want to expropriate their goods so that the rich have time to atone for all their social sins here on earth. The more I beat you, the more I love you, they say in Peru about *amor serrano.* Liberation apostles practice a theological version of *amor serrano:* the more I take away from you, the more I adore you. It's social envy turned into a factor of eternal salvation. Instead of providing economic compensation, the priests offer those from whom they expropriate one of the most precious of all rewards, celestial paradise. Who wouldn't hand over his factory, his mansion, his farm, or even his underwear to a liberationist government in exchange for Heaven? Liberation theology, just like communism, founds the notion of justice on looting your neighbor and abolishing private property. It also searches for a delightful pretext to justify rejecting the Christian premise of God's universal love for their own axiom that represents robbing the wealthy: "Universal love is liberating oppressors of their own power, of their egoism."

The opposite of pillaging is charity. The class-based society created by capitalist exclusivism, unknown to God, is countered by the kingdom of fraternity, a world where charity is the binding element among human beings, the only form of currency acceptable for interaction among bipeds. We're not going to waste time explaining again that you can't divide what doesn't exist and that the desire to distribute what does exist just ends up reducing everyone's quota to minuscule portions. Let's go to another issue: solidarity as a social instrument. In truth, what liberation priests fail to comprehend is that capitalism happens to be the most cooperative system of them all, a world where charity—understood not as a handout but as an attitude, something mystical in human relationships—is infinitely greater than in any other system. This, for example, is the thesis of Francis Fukuyama's book, *Trust, the Social Virtues and the Creation of Prosperity.* (Unfortunately, the phrase "the end of history," which he used in his sensible previous book about the superiority of liberal democracy to alternative systems, caused so many diatribes that his main thesis was lost.) The idea is to ascertain what the keys to prosperity are. Obviously, most of this secret is that capitalism is an economic model that allows the rational pursuit of each individual's interests, the search for personal objectives within freedom. There is also a fundamental component: culture, the union of a society's customs and habits. Within this capitalist culture the key element is trust. Imagine what the capitalist world would be without it. The amount of time and money lost would be immeasurable if the people who participated in the capitalist world didn't have any confidence. You don't need to agree with Fukuyama's argument that societies such as the American and the English, where trust is greater than in France and Italy, have a more robust and prosperous capitalism, carried out by large impersonal corporations instead of family businesses, with less interventionist governments. It's enough to see that capitalism is the only system that requires people to trust someone else's word in order for it to work, necessitating that they be willing to undertake economic activities, confident that they will find a sea of faceless, nameless people who are willing to provide them the necessary supplies and sufficient credit, as well as the indispensable demand required for this activity to survive. In capitalism, everyone works with everyone else. Capitalistic egoism promotes such teamwork that it appears to be the fellowship preached about in the Bible. What is self-indulgent—an angelic way of insulting our Lord—is believing that capitalism has filled the world with Oliver Twists.

Liberation theology's Christ-like charity cannot be more touching: expropriate from the rich, punish the successful, and ruin the well-to-do in order to save them from the egoism that could condemn them to eternal flames on Judgment Day. Ye rich of the world, give thanks because there are caring souls willing to sacrifice themselves to lay hands on your bank accounts and relieve you of your estates with the noble, irreproachable, mystical purpose of not letting Christ catch you with your hands in the cookie jar when he decides to return to this earth. Thanks to those righteous decrees of the revolutionary priests, you will be well prepared—uh, well impoverished—when the time comes to hand out tickets to heaven.

It is a right and a duty to denounce the lack of daily bread as evidence of sin and evil.

The "progressive" Church seems to have learned more from George Soros, the multimillionaire whose investment funds are worth $16 billion, or the French-British Jimmy Goldsmith, so affluent that he financed an entire political party in the United Kingdom, than from the Christian gospels. It just so happens that they loathe poverty. They detest penury, hate material privation, and are

disgusted by destitution. They would like to drink to the last drop from the cornucopia, become bloated with abundance and prosperity. What? Wasn't the
Church an institutional exaltation of poverty, and weren't its ethical foundations
a defense for material nakedness? Didn't they teach us that the poor shall inherit
the Kingdom of God and tell us, with spectacular metaphors of humpback rumi-
nants and metal rods, of the almost impossible prospect of the rich setting foot
in Paradise? Didn't they explain to us that the wallet is the enemy of the Spirit?

No, the "progressives" got tired of preaching poverty. Now—and this they
learned from the best capitalism—they hate poverty so much that they ascribe
to it diabolical elements, an entirely metaphysical dimension of horror and evil
that would delight Donald Duck's greedy uncle. The "people's Church" is tired
of dignifying poverty. Now they see the hand of God's enemy at work in it. Their
theological reading of the realities caused by political incompetence and
mediocre social institutions contains a dangerous fundamentalist germ, not
much different from the Moslems who call on God every time they want to eliminate any human dissent against the norms established by the ulamas or *Shar-
i'ah*. If we approach society with critical eyes for sin and salvation, we become
God, assuming the divine prerogative of pronouncing the final judgment. Thus,
liberation priests exaggerate a little when, upon observing social justice, they see
a factor of the theological battle between good and evil, sin and virtue, God's
cherubs and the Devil's demons. They've made some progress, though. They
agree that poverty must be eliminated and that it's absurd to establish a cause-
and-effect relationship, an equation of equality, between economic poverty and
Christian salvation. The economy is not a theological factor, nor is poverty a
passport to heaven, nor is Switzerland condemned to Hell beforehand, nor has
Haiti secured eternal life.

If we were to establish a relationship between salvation and political institutions or economic policies, the revolutionary priests—although doing a good job
preaching prosperity—would hit the hypogeum head-on, because their economic proposals are old recipes of failure. The influence of the dependency theory that dominated Latin America's political panorama at the end of the 1960s
and during a good part of the 1970s is detectable amid all of the liberation theologian's economic theories. Even literature from Vatican II, the unwitting
mother of the liberationist priests, has a certain trace of the dependency theory
in its central theme: that some poor nations are being distanced from the rich
nations, not because of their own failures but because of the advantages enjoyed
(unfairly, it is to be understood) by the rich. For this reason, the theory calls for
the rich to make the effort, not the poor. Wanting to break economic ties with
its immediate past and its Latin American symbol—*desarrollismo* or import substitution—liberation theology is in fact perpetuating the basic fallacies that were

attributed to the famous "inward development" of the 1950s, so near and dear to Latin America and figures such as Perón. But the shots fired by these theologians miss their target. They believe that the problem with the thesis of inward development was its excessive economism, its lack of political perspective, its overconfidence in the ability to skip steps and modernize itself overnight, and that this was a vision coming from overseas, specifically from international organizations willing to help the peripheral economies develop more. None of these objections is appropriate given where they're coming from. *Desarrollismo's* theory of excessive economism happens to be even more prevalent in the pessimistic view of those who don't believe that development allows steps to be jumped. They forget how fast one's mind and willpower can adapt to a free environment and can therefore boost economies whose typical growth cannot be precisely calculated in economic forecasts. The criticism of the lack of a political factor in inward development is hypocritical because dependency theory doesn't take politics much into consideration either, since it believes that no country can make its own decision on progress but rather is subject to an imperialistic fate. The idea that it's impossible to skip steps, which is quite a different matter if we're talking about the ladder leading to St. Peter, is false in politics. If contemporary experience has shown us anything (taking the Pacific Rim countries, for example, from Chile to Korea), it's that skipping stages is characteristic of capitalism. Finally, concerned about the "imported" nature of the theory of development and its tie to international organizations, they seem to forget that the dependency theory, repeated by both Prebisch and Cardoso, was primarily formulated during the golden age of the ill-fated Economic Commission for Latin America (ECLA), a regional agency of the United Nations of which Prebisch was the executive secretary. They also forget that the birth of the Latin American Association for Industrial Development (LAIA) in 1961—an offspring of Prebisch's theses about the need to unite Latin America in order to defend it from foreign imperialism's relentless pursuit—was inspired by the European Common Market of the postwar world.

Dependency theory, just like the development idea that liberation theologians have sought to overcome, was indebted to the paternalistic vision of the relationship between the government and society and posited authoritarianism and nationalism as the keys to success for Latin American countries. It was also, with a slight hint of class warfare on an international scale, the offspring of Marxism and Hobson's and Lenin's thesis on imperialism. Today, this entire view is rusty and comatose, especially when you see that Latin America's most successful country—Chile—has been the least "Latin Americanized" in recent decades (it even abandoned the Andean Pact) and is the country that internationalized its economy the most. At the same time, countries like Peru, which tried to cut ties with the rest of the world while domestically intensifying the dominant role of the state, are splashing about in destitution.

Capitalism—the object of liberationist hate—is the only system (this word, which connotes a predetermined order, is not very appropriate here) that has been able to expand opportunities and democratize profits, a curious earthly microcosm of the heavenly promise in everything it consists of, from social mobility to ecumenical access. But capitalism doesn't respond to theological virtues. Its saga, slow and painful, dates back to the end of the Middle Ages, with political rivalries between tradesmen and lords, nobleman and monarchy, up to the cyberspace era of the Internet, passing through industrial revolutions and service markets—the distinctive trademark of this century's economy. No one invented, designed, or planned this process. It happened with time and a plethora of individual goals furiously converging and diverging within its— sometimes suffocating, sometimes consenting—legal and governmental framework and its fluctuating love–hate relationship with society. Therefore, to pray to heaven for capitalism would be like asking a few centuries ago for the Nobel Prize to go to the author of *A Thousand and One Nights;* it's impossible because everyone wrote it. Interestingly, capitalism, the individual's paradise, is humanity's greatest collaborative work.

The theological meanderings that the "people's Church" subjects us to (in order to explain its *adieu* to the evangelic exaltation of poverty and its hurrah in favor of prosperity for the destitute) are fascinating. Liberation theology wants to be consistent with the idea that the poor shall inherit the Kingdom of God as long as the second coming of Christ is their entrance to paradise (as you can see, there are more waiting-rooms here than for Louis XIV's *atelier*). The Church should therefore hurry up and save the poor and inflict penance on the rich (and the middle class) before salvation. If the "people's Church" brings salvation to earth, it then parallels those emigrant Max Weber puritans for whom salvation consisted of making oneself rich here on earth. The poverty that the "people's Church" wants is spiritual, not material. Salvation is coming, made reality by revolutionary decrees. Faced with the collapse of the Berlin Wall and a good part of the revolutionary forces in Latin America, one has to ask, could it be that the Devil is about to beat God at His own game, burning God's bread at the oven doors?

The Church's mission isn't to "save" in the sense of securing one's passage into heaven. Salvation is reality acting upon history.

If the road to Hell is paved with good intentions, this statement leads directly to the waters of the river Styx. Liberation theology criticizes—rightly so—the

Church's traditional efforts to develop its role as an official social institution, the bastion of the political establishment. In doing so, the Christian family has divided its functions into the clerical—the Church—and the political—religious parties. This has distanced the Church from the people. This phenomenon was, in those times, intensified by the separation of church and state, secularizing the exercise of political power and dividing the roles even more with the spiritual and ecclesiastical on one side, and the political on the other, contributing to the Church's indolence since the beginning of the eighteenth century and the French Revolution. Liberation theologians believe that, in Latin America, this divorce is both bad and good: bad because on leaving politics the Church simply floats above a predetermined rule of injustice and exploitation; good because the secularization shows that the world belongs to mortals, the here and now, the basis taken by liberation theology to reach the conclusion that one doesn't have to wait for Godot in order to be saved—just go ahead and embark on the revolution.

As evidence of this labyrinthine way of thinking, liberation theology harbors an embarrassing albeit not so secret nostalgia for the old times of the secular state. It yearns for a world where the Church doesn't have an essentially spiritual role but rather a political one. In other words, it wants to have political power. It believes that the overwhelming responsibility of granting salvation on earth comes from the tip of the pen used by ministers and presidents for signing decrees. Liberation theology is then, in this aspect, a Christian reflection of Moslem fundamentalism, no matter how much its methodology may differ. Once in power, the logical consequence of this thesis would be theocracy, a political dictatorship based on the divine word interpreted exclusively by a platonic elite of the all-knowing, "chosen" priests. The fabulous idea of immersing the Church into the clay of mankind (we owe this to the heroic conduct of the Church in countries such as Poland during the terrible years of communism) is distorted in order to restore the theocratic concept of the ecclesiastic role of the State-Church that had eroded in the West a few centuries ago.

The idea of salvation made history, of Heaven incarnate in Man's conduct, is an attractive one. It's also fair. Why condemn the poor to misery with the promise of posthumous redemption if it's possible to accumulate wealth now? The problem is the temptation of fundamentalism. Revolutionary priests reject the existence of two histories, one secular, the other sacred. They think that historical facts, such as the exodus of the Egyptian Jews, represent God as long as they serve as a form of justice on earth. It's a manmade "liberation" from the sin of the Egyptian exploitation of the Jews. So, the Biblical Exodus would be a forerunner of liberation theology, and the Jews in Israel are the theological predecessors of Ellacuría and company. Liberation and salvation are intertwined: Christ came to earth to save us instead of saving us from the other comfortable and shielded world. Christ was also a political martyr (condemned by the Roman state as "King of the Jews") and liberationist forefather of the guerrilla fighter Manuel Pérez or the hooded Subcomandante Marcos. Like Christ, those tonsured guerrillas perform a Passover—they extract life from death. By taking life from exploiters and expropriating from the rich, they liberate the transgressors from their sins and place them on a red carpet at the gates of Heaven.

Standing tiptoe on an indisputable base—the political mediocrity of the traditional Church—liberation theology heads down a never-ending theological serpentine road to the conclusion that socialism is humanity's salvation and revolutionaries, as agents of this salvation, are the second coming of Christ. Dear Lord, deliver us all, amen.

In Latin America, the Christian community should live and celebrate its eschatological hope in a world of social revolutions.

This sentence would be impeccable if the eschatology the liberation theologians are referring to were physiological. Sadly, it isn't physiological but theological. Latin America and revolutions are still drawn to each other like men and women. Since the second Latin American General Bishops' Conference held in 1968 in Medellín—which used the conclusions reached by Vatican II to interpret the Church's role from a revolutionary and Latin Americanist standpoint—Latin America, for liberation theologians, has been a Third Worldist idea. The concept that dominates the Latin American vision of the revolutionary fathers is that of the periphery being confronted by the center, a resounding echo from, yet again, the economic dependency theory. They want to create a Third World Church— an anti-imperialist Church. Here the Third Worldist mythology is dressed in theological garb to explain to us that the Church has the mission to save the periphery from the West. Thus liberation theology, however much it may claim to be Latin Americanist, is actually nationalist, a continentwide nationalism. All of the discussions at Medellín, the cornerstone of the revolutionary proposal from then until now among the members of the "people's Church," is the vindication of a nation—the nation of Latin America's poor—which embodies virtue against a foreign enemy—the rich countries that embody evil.

The new element added to this reproduction of the dependency theses is, of course, eschatology. Salvation is found through liberation, through the revolution. Liberation theologians vehemently reject what they call the old "quantitative" concept of salvation, by which almost all of us (those who pass the test of life to reach heavenly glory) are saved. The revolutionaries are annoyed by this abstract salvation situated in the other world. They want to get there like Fittipaldi. They prefer a "qualitative" salvation, where what matters is that the human experience is one big theater where the question of eternal life is solved. This is the eschatology of the here and now, open to everyone, even to those who may not know Christ. Down this road full of jesuitical curves, one arrives at the very simple conclusion that God is found in the exalted leader of Chiapas or the bearded Abimael Guzmán.

The binding element between God and earth is of course the revolutionary priest, who has abandoned the old views of the Church as a bridge to the afterlife in favor of a bridge to this life. To give Papal benediction to all of this, he goes back to the Council and its definition of the Church as a "sacrament," which he interprets, with an extraordinarily flexible understanding of matters, as a shout for war. By calling the Church a "sacrament," he has abandoned his service as an end in itself and transformed the Church into a "vehicle," a "sign," in other words, a means of transmitting the revolutionary truths of the fighting and screeching masses. This theological nonsense, again, attempts to sanctify the revolution. The revolution is a new epiphany. Eternal salvation can be found at the end of a revolutionary rifle, in an expropriation decree or in a nationalist state.

The "people's Church" has open arms. It wants to put everyone into its bag, even though they may be from other denominations. This call for religious freedom is, of course, not like the one issued by the early Christians, before Christianity was married to the state in the fourth century, but by a congregation of "progressives." This new "ecumenism" is not a reconciliation of different churches affected by the separation of the "Easterners," but a call to a revolutionary alliance, always opposing the class enemy; ecumenism without the bourgeoisie.

Long after the fathers of dependency theory have abandoned their insular mentality (like Cardoso, today the president of Brazil, did) and after some of the fathers of liberation theology have rejected Marxism as a central analysis of Latin American reality (like Gustavo Gutiérrez and others), God's warriors continue to play havoc with Latin American souls.

9

"YANKEE, GO HOME!"

Among all the external characteristics of the Latin American idiot, probably none of them is as distinctive as his anti-*Yankeeism*. It's difficult to become a perfect, well-rounded, flawless idiot unless there is a fundamental anti-American component to the ideology of the subject in question. In addition, a golden rule could be formulated for the Latin American political *idiotology* that would establish the following axiom: "A true Latin American idiot has to be anti-American, otherwise he will be classified as a phoney or imperfect idiot."

But it's not that simple. It's not enough just to be anti-Yankee to qualify as a conventional Latin American idiot. The trait of hating and scorning the United States is not even exclusive to Latin American hotheads. A certain portion of the political right, although for different reasons, tends to share the anti-Yankee language of the thermocephalic left. How is this confusion possible? Elementary, my dear Watson. Latin American anti-Americanism flows from four different sources: the cultural, anchored to the old Spanish-Catholic tradition; the economic, the outcome of a nationalist or Marxist vision of the commercial and financial relationship between the "empire" and its "colonies"; the historical, derived from the armed conflicts between Washington and its southern neighbors; and the psychological, a product of the unhealthy mixture of admiration and rancor deeply rooted in one of human nature's worst characteristics, envy.

This type of Latin American idiot—the most backward on the zoological scale of species—is bothered by the United States' clean and well-kept cities, its wonderful standard of living, and its technological triumphs. For all of this he almost always has an emphatic and absurd explanation: it isn't an organized society, it's a *neurotic* one; they aren't prosperous but *exploiters;* they aren't creative but *thieves of others' intelligence.* The Panamanian press, for example, has begun to report that the clean gardens in the Canal area and the painted houses—later turned over to the Panamanians—weren't part of the Panamanian national culture, thereby justifying transforming them into another gloriously filthy and chaotic way of living—but one that reflects *our* way of living.

For the Latin American idiot, Yankees also assume a ceremonial role from a purely Freudian script: they are the father who must be killed in order to find true happiness. They are the scapegoat to which all blame must be transferred. Because of them we aren't rich, wise, or prosperous. Because of them we can't secure that wonderful place we deserve in the assembly of nations. Because of them we can't regain our rightful power status.

How can you not hate someone who causes you so much harm? "We don't hate the *gringos*," the idiots say, "just their government." Wrong: their governments change but the hate remains. They hated the *gringos* during the time of Roosevelt, Truman, Eisenhower, Kennedy, Johnson, Nixon, Carter, Clinton, everyone. It's a hate that isn't abated or altered when the government changes.

Could it be hatred of the system? Wrong again. If the Latin American idiot hated the system, he would also be anti-Canadian, anti-Swiss, or anti-Japanese; this consistency is completely absent from his repertoire of phobias. Moreover, it's possible to find anti-Americans who are pro-British or pro-German, which contradicts the myth of this being an aversion to the system. What they hate are *gringos,* like the Nazis hated the Jews or the French Le Pen detested the Algerians. It's pure racism but with a distinct peculiarity: this hate isn't the result of disdain felt for someone who is wrongly assumed to be inferior, but for someone who is—also wrongly—assumed to be superior. So, it's not an ideological problem, but a significant pathology, an ailment easily misdiagnosed and difficult to treat.

In any case, throughout this book there are different analyses and numerous references to anti-Americanism originating from twisted interpretations of economic and cultural matters—see, for example, the chapter dedicated to the idiot's "family tree" or the constant warnings of the multinationals' real intentions. So let's focus on the following reflections of the "imperial" conflicts between the United States and its southern neighbors. We'll start with a harsh Latin American saying that is heard repeatedly:

More than a country, the United States is a cancer that has metastasized.

Anyone who glances at a U.S. map for the summer of 1776, following the U.S. declaration of independence, and compares it with another one for the winter of 1898, following the end of the Spanish-American war, could easily reach the conclusion that Washington is one of the most voracious capitals in the contemporary world. In that long century, the United States ceased to be a relatively small country, a little more than half the size of today's Argentina, made up of thirteen colonies located on the coastal Atlantic strip in the middle of North America. It transformed itself in a colossal "sea to shining sea" realm, with territories in the Pacific, the Caribbean, and near the North Pole.

According to a *progressive* reading of the facts explaining this "growth"—a reading our beloved Latin American idiot is so addicted to and which is based on a completely ideological, out-of-context interpretation—the United States, whether by force or intimidation, stripped France of its immense Louisiana territory, declared the Monroe Doctrine in order to dominate the New World, wrenched away from Mexico half of its land, forced the Czar of Russia to sell Alaska, and attacked Spain in Cuba, Puerto Rico, and the Philippines with no other motive than to annex the remainder of the decadent Spanish empire, completely incapable of defending itself. Once having committed this villainy at gunpoint, or through interventions or conspiracy to continue to sustain its economic interest, it assembled and disassembled the Third World—especially Latin America—as it pleased. From this perspective, George Washington, Jefferson, Madison, Adams, and the rest of the country's founding fathers harbored imperialist intentions from the moment the republic was founded.

How much of this prevalent perception of the United States is fiction and how much is fact? The authors of this book are, of course, not interested in exonerating the United States for the abuses that it has committed but are convinced that a victimist interpretation of history—in which we Latin Americans are the victims and the Americans are the executioners—doesn't help to correct the profound causes of the ills that afflict our Latin American societies. On the contrary, it perpetuates them. So, let's have a look at the fundamental milestones of "U.S. imperialism," not with today's eyes but rather with the vision that prevailed at the time and that dictated taking the actions that rattle the moral conscience of our contemporary irascible idiots.

American imperialists began their pillage of the Third World by exterminating, looting, and exploiting their own natives.

It's true—who can doubt this?—that the Native Americans in what we today call the United States were annihilated or displaced by the Europeans. But there are nuances worth examining within this immense tragedy (still in process as much to the south as to the north of the Rio Grande). First to be examined is the laying of the foundation of the supposed European legitimacy that seized the hemisphere discovered by Christopher Columbus.

Spain and Portugal based the legitimacy of their sovereignty over the Americas on the concessions awarded by the Papal authority to some Catholic nations that dedicated themselves to the task of evangelizing. England, whose monarchy rid itself of Rome in the sixteenth century, and France looked for their legitimacy in the rights they derived from the "discoveries" made by adventurers and merchants serving under their flags. Holland, always such a capitalist, attained sovereignty by methodically purchasing territories from the Indians, as we remember the transaction that placed the island of Manhattan under Dutch dominion for today's equivalent of a few thousand dollars. Russia, self-designated heir of the Byzantine Empire, who didn't trust anyone or anything, obtained its legitimacy over land in the Americas through an incessant and severe dominion that in just two hundred years, by simply sending military/commercial expeditions to neighboring borders, slowly yet surely changed the original tiny principality of Muscovy into the largest government on the planet, a phenomenon that persists even today, despite the pruning carried out during the postcommunist era.

This matter of legitimacy is important for understanding the United States' conflicts with Mexico in the first half of the nineteenth century. Let's first of all, however, come to the most obvious conclusion: Americans had as much or as little right to establish a republic in North America as the descendants of Spain did in doing the same in the south. If there was (and is) any difference in how the Indians were treated, it's likely that the Anglos, who didn't enslave them, turn them into forced labor, or try to catechize them through violence or intimidation (although, at times, they didn't hesitate to massacre them or confine them to "reservations"), have been somewhat less cruel than the Spanish or we, the *criollo* descendants, have been.

You say that first the English and French crowns, and later the Americans, wiped out the Indian "nations"? Of course, but it doesn't seem that the Mayans, the Incas, the Mapuches, the Patagonians, the Guaranies, or the Ciboneys had a better fate under Spain or the Spanish-American republics. After all, for each frontiersman who pursued and drove out Indians in the north, something similar occurred in the south that did more or less the same and for the same period of time. Yet no American president sold his own Indians as slaves (a vile act committed by General Santa Anna to several thousands of Yucatan Mayans, whose lives ended on Cuban sugar-cane plantations as punishment for the rebellious nature of that race).

Jefferson took the first imperial swipe at the Third World.

Although George Washington finished his second presidential term with a speech in which he declared the United States' intention not to participate in

Europe's habitual massacres—demonstrating the isolationist tendency that sporadically persists even today in U.S. policy—in 1804 and 1805 there had already occurred what one notable Latin American idiot called "the first imperial swipe of the American eagle on the Third World." Aside from the fact that eagles normally don't have claws but talons, it would help to remember how and why a president so peaceable and pacifist as Jefferson sent his incipient navy to bomb Tripoli, triumphantly credited in American patriotic hymns, almost 200 years before Reagan did the same against Qaddafi and virtually for the same reasons.

Ever since the sixteenth century and until the middle of the nineteenth century, the northern coast of Africa, what today is called the Maghreb (Morocco, Algeria, and Tunisia), was a pirates' den nurtured by local satrapies. These pirates received a good portion of their money by extorting money and goods from sea vessels that dared pass through that western portion of the Mediterranean; naturally, they divided the earnings with the respective authorities. The Americans, subjected to this blackmail, had been religiously paying the tribute since 1796 in order to avoid having their ships boarded and looted, but Tripoli's Pasha, Yusuf Karamanli, decided to increase the tribute and the U.S. government responded with a definite "no." Shortly thereafter, in October 1803, pirates boarded the frigate *Philadelphia* and, after having triumphantly towed it into the bay of Tripoli, levied a heavy ransom for it.

Instead of paying, the American government sent in a commando expedition under the command of Lieutenant Stephen Decatur—a *Rambo* of that time to whom the phrase "my country, right or wrong" is attributed—in order to rescue the ship. Together with eighty-three volunteers, he boarded the sailing ship *Intrepid* (quite so!), entered the bay of Tripoli by night, rescued his companions, and, seeing that the frigate *Philadelphia* wouldn't be able to sail, set it on fire so that the enemy couldn't use it. Decatur didn't lose a single man in the adventure and lived a long life of spectacular military feats.

The second episode of this "saga" took place a year later, in what was undoubtedly the first American intervention to remove a government (Yusuf's) that was deliberately harming the United States' national interests. In fact, U.S. diplomacy succeeded in convincing Yusuf's older brother—at that time exiled in Egypt—to head a military force recruited by the United States to remove Yusuf from power.

And that's how it was: four hundred men, a mix of Arab mercenaries and the first "Marines" in history, departed from Alexandria, Egypt, stealthily marching across the desert for almost two months, until they arrived at the Derma fortress, a military installation situated in the Libyan desert that they captured in just twenty-four hours, and from where they resisted constant attacks for forty-five days. In the meantime, several American frigates bombarded Tripoli until Pasha Yusuf was forced to sign a peace treaty.

The United States is the world's largest predator.

This emphatic statement is attributed to the Argentine Manuel Ugarte. Is there any truth in this sentence? The first United States "metastasis"—the Louisiana Purchase in 1803—was an act that almost took the American government itself by surprise and almost destroyed the delicate alliance among the thirteen states that originally formed the "Union." The tensions produced by this sudden expansion of the nation—the United States doubled in size after this treaty with France—came from two places. On the one hand, the U.S. Constitution didn't include any imperialist provision whatsoever. The document had been drafted with the understanding that the thirteen original colonies would always serve as the basis for the republic. On the other hand, incorporating this enormous territory into the young nation could upset the balance of power among these states, which were at that time and until the Civil War (1861–1865) very zealous about their regional power.

Why France ceded its sovereignty over the Louisiana Territory—an enormous area with unidentified borders, something quite important later on—to the United States for a few dollars says a lot about the prevailing opinion in the world at that time of colonial states and, especially, the nature of "spoils" or "sovereign territory" of those areas conquered by armed forces or political alliances. Napoleon, who in 1800 had wrested control of Louisiana from the Spanish, only three years later "transferred" this territory (six times larger than France itself) to the United States with the fundamental purpose of strengthening an adversary of England, his great enemy.

At that time, Florida, Cuba, Louisiana, or any colony could go from one country's hands to another's overnight without anyone being outraged, simply because the idea of a nation-state still hadn't developed in any of the Western world (this would become established in the second half of the century) and was even less when dealing with colonies in the Americas, territories considered as dispensable attachments of the European nations. That's why Jefferson—more interested in Cuba than in Louisiana—unsuccessfully attempted to buy the island from the Spanish. But give or take a few years later, in 1819, after the wars of "persecution" undertaken by Jackson against the Seminole Indians, Madrid, without too much enthusiasm and after several military skirmishes, decided to "sell" the entirety of Florida to the United States for $5 million. That's why colonies existed: to exploit them as long as possible or exchange them like pawns on the international chessboard of geopolitical battles when no better use could be found.

In 1803 no one knew Louisiana's exact borders since this territory, in the southernmost portion of the United States, was the farthest corner of the Spanish empire in the Americas—the same happened with England in the northwest, on the Canadian border, for the region vaguely referred to as Oregon. Maps erred by thousands of miles, thereby explaining why many Americans, Jefferson included, believed that the almost uninhabited area of Texas was part of the land bought from the French, supposedly a semipopulated area that extended to the Pacific Ocean, a confusion that wasn't cleared up until 1819, right before Spain lost its sovereignty over this almost uninhabited and vaguely demarcated territory when Mexico declared independence in 1821.

Why did Jefferson "force" the limits of the Constitution and buy Louisiana? Essentially, for militarily strategic reasons and not because of any economic imperialist greed, as is assumed by our uninformed idiots. Quite the contrary. As normally happens, the Louisiana Purchase caused a substantial fall in the price of rural property (at that time almost everything was rural), and the Americans' per capita income decreased by 20%. His motives were of a different nature. While Napoleon wanted a strong United States, capable of confronting England, the Americans feared the French and the Indians, because it had been many decades since the latter had abandoned its bows and arrows and now mastered gunpowder and bullets. Even though the Indians lacked complex social and political structures, they were capable of establishing military alliances with the European powers, as was seen during the United States' war of independence, when the French succeeded in enlisting the natives to their side to attack the British.

The Monroe Doctrine is the official birth certificate of American imperialism.

In 1823, President James Monroe, at the end of his second term, placed the cornerstone of what some renowned Latin American idiot has called the "official birth certificate of American imperialism"—a gross analytical error by the idiot. A more careful examination of this "doctrine" and of the causes that precipitated it points instead in the opposite direction: it's an anti-imperialist doctrine.

In that cold December month, when Monroe officially declared that the Europeans were not welcome in the Americas—whether in the southern or northern hemisphere—France, the Austrian Empire, and especially Russia had formed a Holy Alliance to reinforce the absolutist monarchies hounded in Europe by liberal ideas and in the Americas by the establishment of independent republics. This Holy Alliance, headed by the "Hundred Thousand Sons of

St. Louis" contributed by the French, had violently entered Spain to restore Ferdinand VII's dictatorial powers and to remove the liberal government that three
years prior had forced the monarch to accept a Constitution that considerably
diminished the king's authority.

Therefore, Monroe and his cabinet had very good reasons for trying to keep
the Europeans away from the continent. A decade earlier, during the extremely
perilous War of 1812, the English had returned to Washington, now the capital
of the United States, to burn it down. So it wasn't that crazy to assume that reactionary powers intended to destroy the republican nucleus that was inspiring
most of the revolts in the New World. In the end, the Russians, taking advantage of the border confusion in the northern part of the American continent,
descended down the Pacific coast to what is today San Francisco, while the continent's defeated Spanish army regrouped in Cuba, an Iberian colony governed
by martial law under a state of siege. The creation of a great army formed by a
bloc of absolute monarchies trying to reconstruct the Spanish empire in America was certainly more than just a hallucination: it was a real danger for the
United States. Obviously, the Monroe Doctrine—*América para los americanos*
("America for Americans")—which so irritates our contemporary Latin American idiots, was not perceived as such by the liberators of our republics. On the
contrary, it was warmly welcomed by those who saw in Washington a true champion of shared interests and ideals, as well as a natural ally to defend them.

Over the course of time this doctrine was used in a slightly different way than
its original intent, but in most cases it's likely that the end result has been useful for Spanish America, regardless of what may be said by the ineffable idiot to
whom this book is so lovingly dedicated.

Poor Mexico, so far from God and so near the United States.

This melancholic phrase, ascribed to Porfirio Díaz (among others), understandably reflects the attitude of the Mexicans. And this is only natural: between
1835 and 1848 half of Mexico's northern territory became part of the United
States. However, what happened there has a much more complex explanation
than the usual imperialist spasm attributed to this land transfer.

For starters, the borders of the Latin American countries that emerged in the
first quarter of the nineteenth century were not established until quite some
time after Spain was expelled from the South American continent. The perime-
ters we recognize today for Argentina, Peru, Ecuador, Colombia, Venezuela, or
Brazil are quite different from what they were when these countries won their
independence. Central America, which is today made up of five independent
republics, was politically integrated into the Captaincy General of Guatemala,

an entity which at that time was subject to the authority of the Mexican viceroy-alty, but which didn't prevent it in 1821, shortly after the new Mexican state was created, from declaring its own independence.

If this was the situation in the south of Mexico, populated and christianized since the sixteenth century, the north was a scene of absolute chaos, acceler-ated by the disarray and the enormous losses caused by the Mexican War for Independence between 1810 and 1816, a period in which half a million Mex-icans, from a population that barely reached four million, met with a violent death.

In 1819, after the "purchase" of Florida—actually more to ratify the treaty with Spain than because of any real interest, the United States had accepted Madrid's sovereignty over the nearly uninhabited territory of Tejas (later writ-ten with an "x"), as the western border of Louisiana. This was immediately fol-lowed by an upsurge in the number of U.S. immigrants into the region, a phe-nomenon that accelerated after the establishment of the convulsed Mexican Republic two years later. In 1836 when, following a short war, the Republic of Texas was declared, of the 35,000 inhabitants of that enormous region, 30,000 were Americans and many of the 5,000 remaining Mexicans preferred to live under the Union flag than with the continual disorder, rebellions, and attacks by General Santa Anna, who was determined to centralize in the distant capital everything pertaining to that remote and abandoned region.

Not quite ten years later the phenomenon was repeated, but this time the resurgence of the United States' superstitious sentiments of racial and cultural superiority was more evident and would quickly take on the title of "Manifest Destiny." This was the belief that the United States was meant to be the owners and masters of the entire continent, from Alaska to Patagonia, in accordance with a vague divine plan, a belief encouraged by the ease with which the *Tejanos* defeated Mexico, even though it was more or less the same size as the United States, with approximately the same population and an army six times larger. That same year, 1846, Great Britain was obligated to sign the Oregon Treaty and establish the northwest border of the United States at its current location. This confined Russia to the northernmost corner of Alaska, which at that time was lit-tle more than a semi-frozen hunting and fishing preserve and which explains why two decades later (1867) the Czar decided to sell this territory to the United States for a modest price, something, however, that seemed onerous to the Americans who had just emerged from a terrible civil war. They jokingly called it "the icebox purchase."

All that remained then was to draw the southwest border. When President Polk, the only American politician truly imbued with an imperialist view of for-eign policy, admitted Texas into the Union (1846), General Santa Anna declared war on the United States, an opportunity that the Americans took advantage of (they were probably awaiting it with great anticipation) to inflict another resounding defeat on Mexico and impose the surrender of New Mexico and California in the peace treaty, California being an area of the country where the scant Mexican existence was limited to some heroic and reclusive religious advance parties known as "missions." After losing the vital Central American region in the south, Mexico had, in fact, also lost half of its territory in the north, but that was the half that Spain never completely controlled.

The war between Spain and the United States was the confrontation between Ariel's spirituality and Calibán's materialism.

After the Mexican-American War (1846–1848)—the first time that the United States left its borders to seriously fight—and for a half a century later, American "interventionism" ceased almost completely. In the middle of 1898, however, this changed dramatically. It was at this time when the United States navy destroyed the Spanish fleet moored at Manila, the Philippines, and Santiago, Cuba, putting an end to 400 years of European dominion over Cuba, Puerto Rico, and several thousands of islands, islets, and keys scattered throughout the Pacific.

In order to understand these actions—generally ignored or distorted by our idiots—one has to keep in mind, first of all, the international atmosphere in which they occurred and, secondly, the specific technological evolutions that generated a different way of perceiving the "balance of powers," the goal of every geopolitical strategy since the eighteenth century.

The years 1885 and 1886 mark the apogee of European imperialism. England, France, and Germany divided among themselves what we today call the "Third World." In Berlin the powers officially met to determine the exact "influence zones" into which Africa was to be divided. England was experiencing the glory of its Victorian period, and writer Rudyard Kipling proclaimed "the white man's burden" of taking the splendor of civilization and the advantages of development to the dark-skinned, backward people. Practically no one, either from the left or the right, questioned this racist vision. Marx, for example, supported it, since how else can you believe in the final victory of the proletariat in places where the proletariat didn't even exist. It first needed to be created, and this was possible only through the energetic labor of the white homelands, especially of Anglo-Germanic origin.

The United States, which had always automatically considered itself as an improved extension of Europe (and not as anything unique, as did the Spanish

Americans), on the one hand participated in that atmosphere but on the other feared an inundation of imperialism by the European powers in Latin America, a danger that could materialize simply by occupying the delinquent countries in order to collect any unpaid debts.

In those years there also appeared a book on military strategy that every politician had read, written by an American naval officer, Alfred Thayer Mahan, who defended the need to rely on a strong navy—as did England—in order to defend one's trade routes and to "project" one's military power into every corner of the world. But since sailing ships were beginning to be a thing of the past, and the great iron battleships needed enormous quantities of coal, it was vital to have a string of supply bases—"coal bunkers"—capable of providing fuel.

Grosso modo, these essential factors, combined with the aversion that Spain awakened in the United States as a consequence of the horrors that its troops committed in the war against the Cuban insurgents (1895–1898), and the explosion of the U.S. battleship *Maine* in Havana harbor (a mysterious incident attributed to the Spaniards), are what precipitated the confrontation between Washington and Madrid. Everything fell into place: the cause—to expel Spain from Cuba and stop the killings—was extremely popular; the nationalists/imperialists, with Teddy Roosevelt at the helm, saw a unique opportunity to inherit a global empire at an incredibly low cost; and the United States could provide progress, democracy, and justice to the people who had lived an unhappy life, subjugated by the decadent Spanish-Catholic empire. Lastly, this gesture transformed the United States into the indisputable power of the New World but it also imposed on Washington the responsibility of maintaining law and order in its "backyard"—a thankless job, probably impossible to carry out, but fantastically enticing for a young and optimistic power that believed it was capable of doing anything after a history in which it had not known defeat.

The United States has backed every Latin American tyrant.

The euphoria didn't last for long. After the Spanish-American War, the Philippines revolted, gaining its independence in 1946 at a cost of 6,000 casualties. For the first third of the century, right up to Franklin D. Roosevelt's presidency, the United States intervened militarily several times in Cuba, the Dominican Republic, Haiti, and Nicaragua, generally for the same reason: it was "invited" by one of the two factions (or both, as happened in Cuba in 1906) either to establish order in the middle of a national quarrel sparked by fraudulent elections, to prevent a foreign power from collecting a pending debt at gunpoint, or to settle border disputes, a situation that at the end of the nineteenth century was at the point of inciting a war between Washington and London, "thanks" to Caracas.

Naturally, not all interventions were caused by the same situation. The U.S. intervention in Panama in 1903 was undoubtedly an imperialist act, motivated by the United States' desire to communicate by sea with its two coasts. This project was easier to carry out with this weak republic—dominated ever since its beginning—than through laborious negotiations with Colombia, the country from which this isthmus territory had severed itself, taking advantage of an old domestic separatist sentiment. The invasion of Mexico in 1916, on the other hand, was a simple (and useless) operation, based on the "right to pursuit," in order to punish Pancho Villa.

However, the general attitude that emboldened the U.S. government in those years, from McKinley to FDR, was always the same: to discipline those unruly, dark-skinned people in the south, apparently incapable of governing themselves efficiently. Rudyard Kipling was also in charge of the State Department. The U.S. interventionist model assumed that the problem was a lack of adequate legislation that would give rise to solid institutions. Following this diagnosis and based on America's experience, administrators after each invasion laid the groundwork for a modern health system, created some rudimentary mechanisms for tax collections, reorganized judicial power, trained a body of military police, and arranged some precarious elections. From these military police corps emerged young and clever officers like Anastasio Somoza and Rafael L. Trujillo, who later regrettably became two bloody dictators.

After the 1929 crash, and especially after the election of FDR, all of this changed. The Good Neighbor Policy inaugurated by the popular Democratic president was a clear retraction of the past thirty years' policy, not out of some moral reflection but out of fatigue and frustration. The United States found that order, respect for laws, and efficiency could not be imposed by the Marines. On the contrary, the frequent result was that some unscrupulous politicians benefited at the expense of other more or less unscrupulous politicians. Thus the corollary to Roosevelt's diplomatic doctrine was the cynical phrase about Somoza attributed to the Nicaraguan Foreign Minister: "Yes, he's a son of a bitch, but he's *our* son of a bitch." And this complacent indifference prevailed in Washington until the Cold War provoked another interventionist wave.

Imperialism intervened in Central America to defend the United Fruit Company.

The Good Neighbor Policy (a kind of "benevolent negligence," as it has been called) probably would have become the United States' diplomatic norm in relation to Latin America if the Cold War hadn't begun after the defeat of the Nazi–Fascist axis in 1945. Up till then, communists in Latin America, who had become "pro-American" when Stalin gave them the order in 1941, returned to their usual anti-Yankee tradition. It was in this setting of mistrust, paranoia, and—it must be admitted—an instinct for survival that U.S. interventionism took hold during the period between the ousting the Guatemalan Jacobo Arbenz in 1954 and (somewhat) the invasion of Panama in 1989, passing through the Bay of Pigs in 1961, the financing of the armed Nicaraguan opposition from 1982 to 1990, and the invasion of Grenada in 1983. The Haitian situation, as will be seen at the end of this chapter, forms a part of another, different era: today's era.

The most prevalent interpretation of the military coup staged against Colonel Jacobo Arbenz—with whom the Latin American idiot affiliates himself—is that the conspiracy that unseated him was in response to the radical economic reforms introduced by Arbenz himself. But the real story is different. Aside from the fact that the United Fruit Company may have felt harmed by the agrarian reform, what caused the CIA to arrange a military expedition against this legitimately elected government was Arbenz's purchase of Czech weapons and his strong ties to communism, which at that time, by the way, was emphatically denied by the entire Latin American "democratic left"—Rómulo Betancourt, Pepe Figueres, Raúl Roa (later Castro's Minister of Foreign Affairs for more than a decade)—at that time involved in an anti-Communist crusade.

Interestingly, the "success" of the CIA in Guatemala and its inability to distinguish hues—everything was red and everything was the same—were what precipitated the debacle, seven years later, of the anti-Castro campaign waged during the Eisenhower administration, when the officials who had devised the campaign against Arbenz just recycled that same plan of action against a completely different government and leader, leading President Kennedy to his first great fiasco in the famous Bay of Pigs invasion.

"We have to prevent another Cuba"—the watchword after the Cuban missile crisis, a Cold War incident that included Soviet submarine bases at Cienfuegos, on the south side of the island, and even a spy station near Havana (which still exists)—was later the leitmotiv of every U.S. administration's interventionist policy for that area. The "no more Cubans" policy was not based on ideological judgments, as it was in the case of Guyana, a country that lived through a long period of economic radicalism without any commotion and while maintaining normal relations with the United States.

Since the disappearance of the USSR, the U.S. interventionist policy has decreased substantially. In fact, one of President Clinton's not-so-secret "executive orders" prohibits covert actions by the CIA in Latin America beginning in 1995. This doesn't imply that the United States will just stand there with its arms crossed when it believes that Latin America is endangering its "national security," the motive that explains its intervention in Haiti in 1994. Could it be that the Haitian dictatorship was a "threat" to the powerful United States? Of course not. They intervened for two reasons: to prevent the mass exodus of boat people headed straight for Florida's coasts and to weaken the clear ties between the Haitian military and international drug trafficking.

The example of Haiti indicates what the United States' policy will be in the near future in relation to Latin America. They will act only "in self-defense" against the two current "threats" defined by their strategists: uncontrolled immigration and drug traffickers. This was evident in President Clinton's decision to "decertify" Colombia on March 1, 1996, taking away its trade advantages because of the politicians' ties to the Cali cartel and the contributions made by this Mafioso organization to President Samper's election campaign.

⑩

HOW BEAUTIFUL IS MY FLAG!

Latin American nationalism is, just like horses and Jesuits, laws and the Spanish language, a European import. This nationalism, however, has been the most costly product that we have imported. The fact that a philosophy, so extensively circulated around the world, has been invented to justify the isolation of one country with respect to the others, slipping through the borders without respecting mental tariffs, is not the only irony here. In Latin America, nationalism was born with our independence and intensified with the history of the republics, with continuous military music in the background and an undeniable odor of fascism. In the middle of the twentieth century, it came of age when, after we echoed the international Third World trend, the famous theory of dependency emerged.

If what they say is true, that nationalism is a seventeenth- and eighteenth-century French invention (strengthened by Napoleon in the nineteenth century), we Latin Americans all have a Louis XIV crouching in the corner of our souls. Our nationalism quickly jumped from the barracks to academia and from academia to what the snobbish gentility call "the collective unconscious," and after two centuries of political atrocities it's not easy to distinguish between those inspired by nationalism and those that weren't. Our nationalism, which in certain cases has been an expression of political uncertainty, in others evil authoritarian designs, and many times a mixture of ignorance and social complexes about the rich and powerful, has produced fascinating characters, grotesque and solitary figures, and dangerous mental midgets. In every case, it has contributed—sometimes with good intentions and sometimes not—to our passionate love affair with political tribalism and economic infantilism. Nationalism has been the least patriotic of our heroic deeds, even though many Latin Americans have embarked on it with the enthusiasm and faith of the Holy Crusades.

If nationalism is essentially a European contribution to our political behavior, then nationalist *caudillismo* (that is, strongman rule) is one of Latin America's contributions to the world. It has been present since independence, when politics acquired an obviously heroic dimension protected by the military. After independence, several generations of *caudillos* remained in power throughout the nineteenth century, many of them linked to the rural world. There was Dr. Francia in Paraguay; Santa Anna in Mexico, the custodian of his own leg, holding a glorious ceremony in which he made half the country march past his amputated limb; and Juan Manuel de Rosas in Argentina, a perfect example of how the conflict between centralism and federalism that distinguished many of our republics was, deep down, pure nonsense—even de Rosas worked as a provincial *gaucho* but governed like a centralist ogre.

The *caudillo* soon became wealthy because he turned into a constitutionalist, desperate to leave humanity something of his own: not children to prolong his dynasty, but constitutions to perpetuate, legally, the "goodness" of his passage through power. In Peru, for example, Ramón Castilla bequeathed three constitutions. Not all *caudillos* were dictators, though. In Uruguay, José Batlle y Ordóñez was a democrat. With him there emerged another *caudillo*-type characteristic: the welfare state. The *caudillo* is the nation's father, wanting to teach his offspring to read and write, watching over their health, protecting them from the perils of daily life and the uncertainty of old age, providing them with wheels so they can get around. The *caudillo* is a benefactor who spends everyone's money, including the money that doesn't exist (which he discovers one fine day in the form of devilishly evil inflation), to protect the defenseless society. It is also he, of course, who protects society from the charlatans who want to lead it down the wrong path, making sure that all of his possible critics either share the same cozy prison with the most hospitable rodents or have a nice long "walkabout" in exile.

The *caudillo* embodies the state, he personifies it, but he also embodies society as a whole. The *caudillo* is the nation. When the *caudillo* is angry, society is angry. When he's sad, society sulks. When he, the masculine, is happy, she, the feminine, smiles. The greater the multitude of women passing through his bedroom, the more society admires the *caudillo*'s political biceps, the more they fear his phobias, and the greater they enjoy his fascinations. The *caudillo*'s mood is the legal, political, and institutional framework, serving as the country's daily weathervane. Given the absence of solid institutions, the *caudillo* emerges with virile force. The *caudillo*'s long stay in government compensates for the instability of immature societies. The *caudillo* becomes the only permanent thing, a true national project in himself.

While his secret police dissuade the audacity of dissidence with (more or less) friendly methods, they fossilize all of his thirst for grandeur in state-run companies, the Egyptian pyramids of our political panorama. They begin to speak of "strategic areas" and, by applying the military mentality to the economic map of their nations—Vargas in Brazil, Perón in Argentina, Arbenz in Guatemala, Torrijos in Panama, Allende in Chile, Castro in Cuba, all from relatively socialist but especially patrimonial positions—they give a governmental bear hug to all of society's centers of wealth creation. No victim has ever been killed with greater love; the state's embrace is also society's asphyxiation. All of this, of course, with the backdrop of a foreign adversary, aided by the country's domestic enemy. Anti-imperialism is near to the *caudillo*'s heart. The wars between Latin Americans throughout the history of the republics can literally be counted on one hand, but our *caudillos* have waged thousands, maybe even millions, of verbal wars against bordering neighbors, against the enemies of the poor, and against the United States. The *caudillo*'s nationalism is political, military, and economic all at the same time. The theory of dependency of the 1950s and 1960s is the counterpart of our Mirage fighters and tanks.

Caudillismo runs throughout our political geography, encompassing our dictatorships and democracies, political parties and just plain politics. Great liberal *caudillos* like Jorge Eliécer Gaitán in Colombia have been much more *caudillo* than liberal and Haya de la Torre in Peru was such an egocentric personality within APRA (American Popular Revolutionary Alliance) that the only way to establish new leadership was to create a quasi-mystical cult in the memory of its leader. Balaguer in the Dominican Republic has demonstrated that *caudillismo,* after becoming a vested interest for the powerful caste surrounding the *caudillo,* generates an inertia so difficult to overcome that an old blind man can remain endlessly in government without any problems, and not always through fraudulent means (a refined electoral custom to which Balaguer, as well as many of our *caudillos,* is devoted).

Let's have a look at some of the specimens from our vast *caudillo* pantheon, beginning with Latin America's greatest, Simón Bolívar, frequently a victim of the robbers of ideological tombs who unabashedly continue to twist, omit, or simply distort true history.

Simón Bolívar the Liberator is Latin America's greatest antiimperialist, a defender of our native heritage from the cultural invasion of the powerful.

No figure has inspired so many nationalist dithyrambs as Simón Bolívar. But the glowing profile of the hero of Latin America's independence has been reduced to almost a caricature by our patriots' impassioned, misinformed, and at times false representations, with a reading half Carlyle (his fascination with the Providence-man) and half Marx (his proletariat revolution). For starters, Bolívar wasn't born poor but rich, which in a certain respect explains his shield of pride: he didn't wage war in search of fortune, but for power and glory. His ancestors had been well compensated by the Spanish Crown for their contribution in constructing the Guaira port and creating plantations. The Liberator's childhood, like Jefferson's and Washington's, was fanned by slaves (quite normal among the Venezuelans of that period and social condition). This was also the case for his wife, a fragile woman of Caracas ancestry whom he met in Madrid—an obligatory destination for the colonial bourgeoisie—and who died very young of yellow fever shortly after returning to Caracas with her then-unknown husband.

This proto-Marxist Bolívar that our unflagging idiots try to sell us is utterly false. He was obsessed with the race problem. He wanted to avoid, at all costs, the war of classes and colors. Neither in his social upbringing nor in his political philosophy did Bolívar think of doing away with the powerful class. No, his achievement wasn't class consciousness but something else, the offspring of an ideological movement arising essentially among the *criollos,* the colonial children of imperial Spain. Bolívar wasn't the predecessor of the Mexican PRI party or of Haya de la Torre's APRA or of Perón, nor of any contemporary anti-imperialist. His war with Spain was not a battle against anything foreign or against Europe; he owed everything he was fighting for to that world considering that Spanish colonialism was the remnant of a previous era that refused to cede to the passage of time and the liberal ideas of the age of Enlightenment. It wasn't only ironic that the pro-independence supporters rose up against Spain on behalf of Ferdinand VII when he was subjugated by Napoleon; it was also an acknowledgment that Spain's liberal reforms were being threatened by French imperialism and its Hispanic puppets. (The fact that Ferdinand VII, upon returning to power, would give a trapeze-like back-flip, forgetting about liberalism and rediscovering the formidable charms of absolutism, is another matter.) This affinity between Bolívar and the liberals in Spain was evident in matters as significant as the rebellion of the Spanish army that had joined Ferdinand VII in Cádiz to give the independence activists a good beating. The proverbial Hispanic laziness was not the only factor in their refusal to cross the pond; there was also the rejection of the old regime. Even in his military campaign, Bolívar was indebted to Europe and Spain. His armies were full of European mercenaries, as evidenced by the famous British Legion, which participated in many of his battles and not a few of his feats. In contrast, a good portion of the very patriotic indigenous population fought on the side of the Spanish Crown.

Bolívar's supposed anti-*Yankeeism* is also spurious. If there is any song that Bolívar would never have hummed, it's "Yankee, go home!" As would happen to Miranda, his fascination with the United States reached incredible heights after his trip to Boston, Philadelphia, the District of Columbia, and Charleston in 1806, at the peak of his formative years. Most of his beliefs were founded as much on the libertarian ideals of the U.S. Constitution as in the coexistence of its regions within a federal state (reality later showed that he wasn't a very diligent student of both of these lessons, but the blame for that is well shared). Supporters of the independence movement were partisans with strong ties to Great Britain and the United States.

When our illustrious idiots roar against Yankee imperialism, they tend to track the source of this evil to the Monroe Doctrine in 1823, forgetting that Bolívar, along with most Latin American supporters of independence, celebrated Monroe's and John Quincy Adams's policy as a safeguard against the danger of new European interventions in the Americas. In the end, the first foreign power that recognized the revolutionary juntas in full turmoil was the United States, which earned the gratitude of Bolívar and his followers. In Latin America, pro-independence supporters were xenophobic neither in political matters nor in economic ones, as seen by the fact that one of the first measures they adopted, when they succeeded in establishing their dominion, was opening their ports to world trade. Although Bolívar's integration efforts ultimately pointed out the practical outcome of creating an independent power, there is no doubt that the United States was his inspiration, and the Liberator was in many ways much closer to the "Yankee, come home!" motto than the one stating the contrary. Individual nationalism in Latin American countries had, however, little in common with Bolívar's undertaking, which was always for continental unity. Although he focused his efforts primarily on a "Gran Colombia," a territory that was to unite Venezuela, Colombia, and Ecuador, his dream embraced a wider perimeter, as his efforts demonstrate with the Panama Congress convened by him in 1826, to put the Latin American herd once and for all into the same corral. Bolívar's dream, which had hints of continental nationalism (or, as a European commissioner from the Maastricht era would say, supranational nationalism), was put directly into doubt by the petty tyrants who razed Bolívar's castle thanks to their small appetite for power, covered with nationalist poetry. Moreover, much of Bolívar's integration creed came from the fact—of which he was well aware—that national rivalries had kept the Europeans practicing punching and head-butting diplomacy for centuries.

Bolívar was the precursor to the Latin American revolution and the herald of liberation for the Latin American people.

The Latin American idiot believes that Bolívar was something like a proto-revolutionary Marxist. In his dreams he sees the Liberator crouching in the

underbrush of Sierra Maestra, surrounded by sugar canes near the river Mag-
dalena, or setting fire to Somoza's backside. He hasn't bothered to consult the
history books. If he had, he would have discovered, for example, that Marx, a
man for whom the Third World, and especially Latin America, produced hip-
popotamus-size yawns, expressed the greatest scorn for Simón Bolívar, whom,
quoting Piar, the conqueror of Guyana, he called the "Napoleon of retreats." In
a letter to Engels he commented about the Liberator with a passionate ardor
that certainly didn't exclude a bit of racism: "It is ridiculous to see how this cowardly, miserable, ordinary rogue is being praised to the high heavens as if he
were Napoleon." His recounting of Bolívar's passing through the area could have
been endorsed by Ferdinand VII: "He detested," Marx wrote in an 1858 article
for the *New American Cyclopedia,* "any sustained effort, therefore his dictatorship soon turned into military anarchy. The most important matters remained in
the hands of his favorites, who squandered the finances."

Although this isn't a complete falsehood, we are, undoubtedly, witnessing a
manipulation of the facts. It's true that Bolívar lived scattered amid the many
and, at times, contradictory pressures of his achievements, causing him to jump
from one side to the other, frequently from one responsibility to another, depriving him from being able to contribute to the institutional stability of the liberated countries. It's also true that many times he left deputies in power in order
to continue with his political/military wanderings throughout Latin America,
which certainly facilitated the multiple conspiracies he fell prey to by his war
companions, who had a rather transient sense of loyalty. And, last, it's a historical reality that the independent republics were a financial catastrophe, which
cannot be chalked up exclusively to the war, since inefficiency and irresponsibility of the individual governments contributed to this even many years after
the battles had ended. In all of this, Bolívar's responsibility must be qualified:
Bolívar had to travel in order to achieve his goals and had to leave trusted people in power. There were times when the Liberator, in the purest fashion of
Monsieur Camdessus and the International Monetary Fund, fought for specific
financial orthodoxy, as when, toward the end of his life, he dramatically urged
the Colombians to eliminate the huge public debt. In any case, Bolívar, the revolutionary, was looked down on by the father of the proletariat revolution.

If Bolívar was anything, he was the embodiment of what the revolutionaries
supposedly detest, the military *caudillo,* although anyone familiar with his work
cannot deny his political talent. We cannot say, however, that he was the king of
consistency. The same mixture of attitudes that he had about Napoleon (he
admired his creation of the legal codes and his military expertise, but his Cae-
sarism and coronation as emperor frightened him) is reflected in his own biography. Bolívar spoke many times of a government of laws and not of men. In his

famous speech in Angostura he warned against the danger of vesting too much authority in a single man. But this didn't prevent him from "accepting" the nomination of dictator in Caracas in 1812, or in Lima a decade later, when the Peruvians, ancient courtiers of the Incas and the viceroyals, also declared him dictator, adding—just in case—the very finite adjective "for life" to this designation.

It's likewise true that the Liberator immediately expressed his reluctance to being named president of Gran Colombia by the Cúcuta congress. But he didn't make them beg for long and soon resigned himself to taking the mantle of total authority, leaving Santander to govern in his place and going off to conquer the south. The man who used to say that he wasn't "the leader that the Republic wanted" wasn't an obsessive cultivator of congruency between words and actions. In the last years of his life, his democratic modesty, in the turbulent environment of that time, was not resolute. After rejecting San Martín's proposals of a constitutional monarchy, Bolívar proposed governments with quasi-monarchic executive powers and a hereditary Senate, similar to the English hereditary nobility, in which there would be lords plus some sprinklings of electoral representation to blend it all together. He didn't believed strongly in man's ability to freely govern himself by way of impromptu institutions. He had developed nostalgia for some type of imposed order within this labyrinth. Thus it's ironic, in appearance only, that toward the end of his days one of the most repeated accusations against Bolívar, who opposed a monarchy, was precisely that he was "monarchical," and Santander, in the end, accused him of governing "capriciously" instead of in accordance with the Constitution. In any case, Bolívar was as much a pre-Marxist revolutionary or a partisan of class struggle as Fidel Castro is clean-shaven.

One shouldn't underestimate the obstacles that Bolívar encountered in trying to carry out his intentions. There exists the danger of attributing to him, retrospectively, political deficiencies resulting from his opponents' success. Bolívar tried, for example, to institute religious freedom and a nondenominational state in the Bolivian constitution of 1825. He didn't succeed, and the Bolivians made Catholicism the official state religion. In the end, as he himself admitted in a beautiful metaphor, "he who serves in a revolution is trying to plow the sea"; his efforts toward continental unity and constitutional stability came to naught. When in 1826 and 1827 Gran Colombia fell apart, it was clear, as he himself had predicted, that not only had his dream of a union vanished, but also the dream of a region governed according to the rights of civilized and peaceful institutions. There descended a long, dark night of *caudillo* dictatorships empowered by military force. Pro-independence *caudillismo* degenerated into ideals that differed from those of the Liberator, but not all of them were alien to the practice of what the revolutionaries of the nineteenth century had themselves established: the merger of the military and the political, violence and the law. When Bolívar said about Colombia that "this country will fall into the hands of the unbridled multitude and later pass to mini-dictatorships," he was speaking the truth. Let's not forget, however, that there was a notable presence of petty dictators, chaos, commotion, and anarchical crowds during the independence period as well. Bolívar's work, designed to unite Latin Americans, had just the opposite result. What was to be the Liberator's epic—and at times was—had after his death resulted first in a farce and then a tragedy. Latin America's first great nationalist *caudillo* was the first great victim of its nationalism. That era's legacy, mixed with others, brought forth the Latin American republics of the last two centuries. There is something in Rosas, Santa Anna, Gómez, Vargas, Cárdenas, Perón, and all our nationalist *caudillos* that comes from those times.

***Pancho Villa is one of the great founders of Mexican dignity,
a great advocate of the interest of the people, a hero of the
glorious Mexican revolution.***

Pancho Villa is the perfect Latin American macho. He was born weighing seven kilos (15.5 pounds—a good part of which was undoubtedly located south of his belly button) and even though he was short, fat, and ugly, legend has him sitting tall on a horse, elegantly heading up his *golden ones* (followers), who called him "the Centaur." Although he was born in the center of Mexico (no other place would have been favorable enough for the feats of this valiant nationalist), he soon left this land to emigrate north, specifically to Chihuahua, a region conveniently situated directly in the nostrils of the United States so that the hero of Latin America's fatherland could throw out his chest right into Wilson's and General Pershing's whiskers. He learned to read in the prison (a very romantic touch) where Victoriano Huerta, Francisco Madero's right-hand man, had sent him because of his quite unruly and rebellious personality in the chaos that followed the fall of Porfirio Díaz. As any good macho, he had honor, so much honor that he killed the son of a landowner for making a pass at his sister. He was as much a teetotaler as any saint, grotesquely choking down a glass of brandy given to him by Emiliano Zapata the first time they met in Mexico City, the Revolution already underway. He was capable of evoking the indispensable insolence that flames the patriotic imagination of Latin America, such as when he suggested to Venustiano Carranza, who had taken over power in the midst of revolutionary unrest and considered Villa's three thousand men a danger, that they both commit suicide. How macho! And, of course, the myth would be incomplete without his glorious death in Chihuahua in 1923, fighting like a bull against eight hired assassins who fired twelve bullets into his chest and four into his head. (One of the killers was shot down by the brave revolutionary.) The fact that three years later someone would unearth Villa's head so that the people would stop saying that he was still alive is a perfect climax to the quasi-divine biography of the Mexican hero. The country needs heroes, even if a little retrospective touching-up is needed for the exaggerated figure of the mustachioed bandit, who never actually stopped being the highwayman of his youth, and to make a marble statue of him.

Perhaps his only merits were those that were never brought out: his stubborn individuality, which prompted him to fight everybody and made him the enemy of the *caudillos* he had previously helped, once they achieved power; his military skill, since overnight he went from being a captain of fifteen men to a colonel of three thousand; and his skill as a strategist, proving himself a master of railway logistics (a key element in moving the troops in this extensive and rough Mexican territory) thanks to his ability to maintain a constant supply of coal and his zigzagging ability to dodge the enemy's air force fire in the mountains. But all of these military qualities were the product of his bandit background and his practical knowledge of the land, acquired during his intensive childhood schooling as a gunfighter in northern Mexico.

If Pancho Villa is Mexico's dignity incarnate, the country's apotheosis, the Mexicans should start fleeing toward Tierra del Fuego. Much about him was fraudulent, starting with his name (his real birth name—quite inappropriate for the history books—was Doroteo Arango). It's true that he participated in ousting Porfirio Díaz, the old Mexican dictator, and was a supporter of the democratic Francisco Madero (an honest and decent gentleman who didn't know what he was getting into when he decided to call for democracy for his country, bandits coming at him from all four sides to put him in power and then to push him out). But the convictions that motivated Pancho Villa to take Ciudad Juárez, for example, weren't democratic but anarchic and quasigansterish, benefiting from Madero's ascension to power. Fights were his natural element. He was a man who ransacked everything that lay in his path, in accordance with his noble philosophy—worthy of the most lofty canons of corporate management—of needing to keep the boys happy. It was to the point that the revolutionaries themselves had to imprison him for being so rebellious. He wasn't particularly magnanimous with the federal troops he captured, and he had the quaint custom of having them execute one another. Although he was guided by a certain sense of justice in his desire to avenge Madero after his fall at the hands of the revolution's never-ending betrayals, and although there exists the notion that Villa favored restoring the political reforms that Porfirio Díaz had revoked, to attribute to Pancho Villa the sublime principles of politics and economy is like saying that Attila the Hun was a manicurist. In this perpetual revolution, noble invocations of democratic or constitutional governments, such as Carranza's, for example, who confronted the traitor Huerta with the Constitution in hand, lasted for as long as it took to gain power. With little notion of his own brutality—and with a slightly Roman touch—Villa, the champion of the country, allowed himself the luxury of calling the Yankees "barbarians."

Villa's great anti-imperialism, like that of many revolutionaries, requires fine nuances. For starters, Carranza assumed power in complete revolutionary chaos, thanks in good part to Washington's support, which temporarily even occupied Veracruz to help the *caudillo* (who at that time was also supported by Pancho Villa) and because of a strict arms embargo previously declared by Wilson, which weakened the ruling regimen. At one time, Pancho Villa thought it suitable, faced with the enemy's siege, to take refuge on . . . U.S. soil! When he slipped into Texas in 1913, it wasn't exactly to complain to the Yankees about the territory that was lost in the previous century, but to prevent Mexico's federal troops from flinging him like a sack of potatoes back into jail. Nationalist history likes to forget these details, remembering only Pancho Villa's attack on Texas in 1916. That story is also a bit distorted. Villa didn't attack the United States for nationalist reasons. His objective was to discredit his domestic adversaries, Carranza and the commander of his troops, Alvaro Obregón, making them appear weak in confronting the Northern giant. Villa's horizon wasn't international but Mexican, and not even national but regional, particularly the northern part of Mexico, regardless of how much he, just like everyone else, wanted the weight of his importance to be felt in the capital.

Not even his bravery was free from weakness. On several occasions, with his good fugitive sense, he began running cross-country so as not to die like a rat. The most famous of his escapes—but not his only one—was in 1915 in Celaya, when Alvaro Obregón gave him a sound beating and set him racing back to Chihuahua. Lastly, our revolutionary hero was much more given to bourgeoisie activities than proletariat ones. His business-minded appetite emerged very early on, and in 1908 Mr. Pancho Villa, tired of his outlaw escapades, opened up a butcher shop, concentrating all of his efforts there and earning juicy profits (the beef came from the herds his men rustled). When he finally heard the call to battle, at the height of Francisco Madero's revolt, our indomitable *caudillo* was burdened by undying liberation ideals . . . But who would dare say that this degrades his glory? Didn't Machiavelli say that the *condotierri* were the best fighters? Years later, after abandoning his revolutionary wanderings, our revolutionary earnestly dedicated himself to . . . a business in real estate! Señor Pancho, the avenger of *campesinos* deprived of their communal land by Porfirio Díaz and his foreign allies, ended his days, well, as a majestic landowner.

Augusto C. Sandino was a martyr to Nicaraguan national
independence and the interests of the campesinos
and the people.

The word "Sandinista" was introduced into world political discourse in the
1980s, but most people who used the term, including Latin Americans, don't
realize that it comes from a very real person with the same name, Augusto C.
Sandino. Most interesting is that, in his time, he wasn't an unknown figure.
Rather, he was a stubborn thorn in the side of the American mastodon and, for
the international revolutionary movements that shook up the world during the
middle of the 1920s and 1930s, a kind of magical reference, a password among
the rebels. The Chinese Kuomintang party, a devastating power at that time,
though completely incapable of even finding the Segoviana mountains on a map,
later christened one of its divisions with this Nicaraguan name. In Latin America, Haya de la Torre believed that this rough gentleman personified the Indo-
American man of his dreams.

Sandino was the perfect tropical bird. He had a spiritual calling, preferring—
as he *said*—the invisible outpouring of the soul to the obstacles of material matters. Instead of being a Catholic—the religion of the exploiters—he was a
Freemason, a marvelous reincarnation of the lodges that greatly contributed to
bumping off the Spanish empire. To add some exoticism to the colors of his
feathers, he was a semi-Adventist. A dissident of the spirit. Politics and mysti-
cism: the magical recipe to save the nation. He was also, since he couldn't be any
other way, a political romantic, someone prepared to bravely and courageously
offset the drawbacks of a military disadvantage and political solitude. In his biography as the savior of the nation, there is the incident in which, after spending
some time overseas fleeing from justice, he crossed the border into Nicaragua
in 1926 and made his way up to the top of Segoviana to mobilize an army, a handful of men ready to fight like lions against Yankee interventionism and its domestic accomplices. Soon he established his hideaway at *El Chipote,* in the mountains of northwest Nicaragua—the orographic call of Latin American politics is
apparently pathological—and from there he launched his most nationalist and
fiery harangue: "I'm Nicaraguan, my blood is Indian, my blood holds the mystery of genuine patriotism." His rhetoric, that inevitable scarlet touch of any
Latin American peacock, was profuse. For his enemies, he shot off thunderous
comments such as this: "He who wants to enter here should be sure he first
makes his will." The nation's salvation was safeguarded under Augusto C.
Sandino's mountainous highland shield.

Any cursory taxidermist's examination of this species would reveal a reality
less dignified than the image created by the international idiot. It's true that

Sandino had a relationship with the countryside since birth. But there's a slight problem: it wasn't a relationship of a *campesino* with the land but of a landowner and his domain. His father, Gregorio Sandino, was the owner of a not very large property, but big enough to require an unyielding administrator. Who was this administrator? Wouldn't you know? His own son. Sandino's mother was, yes, a servant, Margarita Calderón, but the boy found out soon enough that life was more comfortable on his father's lap. In addition to living out the quiet life of a landowner near Granada, Nicaragua, Augusto decided to exchange his mother's disgraceful servile surname for his father's aristocratic one. So, he stopped being Augusto Calderón and became Augusto Sandino. A small addition came to crown his new life: inspired by the rich collection of classical books in his father's library, Augusto decided to insert the imperial name "César" between the Augusto and Sandino. And that's how Augusto César Sandino was created.

Since this man and his contemporary votaries talk so abundantly about their Indian blood—the hemoglobular obsession of Latin American politics is just as great as the orographic obsession—it's curious to note, with a quick intravenous inspection, that Augusto Sandino had a different blood type than he believed. He wasn't an Indian but a mestizo, and his cultural background wasn't indigenous but "ladino." In other words, he was the result of a crossbreeding of a culture that was present before the arrival of the white man and that which sailed in on those caravels. Sandino's mother and father belonged to that Westernized, especially Europeanized, world that for many years has made up the majority of the Nicaraguan population. His Indian claims against the invading world had, well, little foundation: neither he nor the majority of those who fought with him in the mountains were Indian, nor is Nicaragua an Indian country. Sandino and his followers were mestizos, people who culturally shared much more with their enemies than with the roots of those to whom they wanted to appeal (their specific way of practicing politics reinforces this cultural parentage, by the way). The romanticizing of Sandino should not let us lose sight of his bullying and his proclivity toward weapons. Let's not forget that his first exile in 1920 wasn't for political reasons but rather due to a common criminal act: he wounded a rival with a bullet in a countryside brawl in Niquinihomo.

This icon of emerging socialism in the Latin America of the 1920s and 1930s was also weak when facing capitalism's handiwork. During his extensive travels through Central America in the 1920s, when he was fleeing justice, he worked for major fruit companies—a true symbol of Central American exploitation for the continental idiot—until he ended up, once in Tampico, Mexico, as a well-groomed petroleum executive: Manager of Gasoline Sales for the Huasteca Company. He later returned to his country to take up arms and sink his unsuitable past into the waters of oblivion. But this only lasted for a while. In 1929, after he had spent several years defending himself in the mountains against enemy attacks, he returned to Mexico in search of solidarity and, since he was given the cold shoulder by the very rhetorical yet very practical Mexican revolution, to beg for money from real estate companies.

Sandino's anti-imperialism was an essential part of his nationalist crusade. This anti-imperialism infected him—it can't be explained any other way—on his first Mexican journey. Later, the *gringos'* boundless ineptitude in Nicaragua gave Sandino a fabulous boost. But was he an anti-imperialist to the death, incapable of selling out the anti-Yankee flag in exchange for political advantages, a superman of steadfastness? Or did he have some minor human frailties?

When Sandino erupted onto the Nicaraguan scene, the country had for many years been watching the liberals and conservatives kill each other, establishing coup d'etats and bullets as instruments of the changing of power. Both groups had also used the United States for their respective agendas. The seventeen-year dictatorship of the "liberal" José Santos Zelaya had ignited the fire of hate for conservatives, while the subsequent semidynastic Chamorro dictatorship incited rebellion among the liberals. All of this had come to a head in 1926 in a new episode of Nicaraguan civil wars. Therefore, Sandino's attack on the establishment seems absolutely unquestionable. It was the exasperated, undefiled shout from deep within the country against the political corruption and violence of the country's officials. Up to here fine. But Sandino's initial refusals to ally himself with the liberal opposition soon desisted, since he discovered the virtues of arrangements and deal-making. After his ridiculous attack on the garrison at Jícaro, he took refuge on the Atlantic coast to form an alliance with the liberals. Although Juan Sacasa and his military chief, José María Moncada, didn't trust him, they did ultimately make him a general. These were, however, not true liberals. They had a long history of dictatorships . . . and violence. The most curious thing about this alliance between Sandino and the liberals was not their past but the present when they joined forces. The liberals were in constant negotiations with Calvin Coolidge, the president of the United States, who would ultimately be responsible for working out a Nicaraguan truce. Later, when in 1932 Sacasa was president of Nicaragua, Sandino made a final agreement with the liberals, who had superb relations with the United States, and with the Nicaraguan National Guard, which resisted reform and had been created by imperialism, to stop fighting in exchange for control over a handful of territory. His political vision, aside from asking the *gringos* to leave and renegotiating the agreement to construct an interoceanic canal, was really quite modest. (Of course, during the years of fighting, Sandino, aware that political idiotism isn't restricted to the region south of the Rio Grande, named his own brother as the unofficial ambassador to the United States.) Augusto C. Sandino's anti-imperialist nationalism was a model of pragmatism.

Unfortunately, Yankee blunders in Nicaragua weren't a nationalist invention. Those were what, in good part, gave birth to the myth of Sandino. There isn't a more delectable image in revolutionary mythology than the air raids carried out for years by the Marines against the territories in the rugged Segoviana of the fugitive Sandino. When in 1928 sixteen continuous days of bombing ended not Sandino's life, but the lives of dozens of goats, mules, cows, and horses, leaving—in Sandino's own words—"a sky full of vultures," Washington had created the platform that would propel Augusto into political history. The American press would take care of the rest. Practicing what apparently was an old custom, journalists would often embark on their own pilgrimages to Sandino's wild hideouts, where they admired him, wrapped in patriotic red and black, in awe. An excellent example of an American idiot, Carleton Beals, wrote about Sandino in *The Nation:* "he is completely without vices . . . he has an unequivocal sense of justice." Anyone practicing a little less genuflection would have at least been able to see that the revolutionary had not lost his taste for bourgeoisie attire, arranging it all right up there in the mountain, gelling his hair back like a tango singer and sporting a silk handkerchief, while his troops wore cotton ones (the Ortegas would resuscitate this refined custom many years later).

Blaming the United States for what happened in Nicaragua was quite an optimistic shifting of the blame. Nicaraguan politicians had drawn Washington (which didn't need much encouragement) into its domestic politics, and when the Americans left, around 1930, defeated by a Central American chaos sufficient to depress even the most enthusiastic imperialist, it was the Nicaraguans themselves, particularly those in the Nicaraguan National Guard with Somoza already emerging into the limelight, who plunged the country into that political morass. It was this same National Guard who killed Sandino in 1934 as he was leaving the presidential palace, after he had given up using weapons (he only retained a small group of personal bodyguards) and had become a politician in the bourgeoisie system, lobbying for his causes. No less important in all of this was the weakness of the liberal government in confronting the military's villainy.

Perón turned Argentina into a modern, free, and proud nation.

If Perón is, as his supporters believe, the soul of Argentina, what Argentina hastily needs is an exorcism to remove such demons from within. Of all the figures of Latin American nationalism, probably none has generated so much quasi-mystical fanaticism, nor intrigued the world with the dark recesses of its system of power, as has Perón. Therefore, it isn't enough, as Borges wanted, to just eliminate his name to banish his memory. If every Argentine has a Perón in the depths of his soul, it must be excised, with a benign cross if possible, and if not, then with a sharp scalpel.

At the beginning of the twentieth century, the Argentine nation was Latin America's happy story; a case—though not without its own political atrocities, true—of prosperity and modernization. After Perón left power in 1955, savagery had returned to the center of the political stage and the economy slid down a slope that was slicker than the general's styling gel.

It's particularly interesting that incense is burned for Perón because of his nationalism, when, as with most Argentines, his roots were European and, what is even more significant, he himself made sure that those roots were recognized at the appropriate time. He wanted to flaunt not only his Spanish and Italian origins but also that his great-grandfather had been the senator of Sardinia. Some wag reported that the name Perón was actually Peroni. Just as curious is how he tried to change the social origin of his surname into a proletariat legend. In his day, his father had lived with him on a sheep ranch near the Atlantic coast of Buenos Aires province, the perfect bourgeoisie culmination of a life of constant work.

According to legend, he had the strength of Samson and the determination of Ulysses—the perfect Latin American macho, the powerful virile incarnation of the Argentine nation. Perhaps he was in his spare time, but he certainly wasn't all the time. Some key episodes in his biography reveal a much more fragile and indecisive character. When in October 1945 he resigned from several of his positions in the military government he was serving, Mr. Juan Domingo Perón, who had tried to escape by crossing the river, was imprisoned on the island of Martín García. After a few hours he began his deafening complaints of pleurisy, writing imploring letters to the president and asking to be sent into exile. It was Evita who stopped him from negotiating any type of abandonment of principles. This is no minor detail: the story of his triumphant march into Buenos Aires on the shoulders of the working people and his immediate election victory, which changed the course of Argentina, could have been avoided if Eva hadn't blocked this surrender. On the other hand, in 1951, at the height of his government, rumors of a coup d'etat caused Perón to leave the Casa Rosada (the executive office building) seeking asylum in the Brazilian Embassy, from where his wife had to grab him by the ears and take him back to his office.

Latin American nationalism has always had an essential military component. Perón was a devout heir to that tradition. He had a military education at a very young age, but, unlike what happens in civilized countries, his climb up the military ladder wasn't based on merit but on uprisings and confraternities. When he finished his military studies and entered the Ministry of War he held the rank of captain. Thanks to the coup d'etat against Hipólito Yrigoyen, it was possible for Perón to receive more military stripes on his sleeve in the 1930s and, later, in the 1940s (thanks especially to a military man with a name worthy of vaudeville, Edelmiro Farrell, the Minister of War who, like any good Latin American, decided to line up the cannons against his own government coup and grant himself total power). Politics was inseparable from the military in the delicate Peronist sensibility and the military inseparable from the fascist organization, with a mix of drama, corporatism, and populism. His European examples were Mussolini's Italy, Nazi Germany, and Franco's Spain, countries he opportunely visited, and his exercise of power demonstrated that his horrifying statement— "Mussolini is the greatest man of this century"—should have been taken seriously. When in 1946 Perón took over with 56% of the vote, he set into motion his most enlightened authoritarian instructions and took control of the press, created a judicial branch that supported his regime, flooded the public schools with a cult to himself, and gave a nice imperialist look to his band of thugs so that they could handle any challenge from dissident elements. All of this mixed with half-mystical, half-military fraternal orders and a thick occultist atmosphere. The nation's defense was a fascist-inspired dictatorial regime (with a touch of *milonga* and *porteño* magic).

The central element of Peronism was the workers and their unions. This proletariat angle also echoed, of course, fascism. Until then Argentina's history as a republic had been, to a certain degree, one of centralist *caudillismo* against regionalist *caudillismo*. Perón changed the terms of the battle and replaced this conflict with one between the city and the country. In the military dictatorship preceding his government, the one in which he served, Perón had already created an extensive social base from that position of power. To this he added the cataclysmic Eva, a radio actress, well versed in the instruments of unrest and propaganda. Once president, Perón accelerated the process, unleashing an insolent and onerous demagogy in favor of unionization (Perón's fiscal good sense was inversely proportionate to the capacity of his salivary glands), which, for example, increased the CGT union membership from 300,000 workers to 5 million! A military and social alliance hadn't previously existed in those terms in Latin America. It was a Peronist creation. The general forgot his calculator and began increasing wages left and right. In the excitement of collective bargaining, he encouraged the workers to attack management and gave them a privileged status in his corporatist organization of power. In the long run, however, this scheme backfired: the proletariat threat scared the pants off the military and in 1955 the military decided to send Perón into exile.

Populism and corporatism inflicted the most patriotic misfortunes on a country that during World War II had attained enormous wealth thanks to the frantic demand for beef and wheat throughout Europe. Perón's nationalism was such that his agrarian policy caused beef to disappear from the nation's menu for fifty-two days, the countryside was spent, and all the reserves accumulated during the bustling wartime trade were depleted. Nationalizations, emblems of a Latin American period that united political nationalism with economic statism, reached incredible levels with Perón. When he assumed power, 60% of the industries depended on foreign capital, and one-third of the money earned by those companies left the country as foreign remittances. International confidence in the Argentine economy, however, was seen as a superb imperialist affront. Therefore, the general expropriated the gas, electric, and telephone utility companies, the Central Bank, the railroads, and anything else that had the mark of being foreign. He accompanied these acquisitions, designated to swell the patriotic booty, with stimulating nationalist rhetoric. From the *gringos* he seized the telephone companies. (He had already humiliated them once before with his electoral victory, following the incredibly opportunistic intervention of the United States through an intermediary, the Undersecretary of State Spruille Braden, who thought to present a colossal anti-Peronist tome of 131 pages known as "the blue book" right in Buenos Aires; but anyone slightly familiar with the intellectual coefficient of Perón's advisers could easily have attributed this text to his own campaign staff.) From the British he took the railroads. Even though U.S. imperialism was the great ogre, Argentina felt, because of its history, a particular debt of hate against England, since it had dared to trade British coal, oil, and machinery for Argentine beef and wheat. The famous import substitution and trade controls left the industry powerless to import supplies; the lack of competition dried up the manufacturers' creative energy; and inflation, a product of a social spending policy turned into a continual Christmas, soon turned the little industrial growth produced at the beginning of Perón's government into dust as an immediate reaction to a Keynesian stimulus to demand. Price controls, which had ruined the agriculture sector, also tied the industry's hands. The great nationalist leader reduced the nation's economy, which a few years prior hobnobbed with the largest in the world, to Third World proportions.

Perón, in honor of the *descamisado* masses, denuded all of Argentina. Neither the enormous palatial balcony speeches, nor the cries demanding a seat in the Security Council of the United Nations, nor the distant memory of the young Perón who, as a military attaché in Chile, tried to steal military secrets from Chile for his country, nor the 500 million pesos that he distributed for social housing (Peronism was a firm devotee of the Homeric epithet that has since become generalized) could save the nation. In 1974, when the general died—and with him his short return to the presidency after a lengthy exile in Spain—his country, choking from so much national glory, had been suffocated.

General Velasco put an end to the bourgeoisie sell-outs that
had always dominated the Peruvian republic.

Behind Latin American nationalism, as we have already noted, there always tends to be a pair of boots, epaulettes, and martial music. In the twentieth century, Peruvian nationalism was embodied by general Velasco Alvarado, about whom it was once said that when he opened a cabinet meeting he said: "I think that . . ." and his ministers, overcome by the prodigious event, burst out in applause. Velasco was neither an extremely gifted leader nor a man far evolved from the rudimentary levels of *Homo sapiens*. Therefore, the existence of his regime is due more to complex factors than to his ability to lead. In large part he embodied the "new" Latin American militarism with a "progressivist" tendency. What's interesting is that the Peruvian soldiers who carried out the attack against President Fernando Belaunde in 1968 were the same ones who only shortly before had mercilessly wiped out the pro-Castro guerrilla forces in the highlands. First they destroyed the guerrillas. Then afterwards, to complete the mission of rescuing the nation, they destroyed their democratic president and his constitutional government.

With an acute sense of national dignity, they established a dictatorship that expropriated newspapers, gagged the unions, reduced judicial power to a farce, jailed and exiled the opposition, and carried out a socialist economic policy well greased with populist and military rhetoric. Certain gestures of sublime patriotism distinguished this particularly touching period of the vernacular crusade: the official abolition of Christmas and the banishment of the most feared enemy of the country—Donald Duck.

A good example of that strange Peruvian characteristic of never giving oneself over to any cause with too much consistent enthusiasm, Velasco didn't dare commit to communism. He flirted with it, giving it a privileged place in his government, conferring on it two areas that occupied a remote position on his list of priorities—culture and the press—and even establishing relations with Cuba, despite the fact that only a few years earlier that country's government had planted guerrillas in Peru's mountains. He also expropriated ranches to carry out his agrarian reform, orchestrated by bureaucrats full of patriotism, causing a million Peruvian citizens to flee from the countryside to the city, swelling the size of the city's poor districts. He didn't, however, completely abolish capitalism because Peruvian businessmen, including those who had been hardest hit by Velasquism, found a way to negotiate their survival. Marianito Prado, the distinguished representative of Peru's oligarchy, whose industries were expropriated by the regime, showed up at the wedding of the general's daughter with a gift even bigger than Velasco's patriotically embannered red-and-white thorax, and subsequently Velasco slightly restrained his revolutionary impulses. The group that currently controls Peru's first bank, for example, owes its initial success, although it was later consolidated, in good part to the period of the revolutionary military dictatorship.

Velasco created close to two hundred state-run enterprises, which at the beginning of the 1990s was still costing the Peruvians $2.5 billion annually, and thereby destroyed the fishing and mining industries, two areas in which Peruvian capitalism had been successful. He was a firm believer that one's love for his country has to be expressed by the number of state-run enterprises established: each public company is an offering, an oblation, on the nation's altar. With so many offerings, Peru suffocated from the incense.

Velasco's patriotism became a symbolic expression. A patriotism that did nothing more than take over the government by expropriating the Brea and Pariñas oilfields, which were owned by the International Petroleum Company, a subsidiary of Standard Oil of New Jersey, a favorite obsession of Incan anti-imperialists. Velasco's tragedy was that he found himself confronting Nixon's and Kissinger's White House, which, too pragmatic to create another Castro in South America, treated the Peruvian regime with ironic condescension. So, despite the outcry from Standard Oil for Washington to sanction Peru, Nixon's advisers didn't take the hint and dashed Velasco's hopes. Desperate for them to notice him, he detained two Yankee ships that he accused of having penetrated Peru's "200-mile territorial waters" and then refused to receive Nelson Rockefeller, sent by Nixon. The only thing he succeeded in receiving was idle American pressure, some public threats, and a secret negotiation in which his government finally paid the *gringos* for the expropriation. This furious anti-imperialist ended up being a gentle little dove. The man who had accused Belaunde of selling out to the International Petroleum Company (although Belaunde, in tune with the times, was in the process of "renationalizing" part of the economy) ended up passing imperialism a small check under the table. Imperialism, of course, returned the favor by expressing understanding for Velasco's socialist measures.

The country was saved and the Peruvian people were ruined. Another patriot averse to Velasco's style took over in 1975 and began—as slowly as possible, so that things wouldn't go awry—the march toward democracy, which would come in 1980.

THE IDIOT'S FRIENDS

Our perfect idiot is not alone. He has friends. Powerful and influential friends in the United States and Europe who take the Latin American idiot's ineptitudes, fallacies, interpretations, excuses, and illusions, disseminate them in their respective countries, and then return them to Latin America duly stamped by the world's conscience. It seems incredible that these gruesome lies, homemade by our rustic populist, our friend the idiot, come from the largest centers of the cultural universe with a certificate of authenticity, just like wines. But it happens. And it has always happened with the fables originating in Latin America, perhaps even since the time of Christopher Columbus.

Who are these international friends of the perfect Latin American idiot? Other idiots? No, not necessarily, except when referring to our Latin American continent; then they usually turn into spokesmen with their news stories, editorials, written and televised reports, essay tomes, political declarations, or diplomatic interventions. They can come from any field but are primarily journalists, although not exclusively from leftist newspapers, who for ideological reasons, are fatally inclined to share the same irrationality as the perfect idiot. And for some unknown reason they also find space and permission to insert their ineffable stupidities in some of the most respected newspapers like *Le Monde, The Times, El País, The New York Times,* and *Il Corriere della Sera.* There are, however, philosophers, sociologists, politicians, and diplomats whose view of Latin America is as incredibly far-fetched—typically founded on stereotypes and fairy tales, distortions and dangerous simplifications—as was the case sixty years ago, for example, concerning the Soviet Union during the brutal period of Stalinism. The world changes, but these cases of political color-blindness are tirelessly repeated, especially in anything referring to Latin America, which because of this group of idiots has become a paradise for disinformation.

How does one explain that educated people, doubtless capable of minimizing disparities when speaking about their own countries, lack all critical discernment when discussing the Latin American continent? Perhaps Revel and, among us Latin Americans, Carlos Rangel are two political analysts who, digging through all possible explanations, have found the shrewdest and most profound ones. According to them, our continent has always been considered by many Europeans to be a repository for those dreams and utopias unattainable in their own lands. "Most foreigners, Europeans in particular," says Revel, "are largely responsible for the myths about Latin America. . . . Our perception [of this Latin American continent] belongs almost exclusively to the category of legends. Since its beginning, the desire to become acquainted with its societies, to understand them or to simply describe them has been overwhelmed by our need to use them for our own hallucinations. The evil would not be so great if our legends had not been, throughout history, the venom that nourished the Latin Americans."

In the twentieth century, there was a period of time (in many ways marvelous) during which, on both sides of the Atlantic, there flourished student uprisings, revolutionary utopias, and the most radical challenges to the current system, all at the same time. It was the era of the 1960s and that generation's plans for the following decade. With romantic postcard images of Fidel and his bearded followers descending from the hills and entering Havana, with Che Guevara dying in Bolivia, and of hundreds of young men joining guerrilla *"focos"* (military units) in the jungles and mountains, Latin America, in those years, became a fashionable continent for Europeans and Americans. Here there seemed to materialize the dreams of that new generation that let its hair grow out, sang Beatles songs, rejected the consumer society together with the hippies, protested the war in Vietnam, and erected barricades on the streets of Paris during the well-known May of 1968.

But all of this vanished like smoke, so that those who were twenty years old then had to in time resign themselves to keeping their hair trimmed and dressing in a conventional manner, and passing monotonous hours in the office, factory, cafes, metros, or editing rooms, enduring those modest and quite unexciting prospects of an industrialized society. For these frustrated rebels, Latin America would once again represent the only place on the planet where, according to them, because of the poverty, inequality, arrogant capitalists, and landowner privileges, the revolutionary chemistry of their youth is still kept alive. That's how they turned Che Guevara into one legend and Castro into another. Instead of seeing Cuba as an atrocious reality that the Cubans suffer, they continue to see it as what it represented for them—and for many of us—in those golden years of the 1960s, clutching all those Third Worldist lies and excuses as truths.

Mesmerized by the myth of the "good revolutionary," just as their compatriots were centuries ago by the myth of the "noble savage," their travels to our Latin American continent help very little, since there they only see what allows them to confirm their beliefs. And, incidentally, they want us to accept conditions in our countries that they wouldn't tolerate in their own. It's true, for example, that neither Régis Debray, Günter Grass, nor Harold Pinter would allow France, Germany, or England to accept the Communist Party as its only legal party, or permit only those who professed faith in Marxist Leninism to write for newspapers, or prohibit strikes, or have someone's critical opinion of the government constitute a crime of "counterrevolutionary activity," punishable by arrest or imprisonment. It's interesting, though; democrats and, more specifically, social-democrats (as they are called in Latin America) barely cross the Atlantic and suffer the first bite from a tropical mosquito, when they discover that in Latin American countries their own values and democratic principles are pure formalities and that it's necessary to abandon them in order for children to eat and get an education, or for the sick to receive medical attention. For Latin Americans, democracy is, well, a luxury of rich countries. What a curious form of ideological colonialism!

The same litany can be heard from a government official, while smugly filling the air with his cigarette smoke, from Felipe González's party in Spain or a French socialist friend of Mr. Mitterrand, a German socialist or a leader of the Italian PDS party, not to mention that vast fauna of reporters sent by European television and press who, impregnated with the same Third Worldist visions, arrive at our paradises to illustrate the stereotypes they are already carrying in their heads. They will always see our world, like the old banana republics, divided into the very, very rich and the very, very poor; the whites and the Indians; monstrous military thugs and brave guerrilla fighters; the exploiters and the exploited. If we Latin Americans, with this same kind of irresponsibility, were to do likewise, we would be able to paint a horrifying picture of France similar to what they portray about our societies, presenting the startling contrast between the opulent diners at Maxim's and the beggars in the metros, the workers and students parading in the streets and the police mercilessly beating them, which at times does happen. The drastic polarization of our political and social landscapes, which ignores any nuances or interpretations that differ from those given by Third Worldist explanations, makes us victims of the only colonialism that they themselves do not denounce and which they are responsible for: disinformation.

The countries these European journalists describe, according to their inventions and preconceptions, do not correspond to the countries we live in. Frequently, these happy travelers supply their opinions as news events, defending them with a generous use of the conditional (*as is said, it seems that*, etc.). They always talk about government repression and not of terrorist rampages. Members of armed groups who still attack, kill, and kidnap are piously called "insurgents," and if any are ever killed or arrested then they become defenseless *campesinos* or students whose disappearance or imprisonment is denounced by human rights organizations. They never seem to remember that our governments establish legitimacy at the ballot boxes: for them our democracies are pure façades, mere caricatures. Wherever you find guerrilla soldiers, the government assumes the role of authoritarian villain fighting the idealist rebels, with the help of ominous *paramilitary groups.*

The most faithful archetype of this kind of "expert" journalist in Latin America is the Italian Gianni Minà. The author of a torrential interview with Fidel Castro (who, according to Minà's compatriot and colleague Valerio Riva, deserves to be listed in the *Guinness Book of World Records* for the longest interview in the history of journalism made while kneeling), Minà prides himself on having made more than thirty trips to the Latin American continent—with the mandatory layover in Havana—and feels that, thanks to them, he has a profound understanding of our problems. Or maybe his publishers, the editors of those newspapers in which hundreds of articles appear or the television stations where he usually shows up, believe this. What is pathetically certain is that those travels of his have only reinforced his fables, since his usual interlocutors in Europe and on the other side of the Atlantic are only Latin Americans who share these fables. Thus his dialogues are nothing more than variants of the same liturgical monologue. He's a survivor of an extinct species of dinosaur that dreamed, thirty years ago, of seeing the Andes Mountains become an extension of the Sierra Maestra, and therefore his latest book carries the distressed title *Continente desaparecido* ("The Missing Continent"). (In reality, the continent that is missing is his, his continent of fables, not ours.)

If we mention him in this chapter, it's because his book, published in Italy in 1995, deserves our sincerest gratitude, because it gathers a very complete sampling of all the adulterated ideas about Latin America that our idiot's friend propagates overseas, so much so that the name of our book should belong to Minà's as a more fitting title. It's an extensive grassland of clichés, from which a chorus of pained voices repeatedly reminds us of the poverty on the Latin American continent and of the millions of children who die there from malnutrition and the lack of medical attention, and identifies the one and only culprit: the market economy. And although it may seem outlandish, it also provides the one and only solution: socialism according to the Cuban model. Rarely has a more daring work of fiction been seen, a true Disneyworld, or rather a *Jurassic Park,* a political literary work about Latin America. Let's have a look at its entertaining attractions.

Barely crossing the threshold of the book, we hear the bellowing against the World Bank, that famous establishment for which a gentleman named Pierre Galand served as its adviser for three and a half years. Introduced by Minà as the General Secretary of the so-called OXFAN Belgium, Mr. Galand's position of international technocrat seems to give an appearance of credibility or a seal of nobility to the diatribes hurled against the World Bank and the International Monetary Fund by our friends, the perfect idiots, far and wide on the continent. Except that in his letter of resignation of his consultative functions for said Bank, Mr. Galand uses the same threatening language that our populists use in open forums. Let's hear what he says:

According to your point of view, the only good governments are those that allow their economies to be prostituted by multinational interests and by the interests of omnipotent international financial groups. . . . Africa is dying and the World Bank is getting rich. Asia and Eastern Europe are seeing their wealth plundered, and the World Bank is supporting the initiatives of the Monetary Fund and GATT, which authorize the plundering of their material and intellectual wealth. . . . In its speeches, the World Bank talks about the unavoidable sacrifices that structural stability demands of nations in order for them to enter into a globalized world market, as though one were talking about a desert that must be crossed to reach the promised land of development. I do not want to be an accomplice to this inexorable fate. I prefer to continue supporting organizations for landless campesinos, children in the street, women in Asian cities who do not want to sell their bodies.

After reading this letter in the boardroom—that is, if they even read it—the executives of the World Bank must have been stunned, as if in the middle of winter a boisterous macaw from the tropics had just flown through the window. We've already seen the foolishness of portraying international companies as modern-day versions of the buccaneers—who ravaged the Caribbean in the seventeenth century. And we've seen that Ethiopia and several other African countries are starving to death not because of the actions of the World Bank but because of petty barbarian dictators who share Mr. Galand's Third Worldist theses, precisely because it gives them an alibi, diverting public attention from their own dishonesty, greed, and incompetence and blaming others for the evils caused by them. It isn't the presence of international companies in their territories that is ruining them but just the contrary: their absence. Their national and foreign investments are very weak, and there is no savings or development of private enterprises. It isn't the IMF's technicians who are plundering their supposed wealth but the political, military, and tribal factions, corrupt and perfectly inept, who, to top it all off, are generally inspired by Marxism, oppressing their impoverished citizens.

Not even the poverty of some Eastern European countries can be ascribed to the World Bank or the International Monetary Fund as the colorful Mr. Galand seems to believe. It's the consequence of that more than forty-year-old nationalized economy that he and Mr. Minà seem determined to recommend to us as the ideal alternative. One has to again revert to the patience of a Franciscan priest to remind them that the interventionist state has only spawned poverty among us, not wealth. The World Bank hasn't done anything but proven a sad truth: our governments cannot fight against poverty unless they themselves change; unless they yield back space to the private sector to better administrate what governments administrate poorly, disorderly, and inefficiently; unless they shape up the finances by correcting the mistakes and excesses in public spending, inflation, and irresponsible money distribution; and unless they turn to private businesses to straighten out directionless state enterprises. In other words, the truism that so offends the perfect idiots of both continents is that without economic development there is no possible chance of eradicating poverty, and one of the essential conditions for this development to take effect in the medium or long term is the regulation of public finances.

To our friends, all of this seems like an unbearable crossing of the desert, to use one of Mr. Galand's expressions. It would surely be better for them to save their energy and just take heaven, in other words, utopia, by storm, which in the name of the Redeeming State offers bread, land, shelter, and prosperity, as if all of this were possible through a decree, a law, or an armed takeover of power. This road, in reality, doesn't lead to Heaven but to Hell, and that's where Mr. Galand will be, far from the accursed World Bank, standing with the landless *campesinos,* the street children, and the women who, to Mr. Galand's dismay, have to sell their bodies along Malecón Avenue just to be able to eat, just like in the Havana of his dreams.

In Latin America, 180 million human beings out of 400 million live on the verge of poverty and 88 million in abject misery. Cuba is the exception. **(Gianni Minà, Continente desaparecido ["The Missing Continent"])**

After a hundred years of effective hegemony of the market economy in Latin America, the panorama is devastating. Seventy percent of the population lives below the poverty line and 40% (of them) in misery. One million malnourished children die every year on the continent. Cuba has dared to dismantle this mechanism that made this continent, as well as Africa and Asia, necrophilous continents. In our countries one is born to die. But not in Cuba. (Friar Betto, *Continente desaparecido* ["The Missing Continent"])

Friar Betto is a Brazilian Dominican priest, an apostle of liberation theology and a friend of Castro who also conducted just as famous and torrential an interview with him as did Minà (and, as an aside, also on his knees). In a few sentences—this must be noted—the bearded Dominican priest synthesized not only the central thesis recited one hundred times in Minà's book, but also the opinion of countless "divine left" or "caviar left" European intellectuals about Latin America. All are grieving over the poverty, the quite obvious and unbearable poverty, that they find in Latin America. The perfect Latin American idiot knows this and takes advantage of it to attract their attention, like a beggar with his wounds, and in fact sells them a false diagnosis and treatment for the ill. And there's no doubt that he gets what he wants. Those intellectuals, journalists, sociologists, anthropologists, movie directors, and songwriters from the European left not only vehemently allude to our poverty in essays, reports, statistics, images, poems, and songs; with a mixture of candor, ideological alienation, and crass ignorance, they also decide that all we can do, the only way to redeem ourselves, is to accept Castroism, Sandinistaism, Zapatistaism, Maoism, and even Shining Pathism, anything, except for that silly democracy that they themselves have at home or even that vile capitalism—a synonym for exploitation.

Such stupidity, obviously, doesn't hold up to even the slightest analysis. First of all, it's not true, as Friar Betto says, that the market economy has been in power in Latin America for a hundred years. With the exception of the timid liberal attempts that were only recently introduced to the social and political economies of some countries, we haven't had either a true market economy or an actual open society of a liberal persuasion. What has been in Latin America until now is mercantilism or patrimonial systems. In other words, noble brother Betto, a system in which a bureaucratic political class, its electoral cronies, and their allies—overprotected businessmen and a unionized elite tied to state-run enterprises—manage the country as if it were their estate. In this supposed welfare state, generator of disorder, waste, inflation, and corruption, you will find the key to both your and our concern about the poverty of large segments of the population. So, don't try and sell us a solution that is the cause or at least part of the problem!

Second, and in honor of the bitter truth, it's not true that our poverty continues to worsen as our idiots, and foreign idiots alike, continue to repeat that prayerful refrain in chorus. In spite of fallacious development models, populism, and inefficient, corrupt, and politically brokered governments, our continent has in the last fifty years sustained an average annual growth of 5%—not achieved, as Revel reminds us, by any European country—thanks to the commercial spirit which amid so many difficulties has managed to forge its way through. But he says, "it's a growth with razor-sharp teeth, with enormous differences depending on the year, and a very unequal distribution among countries, and among social regions and levels. . . . This growth does, however, exist. From 1950 to 1985, real per annual capita income, in constant dollars, has doubled from $1,000 to a little more than $2,000 (which was the level in Western Europe in 1950) and is triple the income of poorer African and Asian regions." The conclusion: "The disparities in the standard of living, the impoverishment of one part of the population, the resounding bankruptcy of public finances, the inflation that disrupts daily life and neuters investments are not from a fundamental underdevelopment. Rather, these ills are derived from politically originated wastefulness."

However, the greatest inanity held by Friar Betto, Minà, and many leftist Europeans is setting Cuba—the poorest country in Latin America after Haiti—as an example and a solution to these problems. The chapter on the Cuban revolution responds to their hallucinatory ravings on that experience, so it won't be repeated here. We'll only add this: it's a shame that all of them travel to the island as Castro's guests. By enjoying his hospitality, which places them on the privileged level of that system and not that of the average, modern Cuban, they can't know how serious this average Cuban's poverty is. It must be sad, Friar Betto, not to be able to drink a beer when the heat becomes unbearable while you're on the beach, because that kind of pleasure can only be enjoyed by dollar-toting tourists. (The dollar that you so detest as a symbol of imperialist power is, in fact, king of the island.) It must be sad to watch tourists eat in the Bodeguita del Medio whenever they please while the people of Havana have to limit themselves to a plate of rice or black beans and a glass of sugar water on their table at home, predisposing them to vitamin deficiency and optical neuritis because of so much frugality. It must be even sadder to see how this average Cuban's sister or cousin has to walk the street of the Malecón at night, offering herself to some tourist, because her family cannot survive on a salary equivalent to $5 a month. It isn't sad but pathetic not to be able to say aloud what you think, not even in your own home, for fear of microphones, accusations, or punishment; or to be beaten, as the poet María Elena Cruz Varela was, by State Security henchmen for having signed a manifesto petitioning for an open democracy, taken by the hair, dragged down a set of stairs, and forced to swallow newly written poems to the shouts of "I hope your mouth bleeds, damn it, I hope it bleeds!" It must not only be sad but humiliating for Cubans on the island to know that foreigners and even their own exiled compatriots can establish companies in Cuba, but that they can't, which makes them second-class citizens in their own country, something that has never happened anywhere else, except in South Africa with the colored population during apartheid. Faced with all these terrible and verifiable realities, one of your comments, Friar Betto ("Cuba is the only country where the word 'dignity' has any meaning") has a completely different definition than the one you gave it. Dignity for the Cuban people is being able to confront the humiliation inflicted upon them by the Castro regime.

The uprising in Chiapas demonstrates that the armed way has not ended. **(Gianni Minà)**

Since all previous political and ideological experiences have not produced permanent or significant results, we maintain that the only ones who can help Latin America take a significant step toward a different, more equitable, more honest and more humane world would be the indigenous people because they were the first on this land. **(Monsignor Samuel Ruiz, Bishop of Chiapas, Mexico)**

Have you noticed? There's no curing our friends, the protagonists of this book. They keep going around in circles; their utopias, made of stainless steel, resist the glaring evidence that contradicts them. With communism having disappeared from the former USSR and Europe, Castro's orthodoxy being destroyed because the dying Cuban economy needs a little capitalist oxygen, Sandinistas having drowned under the weight of their monumental errors, the Maoist illusion having suffered a fatal wound in Tiananmen square, and communist Vietnam having converted to the faith of the market economy, the Chiapas uprising came providentially to their aid. "It's the first war of the twenty-first century," predicted with unbridled joy our friend Carlos Fuentes, a Latin American replica of the *gauche divine* that the French talk about, or the "caviar left," as it is called in Spanish. Whatever the case, he shares their erudition and ideological flirtations; in the sophisticated world of European intelligentsia, this provides him an elegant safe-conduct. Echoing this, Minà, journalists at *Il Man-*

ifesto, and other orphans of Latin America revolutionary fantasies are hopping up and down with glee on one leg. "Armed conflicts have not ended nor have they been destroyed; just like we said," they write. The great Emiliano Zapata has been resuscitated.

Based on an undeniable reality—the poverty and abandonment of the indigenous people of the Lacandón and Chiapas rain forests in Mexico, victims of exploitation by cacique-like politicians belonging to the PRI party—another fable has yet again been conceived and celebrated by our perfect idiot and his friends in Europe, those incessant producers of myths about our continent. In Chiapas there wasn't, as they hasten to say, a spontaneous and unexpected uprising of the landless indigenous people like the great agrarian revolts of the past. Rather it was a political publicity campaign carefully prepared long beforehand by members of small leftist groups, which, like the so-called Subcomandante Marcos (a professor at the University of Xochimilco), don't have a single Indian or *campesino* hair on them; they have deceitfully sought to present their adventure—with the aid of the fax machine—as a populist revolt against the supposed "neoliberal policy" of the last two Mexican governments and especially taking advantage of the fatigue produced in the country from long political dictatorship by the PRI party.

This is, of course, a blatant distortion of the truth. First of all, because if anything is contrary to liberalism it's the PRI's political structure and its venal practices. Second, because the poverty of the Lacandón Indians isn't due to any liberal or neoliberal policy; it's due to the corrupt statism that has reigned in Mexico for more than fifty years, a reign in which one of its consequences, as in the case of the Chiapas region, was allowing government officials and caciques or timber-industry businessmen linked to the official party to get rich, with impunity, by exploiting the indigenous people and deforesting their natural environment. But in this case, unlike in the others, the instigators of this adventure (the perfect Mexican idiots and their global counterparts) have not only been able to give a new spin to the old stereotype of armed revolts of the landless *campesinos,* but have, in fact, also demonized the liberal model, presenting it as the source of these social injustices. Also, thanks to this fortunate episode, Carlos Fuentes can present himself in U.S. think tanks as a sophisticated defender of the dispossessed Indians and a critic of savage capitalism. Parroting this, both Régis Debray, who has yet to finish paying his dues for his continual errors concerning Latin America and the Cuban revolution, and the English writer John Berger again occupy privileged positions in the European press presenting Marcos as the new Robin Hood and discovering, amazed, a new literary talent emerging from the continent with his poor Third Worldist rhetoric. Nothing can be done: theirs is a senile return to their childhood stories.

They are lechers from Latin America's revolutions, infatuated with their dusty passions. If instead of pursuing such myths they studied what is happening in Mexico, they would realize that Marcos is taking advantage of the Lacandón Indians in order to get his political message out into the world, not doing anything concrete to solve their most pressing problems or aspirations, something which would be feasible if the future of these indigenous people were his real concern. After all, aqueducts, schools, and health centers are of little importance to him in a remote jungle if the project that he's pursuing is impregnated, as were Abimael Guzmán's or Father Pérez's in Colombia, with ideological delusions and outlandish dreams of liberation. Those ideas, and we have seen more than enough of them, leave our continent with the usual turmoil, blood, and poverty.

Monsignor Ruiz's fantasy is of a different order: it's seraphic. Since the myth of the "good revolutionary" has failed—as he seems to be telling us when he says that "political and ideological experiences" haven't attained "permanent or significant results"—let's go back to the myth of the "noble savage," the kind extolled in France by Montaigne and later Rousseau. "There [among the Indians]," said the former, "are no rich or poor people, no contracts, no inheritances, no stockholdings. The very words that mean 'lies,' 'deception' and 'greed' are unknown." The Monsignor must have believed this fable and proposed to return us, at the hand of the Lacandón Indians, to that healthier, fairer, more humane, ideal society so that we could see what it's like. Being a minister of liberation theology, he proposes a return to the Golden Age (actually the Stone Age) as a paradoxical advance, jubilantly hailed by Mr. Minà; this does presuppose, however, that he has at least stopped believing in Marxism as a means of reaching a world free of oppressors and the oppressed. (Friar Betto and Marcos himself probably don't concur with this.)

It will undoubtedly be difficult to bring this new, yet ancient, utopia to reality. We greatly fear, however, that the average, modern Mexican will not agree with Monsignor Ruiz much in replacing Harvard economists with natives from the Chiapas rain forest, placing the national economy in their and Mr. Marcos's hands. It's possible, nevertheless, that this idea will seduce some Mexican intellectuals, their "caviar left" European friends, and journalists like Minà, who consider us as more than just exporters of coffee, sugar, and bananas, but also exporters of dreams. How would his life have been and with what would he have fed his uninspired imagination—after Castro donned a tie to visit the Élysée Palace—if on January 1, 1994, that incident hadn't happened in Chiapas?

I know it's embarrassing for everyone to discover in the 1993 Amnesty report (after having talked for so many years about

the Cuban gulag) that, aside from Costa Rica, Cuba, with its
300 prisoners of conscience—I am quoting directly from the
book—and several political opposition detainees (often just
interrogated by the Security forces), probably has the fewest
incidents of human rights violations on the continent. (Gianni
Minà, *Continente desaparecido* ["The Missing Continent"])

This claim doesn't, however, come from Amnesty International but from Mr.
Minà himself, who found a way to attribute this information to the aforementioned human rights organization, which never said it. Amnesty International
has denounced the abuses committed by Castro in its reports to the point that
Castro has prohibited its members from coming on the island. It's Mr. Minà
who, believing the number of political prisoners to be quite modest, has established a not-guilty verdict for Cuba, putting it in second place among the hemisphere's countries that hold the greatest respect for human rights.

The idea is simply outrageous. If there is any one country that has for more
than thirty years flagrantly and constantly violated, and continues to violate,
human rights it's Cuba, and Armando Valladares's disclosures as well as other
horrifying testimonies written by many who have been in Cuban prisons prove
this. Nowhere else in the hemisphere does expressing an opinion or criticism, or
attempting to request a pluralistic form of democracy, continue to legally constitute a crime, punishable as a counterrevolutionary activity, as it does in Cuba.
Could there be anything more outrageous than the public trial that culminated
with a death sentence for General Arnaldo Ochoa, Tony de la Guardia, and other
government officials—a sinister masquerade reminiscent of the pogroms in
Moscow and Prague during the Stalin era? With such realities, the idiot's international friends, parading as defenders of human rights, appear to be covering
up or excusing appalling abuses. Here you will not find candor but blatant dishonesty.

The aspirations of the boat people, despite the social and work
situations of their country, are the same as thousands of
Mexicans and Latin Americans who try to enter the United
States, which frequently rejects them. But no one dares to think
that those undocumented immigrants are crossing the border
for political reasons. (Gianni Minà, *Continente desaparecido*
["The Missing Continent"])

To believe that Cuban boat people are abandoning the island for reasons that
have nothing to do with the Castro regime is just another blissful folly. Just lis-
ten to what they say, or said, when they enter U.S. territory after their terrible

odyssey. Everyone knows that they're escaping from Castro and what he represents to the Cuban people, not only in terms of hunger and poverty but also political repression. They're searching not only for a means of survival but also for something else that they've lost on that island of misfortune: freedom.

Of course, many other Latin Americans try to enter the United States, whether legally or illegally. In their countries of origin, however, no authority is preventing them from having a passport and traveling overseas whenever they want. Except for the Haitians—and only because of their destitution—the rest don't have to make use of four wooden planks and a tire and defy the voracity of sharks in order to leave. All of them do just what Mr. Minà does: take a plane. *Voilà la petite différence.*

Why are we so surprised then? Fables about us have existed in Europe for more than five hundred years. Columbus saw mermaids in the Caribbean and believed that he had found heaven on earth at the mouth of the Orinoco. Five centuries later in that same sea, another Italian, Mr. Minà, doesn't see desperate boat people but ingrates in search of fortune, leaving behind a different paradise discovered by him. Nothing can be done: the international idiot is an incurable dreamer.

(12)

HERE COMES THE BIG BAD WOLF!

"A specter is haunting Europe," Marx said in his famous *Manifesto* referring to communism. Today, the specter that incites fear, hate, and criticism in the perfect idiot's universe is liberalism. And what a deluge of insults it gets! It is being condemned—all of them using the exact same reasons—by communists, social-democrats, and Christian democrats; heads of state as diverse as Castro, Rafael Caldera, and Ernesto Samper; supposedly well-informed journalists like the editor of *Le Monde Diplomatique,* African tribal colonels, and sophisticated writers like Carlos Fuentes; leftist guerrillas, academicians, sociologists, economists, congressmen, and union leaders; bishops of liberation theology and Maoist youth; octogenarian widowers of the CEPAL policy; and of course the Galeanos, Benedettis, Dorfmans, and any of our perfect idiot's other evangelists, not to mention his latest emblematic figure, Subcomandante Marcos. All raise their voices in a unanimous chorus of diatribes against this modern-day heresy.

What is it that infuriates and horrifies them so much? The obvious; things that ultimately are so self-evident that even at first glance they don't deserve to be demonized; things brought up in this book in response to the perfect Latin American idiot's fables. Responses such as the government isn't the one that creates wealth but individuals; that a country's wealth is made or can be made by savings, effort, national and foreign investments, creating, developing, and pro-liferating companies within the framework of a market economy; that state-run and private monopolies are the source of abuse and that free competition is the best way to regulate them and protect the consumer; that excessive regulations, foreign exchange controls, import and export controls, tariff barriers, and subsidies generate corruption and illegitimate privileges. All of these and more, contributing to the liberal model for Latin America, arise from our own experiences on this continent and not merely from Mr. Adam Smith's texts. In other words, they are endorsed by reality and are proliferating in view of the failed patrimonial system that we have had until now and, too, of the disasters caused by populist and revolutionary adventures.

If this were strictly a technical problem, without any ideological interference, even the perfect idiot would end up accepting as evident that the liberal model produces better results. But ideology, like religion, thrives on dogmas of faith. It's an intellectual dispensation, a way of explaining the world and society with comfortable theoretical suppositions, but not subjecting them to tests. When one questions this dogma, however, (which serves as the basis for an entire code of interpretation that has until now been irremovable as well as the foundation for everything that this code has planned for an individual's destiny or the destiny of a group or party) the response is virulent; just like, by the way, what happened when Galileo revealed that the Earth was round and that it circled the Sun. Burn the heretics at the stake! Repeating this damnation to exhaustion is, almost liturgically, one of the most valuable contributions that Stalin gave to Marxist Leninism and which through contagion has been spread to most of the left. Following these guidelines, the insults hurled at liberalism—or at neoliberalism, to use its demonic name—are vicious. A few, however, only by being hammered in daily, actually stick in the public's consciousness, quite to the joy of our idiot. So, let's see what we've got here:

Neoliberalism represents savage capitalism. We should
oppose it with a social state.

It's just a simple charade of masks to cover up reality. The gruesome mask is ours and the nice one is given to the interventionist welfare state, which has produced nothing but disasters on this continent. This social state was to be represented by Perón's *justicialismo* doctrine with, for example, his famous "third way," equidistant from heartless capitalism and Soviet communism. In the chapter on *caudillos* and nationalism we observed the disasters resulting from this experiment: a country that in the first decades of the century had a standard of living comparable to Canada's, but which in less than twenty years experienced a dramatic involution to a Third World underdevelopment. Argentina's situation, after Perón and the barbaric military dictatorships that followed, was no better than that of a country like postcolonial Algeria.

Peronism definitely represented the apotheosis of the so-called social state, in other words one that sacrifices development for a redistribution policy, believing that this will remedy social injustices and inequalities. We saw how Perón succeeded in creating an enormous fiscal deficit where previously there had been a considerable amount of capital from its own funds and from monetary reserves accumulated during the years of the Second World War. That catastrophe was precipitated by a policy encouraging consumption, nationalizing flourishing public service enterprises like the railroads, creating completely unproductive state companies, and, above all, flattering the Argentine unionist establishment by giving it anything it asked for. In the meantime, Evita, his wife, turned the government into a charitable organization—in the name of so-called social justice—giving away houses (5,000 in just the first six months of 1951) and millions of packages of medicines, furniture, clothing, toys, and even false teeth. The Peróns behaved like heirs who were impetuously squandering a large inheritance. This entire carnival of illusions represented by the social state ended in corruption, economic bankruptcy, runaway inflation, poverty, and, as a response to this, bloody military dictatorships.

The basic idea of those who suggest this monster is that the ultimate reason for our economic and social problems lies in the unjust relationship between those who have everything and those who don't, and therefore it's the state's duty—that famous social state, synonymous with the welfare state—to eliminate these injustices with redistribution laws and, by way of nationalizations and controls of all types, increase the power and span of the government sector. That was what General Velasco Alvarado and Mr. Alan García, each in his own time, did in Peru with the results we've described earlier. The Sandinistas also obeyed the same concept of the social state, and what they succeeded in doing was to financially ruin Nicaragua. The standard of living of its population in 1989 was almost as impoverished as Haiti's; consumption had decreased 70% in those ten years of Sandinista policy; the Nicaraguan people's buying power dropped 92%; and inflation rose to astronomical levels. Bolivia finally saved itself from a similar situation because President Víctor Paz Estenssoro, free of ideological nonsense, turned the state and the economy around 180 degrees by adopting a liberal model, replacing the one flying under the emblematic "social" flag that was promoted with disastrous consequences by idiots from his own country. His, by the way, is one of the valuable cases of intellectual honesty known on this continent; he was once a historic leader of the so-called MNR Bolivian revolution, whose formulas, applied outside this particular context, served as a model for disastrous governmental and nationalist experiences.

Which, then, is savage capitalism? Could it be the system that has dominated until recently, that "patrimonial system" as Octavio Paz called it; or is it what we liberals have wanted to implement? Even the Latin American countries that didn't live through the disastrous populist experiences of Argentina and Peru have had their own inward development models and interventionist economies spawn mercantilist skeletons and their consequences: monopolies, privileges, corruption, all types of obstacles, bureaucracy, costly and inefficient public service enterprises corroded by political clientelism, and, as a corollary to all of this, inflation and the impoverishment and extortion of defenseless consumers with exorbitant rates and taxes. Anyone who honestly examines such a state of affairs will understand that what is savage is not changing the old system for privatization proposals and policies of openness, but maintaining it.

There are new, positive experiences in Latin America from the liberal model: those in Chile, and even those beginning to make headway in Bolivia, are developing under good auspices and seem irreversible. Of course, these being paths toward development and modernity, the benefits will only be appreciated in time. Only populism offers immediate and deceptive cures for poverty and backwardness. It's a simple act of demagogy, because no one can show laudable examples in our continent of the social capitalism they propose. No matter how long one looks on a map or at the continent's history, he will only find a collection of disasters in this pomposity, in these disguised obsolete ideologies and demagoguery, both in the past and the present. Is it social capitalism or social market economy that Castro is trying to introduce into his unfortunate country? Is the octogenarian Dr. Caldera's agonizing experience in Venezuela a good replica of liberalism? Where in Colombia, a country crucified by political clientelism and the corruption that it entails, can one see convincing signs of that savior, social capitalism? Isn't it the same old tune trying to pass itself off as a new beat?

Neoliberalism not only represents eternal dependency, the fragmentation of our countries and ever-increasing poverty, marginalization, the loss of natural resources, unfair exchange, and the technological and scientific gap. It also represents political systems in which the participation of the people in decision making does in fact not exist, or it rests on such terrifying social injustices that these systems become vulnerable. **(Declaration of the Fourth Latin American and Caribbean Conference held in Havana in January 1994)**

Presided over by Fidel Castro, this conference included not only representatives from the continent's communist parties and other organizations of the same ideological profile among its participants but also leaders of guerrilla organizations such as Colombia's Camilist Union–National Liberation Army (UC–ELN) and Coordinadora Guerrillera "Simón Bolívar" who have incorporated terrorism as a weapon of battle, and kidnappings and an alliance with drug traffickers as a very profitable business. Their attacks on oil pipelines have caused extremely harmful ecological damage. Obviously, for these horrifying orphans of communism, all of the evils that they assign to neoliberalism have been rooted out in Cuba by the Maximum Leader. No increase in poverty has been seen there, only the most complete well-being, and the political system—based on a single-party plan, a president for life, and the total absence of any opposition—is for them the only system that truly represents an effective participation of the people in decision making. Since they are happily driving the wrong way down the road of reality, and because when they say white it should be interpreted as black, these sympathies of theirs are, ultimately, highly rewarding. They deserve a place of honor on the altar of the perfect idiot.

The market tends to produce more luxury items than basic necessities. Therefore the production of these staples will not be sufficient and needs will not be met. Needs that must be satisfied but cannot be paid for do not exist in the market. The market only produces what generates private profits, regardless of the social benefits. (Juan Francisco Martín Seco, La farsa neoliberal ["The Neoliberal Farce"])

After producing such an affirmation, Juan Francisco's brain must have become just as dry as his second surname implies in Spanish. This gentleman from the Mother Country, with his pamphlet against liberalism, went much further than our modest Latin American idiot. He deserves to be his godfather. According to what appears on the book jacket, he is a professor of Economic Sciences at the Universidad Autónoma and a columnist for *El País* and *Cambio 16*. He has also been a functionary in Spain's socialist government, which perhaps explains his curious theory about the market. Living in Madrid and noticing in his daily strolls that the city has no shortage of *chorizos,* Spanish tortillas, olives, *jamón serrano,* coffee, wine, bread, milk, toilet paper, or other basic items, this illustrious critic of liberalism must certainly be convinced that, if it weren't for Felipe González and the reforms that Spain's socialism must have carried out on the barbaric market economy, all of these things would be missing in Spain. Certainly in London during Lady Thatcher's era, or in Reagan's United States, or in Taiwan, New Zealand, and Chile, where the government doesn't fill the role of a savior as called for by Mr. Martín Seco's mentor, Mr. Keynes, those store windows previously offered and still continue to offer only Cartier perfumes, Rolls-Royces, suits by Armani and Valentino, as well as other luxury items, but no essentials. Professor Martín Seco has dusted off that picturesque theory in which anything that implies social benefit is not profitable and therefore scorned by the market economy and its infamous law of supply and demand. Only the state is interested in putting bread and butter on everyone's table and everything else needed to survive. And if you don't believe that, just ask the Cubans.

It would be worthwhile suggesting that our friend, the idiot, read his book. It might be another bible just as convincing as Galeano's. All of the dogmas are repeated there. He'll see how the state and only the state "has also assumed the role of correcting the inequalities produced by the market, by distributing profits" and how "the state takes responsibility for the smooth running of the economy, which is directed by its economic policies, and even intervenes directly as a business." ("That's what I've said before," the Latin American idiot will say at this point.) He will also see how, according to the author of this libelous piece, "the consumer is the new proletariat of our time," divested of his salary by slick multinational advertising, which induces him to purchase chocolates, detergents, vegetable oils, soaps, dog food, deodorants, soup, and other such trivialities. Like Don Quixote on Rocinante, the ineffable professor rides his book of dreams and insults.

In France there are also heated diatribes against liberalism. Concerning the strikes that paralyzed France in November 1995, the editor of the well-known newspaper *Le Monde Diplomatique*, Ignacio Ramonet, wrote an article published in December 1995 in the newspaper *El País* under the title "La chispa francesa" ("The French Spark"), with the following comment:

Of what importance is this unusual uprising? It is the first collective protest against neoliberalism, on a countrywide scale. And that's historic.

It wasn't the first time, and obviously won't be the last, that crises provoked by a welfare state (*L'État providence* in French) are joyously attributed to liberalism. The mass mobilization of workers and government officials, which left France without transportation and mail for two weeks, actually had the trademarks of a protest against a plan proposed by Prime Minister Alain Juppé to reform social security and government pensions. But not even Juppé, or President Chirac, or the reform proposal—quite on the cautious side—deserves to be described as liberal. At best, this was a desperate act of emergency taxation, thoroughly insufficient to save a welfare system whose exclusively statist creation, bordering on financial catastrophe, was not questioned by the French government.

Considered by the vast majority of French citizens to be a permanent societal victory, France's social security system, as is the case in many other developed countries in the West, is more and more onerous, more and more complex, and more and more voracious. Its deficit today totals the astronomical figure of $50 billion (200 billion French francs). The quality of its services is deteriorating and dehumanizing. The system, which is growing uncontrollably, generating a tentacular, abusive, and wasteful bureaucracy, incessantly exceeds its source of financing, obligating the state to every so often impose new taxes on the so-called company payroll. The tax burden that any new job creates in itself is so high for workers and businessmen that the latter, especially when they are small or medium-sized business owners, think twice before hiring another employee or worker. The high, unwieldy rates of unemployment—this specter that today rightly alarms industrial society with consequent crime and lack of security—are in no way unrelated to France's stifling tax system and other factors that discourage production activity and hinder momentum for technological advances and competitiveness from many of the country's industries, with the resulting loss of markets and an increase in the excluded and marginalized sectors of society.

French politicians, whether from the left or right, offer something virtually impossible in their election campaigns: reduce taxes, fight unemployment, and at the same time maintain and even increase social security benefits. Faced with the reality of a monumental deficit, forced to create new methods of taxation, desperate concerning the impossibility of slowing down the unemployment that is particularly hitting those young people just entering the workforce, they are aghast, witnessing their popularity in the government drastically erode, opening the door to their opposition. The pendular movement between left and right doesn't solve anything. It only creates fleeting illusions of change, quickly debunked, which incite skepticism about the political establishment as a whole in the civilian society, at times causing it to favor xenophobic initiatives or naive ecological movements, only because they represent something different from the traditional party lines.

In short, what analysts like Mr. Ramonet do not want to see is that the welfare state has created a metastasis and its welfare programs have no possible cure, simply because there is no way to pay for it all. The "philanthropic ogre" causes much more harm than good: what it gives out with one hand, it takes away with the other and more, taking it from the taxpayer's pocket and then imposing on him the additional cost of its prodigal borrowing and voluminous bureaucratic systems. The liberal analyst José Piñera Echenique, author of Chile's successful tax reform, has explained the nature of this crisis very well: "The duality of this criterion—to be liberal in economic policies and nationalist in social policies—compromises the efficiency of assigning resources to fight poverty just as it compromises the stability of any advances made on the economic level by maintaining a permanent tension managing both public affairs criteria. Probably the best example of this duality is the existence of markedly declining national social security systems in countries with a long tradition of market economies."

Mr. Ramonet along with many detractors of liberalism try to place this debate on an ideological plane instead of on reality. On that ideological level, they very comfortably proclaim to the four winds that every citizen has a right to full social protection via the state, to every form of subsidy, including for strikes and unemployment, and they present liberalism as a ravening wolf that doesn't recognize these benefits deemed by the working majority to be irreversible conquests. Repeating this type of discourse ends up generating, roundabout the welfare state, a collective culture and mentality, similar to that expressed by those who live on public assistance. Those who stage their social protests as a response to liberalism never take the time to present their own alternatives to the wide range of insoluble problems found within the framework of the welfare state: such as the deficit in the social security program, the ruthless tax system, and growing unemployment. All they do is shout through loudspeakers complaining about the deaf "philanthropic ogre," in the name of their ideological illusions, trying to square the circle.

What, in their opinion, is liberalism to be blamed for in countries where a true liberal option remains untested? For presenting these truths and not participating in the deceit of those who, like them, are storming heaven. In other words, for not pursuing social utopias or the fables of the welfare state. And because of pat political or ideological maxims, any other alternative of a liberal nature is the object of derision. Yet it does exist in other latitudes. The tax reform in Chile, for example, has allowed the citizens of that country to freely choose their health care and retirement systems as each pleases. Only 10% of them have remained with the old state social security system, leaving the management of their pensions in the hands of the government sector. The rest, in other words 90% of the workers and employees, opted to trust private companies with their pensions, with results so markedly more advantageous that no one wants to return to the old system, the one that still exists in France. It's an irreversible privatization. Thus, for this problem, liberalism has provided a solution that the welfare state is incapable of giving. Once again reality, and not the ideological fables of our perfect idiot, has had the final say.

⓵⓷

TEN BOOKS THAT "SHOOK"
THE LATIN AMERICAN IDIOT

As a general rule, every Latin American idiot has a specific political library. The idiot is usually a good reader, but typically of bad books. He doesn't read from left to right like Westerners, nor from right to left like Easterners. He reads from left to left. He practices ideological inbreeding and incest. And it's no wonder that, frequently, his readings give him a certain air of intellectual superiority. Those who don't think as he does are considered victims of a type of congenital stupidity. This type of arrogance derives from the dogmatic vision that is inevitably forged into the minds of those who use only a single moral lobe to formulate their critical judgments. Any liberal, conservative, bourgeois, or other literature contrary to his revolutionary postulates seems a waste of time, a sign of irrationality, or a simple pack of lies. It's not worth looking into.

What does our legendary idiot read? Many things, of course. An endless number of books. It's possible, however, to examine his well-stocked bookshelves and select various illustrative titles that encompass and summarize the essence of the rest of his library. The following, not in any strict chronological order, does exactly this: select the idiot's favorite collection, so that if a reader of our book wants to join the clan of political mental retardation, after a week of intensive reading he'll be able to deliver a lecture to some prestigious audience, preferably in American or European university circles. There are still people who are dumbfounded when they hear this nonsense.

One last note: after reading the selection of the ten books that have "shaken" our dear idiot, you will observe three categories that join and reinforce these texts. Some establish Latin America's fatal diagnoses as democracy, the market economy, and treacherous Western values; others provide guidelines and violent methods on how to destroy the foundations of that despised system; and the last category supports an enlightened plan for the future, based on the generous and efficient qualities found in the Marxist-Leninist model. This last one is a curious aspiration, because in those years when the idiot reached his greatest historical glory—from the mid-1950s to the end of the 1980s—it was already quite well known that the proletariat paradise was nothing more than concentration camps enclosed in barbed wire.

History Will Absolve Me
Fidel Castro, 1953

According to a very well known legend—spread by Cuban propaganda—this is the speech that Fidel Castro made in his own defense at the trial following his failed attack on the Moncada military barracks on July 26, 1953. Those who haven't read the text are usually satisfied with the quote of the last sentence, "Condemn me, I don't care; history will absolve me," a statement, by the way, that Adolf Hitler used under similar circumstances when creating the Nazi party. There are, of course, hundreds of printings of this work, but in this review we are using the second edition from Ediciones Júcar, Gijón, Spain, January 1978, fawningly introduced by the indescribable Ariel Dorfman, who we'll talk about later since he too authored one of the classics rightly venerated by our highly educated Latin American idiots.

We'll give the reader the true story. On the morning of July 26, 1953, a young, inexperienced lawyer, only twenty-seven years old, and a candidate for congress in the thwarted elections of June 1952 (aborted by a military coup carried out by General Fulgencio Batista in March, three months before the elections), led the attack on two Cuban military barracks located on the easternmost side of the island: Moncada and Bayamo. His troops consisted of 165 unskilled fighters, poorly armed with shotguns, 22-caliber rifles, pistols, and maybe a decent machine gun here and there. Twenty-two soldiers and eight assailants died in the attack—proving the bravery of the group headed by Castro—but Batista's army and police succeeded in taking control of the situation, arresting most of the revolutionaries and immediately brutally torturing and killing fifty-six defenseless prisoners. Fidel, along with a few survivors, managed to escape and take refuge in the nearby mountains. Thirst and hunger forced them to surrender. Prior to this, however, the bishop of Santiago de Cuba, Monsignor Pérez Serantes, had secured from Batista a promise to spare Castro's life and give him a fair trial along with the rest of his companions.

There occurred, in fact, not one but two trials, and neither of them would qualify as "fair." In the first trial, Castro, in his capacity as a lawyer, was allowed to speak in defense of his compatriots, a situation that Castro took full advantage of, very adeptly attacking the government and proving the crimes it had committed. Faced with this public discredit and wanting to avoid greater damage to his diminished prestige, Batista declared Castro ill and ordered him to be tried behind closed doors in the Civil Hospital, before an ad hoc tribunal, completely subject to the executive power. This happened in mid-October 1953, and it was before this court where Castro improvised his defense for five hours. Everything he said there is supposedly what makes up his famous speech known as *History Will Absolve Me.*

But it doesn't. There is a world of difference between what Castro really said and what was later published, which shouldn't surprise us, since we are referring to a person who has no qualms about rewriting history according to his latest needs. What did happen was the following. Once in the Isla de Pinos prison, where he was sentenced to fifteen years for military uprising, Castro, with all the patience in the world, wrote the first version of his speech and through Melba Hernández, a fellow-fighter, got it into the hands of the brilliant essayist Jorge Mañach—also Batista's opponent. Mañach organized Castro's ideas and improved his syntax, enhancing the text with scholarly quotes, Latinisms, and even pronouns completely foreign to most Cubans (such as the "os," which Jorge, who grew up in Spain, was so fond of). Balzac, Dante, Ingenieros, Milton, Locke, and St. Thomas, all of whom parade through the work, don't belong to Castro but to Mañach, as do the lengthy quotes from poems by Miró Argenter and Martí that are interspersed throughout the speech. This is quite believable to anyone who is familiar with Castro's speech, common and effective, but always repetitive, devoid of learned expressions, and lacking appreciable intellectual gems.

This book isn't really what Castro said in his defense after the Moncada attack but what he would have liked to have said if he had Mañach's prose, although the basic ideas—not the way in which they were expressed—do indeed belong completely to him. In any case, *History Will Absolve Me,* as it is known, is not a testimony before a few judges, but the debut of a politician and his government program in Cuban society. It was, under the pretext of a legal defense, a "launch" into public life by someone who, until that moment, had been seen as just a rebel, always linked to violent acts. So what did the former apprentice Comandante say (and later write) in this "pseudo-oratory" piece, making his book the lead in the Latin American idiot's small library collection presented here in our work?

He said a variety of things. First of all, he explains the reasons for his defeat, justifies his retreat and surrender, and reveals what he was planning to do if he had captured the barracks: arm the people of Santiago de Cuba and Bayamo in order to defeat Batista in a pitched battle. Then—from a frankly petit-bourgeois perspective—he defines who his political constituency is: the poor, the farmers, the professionals, the small businessmen, but never the rich capitalists. Afterward, he immediately declares the five measures he would have taken had he succeeded: (1) Restore the Constitution of 1940; (2) give the freehold land to the *campesinos* living in smallholdings; (3) pay 30% of company profits to the workers; (4) give plantation workers a greater share of the sugar earnings at the expense of the plantation owners; and (5) confiscate ill-gotten assets from dishonest politicians.

After this election campaign disguised as a legal appeal, Castro presents a picture of abject poverty and offers a populist recipe for ending it: nationalize the industries, grant the state a primary role in managing the economy, and forever distrust the market, free enterprise, and the law of supply and demand. Castro is already the perfect Latin American proto-idiot interwoven by an old populist trend. He's so Latin American that, with great pride, he calls himself a "revolutionary." But he also belongs to an even more dangerous, very deeply rooted, and feverish Latin American tradition: Castro is also an *arbitrista*, someone always capable of contriving simple and easy solutions, instantly solving the most complex problems. At the tender age of twenty-seven without the least bit of work experience—to say nothing of corporate or administrative experience (since he hadn't worked a day in his life)—Castro knew, in the blink of an eye, how to solve problems in housing, health, industrialization, education, nutrition, and the creation of instant wealth. Everything can be done quickly and efficiently with a few decrees issued by kindhearted men guided by higher principles. Castro was a revolutionary, and what Cuba and Latin America needed were men like him to take the continent out of its hundred-year paralysis. Forty-some years after that spurious speech, it's painfully easy to walk through the crumbling streets of Havana and see—once again—how the road to Hell tends to be paved with marvelous intentions. The intentions of revolutionary *arbitristas*.

Finally, after this childish string of simplifications, half-truths, and utter foolishness, Castro concludes with a moving description of how his companions were killed and describes the legal foundations that justified and condoned his rebellion against tyranny. At last, we now know that history will not absolve him, but rather, as Reynaldo Arenas said, it will "absorb" him. But our idiots probably don't fully realize this. They love their myths too much.

The Wretched of the Earth
Frantz Fanon, 1961

Fanon's life and work comprise several painful paradoxes. This black doctor was born in Martinique in 1925 (he died of leukemia in 1961, the same year that this book of his *Les damnés de la terre* appeared in Paris) as part of a very refined French culture. With this work—read by every political leader in the 1960s and 1970s—he provided the revolutionary radicalism of the then so-called Third World with an anti-West gospel, whose aftereffects are still very much alive and kicking.

After writing the essay entitled *Black Skin, White Masks* in 1952 (where he put forth some of the theses that he would later defend in *The Wretched of the Earth*), Fanon, who had studied psychiatry in Martinique and France, moved in 1953 to Algeria, which was at that time at the height of its nationalist movement. From the hospital where he was working, he was drawn into the independence movement, and in 1957 he became the editor of one of the group's publications. In 1960, shortly before his death, the ruling Algerian government named him Ambassador to the African Republic of Ghana. It was during the tumultuous decolonization period in Africa.

Two factors gave *The Wretched of the Earth* the great start it initially experienced. First was its appearance during a time when Algeria's war for independence against France was shaking both countries—to the point where France's institutional stability was threatening to fall apart. Algeria was making the headlines everywhere, but the world was showing no sympathy to either Paris or the *pied-noirs*, but rather to the humiliated and exploited Arabs. Second, the work was graced with a laudatory and assenting prologue from Jean-Paul Sartre, the undisputed head of Western intelligentsia at that time. Our edition is the twelfth printing by the Fondo de Cultura Económica in Mexico in 1988; the first version appeared in 1963, slightly modified by translators two years later, when they settled on a definitive text.

Interest in Sartre's preface can be summarized in two points, the most intriguing of which is the book's target audience. Sartre speaks to the Europeans who might read this book. Fanon, however, addresses the non-European, the "wretched or accursed of the earth." Sartre speaks to the victimizers; Fanon, to the victims. Sartre could have called his text "a foreword to the colonizers," just as Fanon could have called his "a guide for the colonized people in search of their true identity." Sartre warns the Europeans that a just retaliation has materialized by those exploited in the Third World and he congratulates them, or at least accepts the moral reasons given, while Fanon tells his readers how and why the bloody separation is not only necessary but unavoidable. Fanon justifies the anticolonial violence. Sartre legitimizes it and assumes the shame of the white man consumed by remorse.

The primary and greatest paradox in Fanon's work is that Fanon, perhaps inevitably, gives us an anti-European, or anti-West, analysis based on Western standards. His profound thoughts on individual and collective identity refers us, without his directly saying it, to psychoanalysis and Freud, something quite pre-dictable from a psychiatrist educated in the 1950s. In any case, his defense of violence as an element of exorcism and as a catalyst in history is deeply rooted in Marx and Engels, while his exaltation of nationalism has definite echoes of the motherland he is fighting. Fanon wants the people of the Third World to cast off the false cultural skin that they have been covered with by the white, arrogant invader, but his wanting to do this, aside from being an instinctive tribal rejec-tion, can only be rationalized from a perspective which is ultimately that of the dominating power.

At the same time Fanon, a gifted man capable of foreseeing the consequences and the outcomes of his proposals, at the end of his beautiful yet distressed book tells his comrades-in-arms something that doesn't appear feasible: "The Euro-pean game has ended for good; we have to find something else. We can do any-thing as long as we do not imitate Europe, as long as we do not let ourselves become obsessed with the desire to emulate Europe." He later adds: "Dear friends, let's not honor Europe by creating states, institutions and societies inspired by it."

When the Latin American idiot discovered this book, he fell to his knees stunned. Here was the ideological key to raising one's fist in fury against those bastards of the developed world. *We* don't have to be like *them. We* have to rid ourselves of *their* influence. Yet our beloved individual doesn't realize that the only ones in Latin America who can use this argument are the few Quechuas, Mapuches and other untainted pre-Columbian indigenous people who are just barely surviving in this part of the world. It just so happens that "we"—the mes-tizos and blacks, along with the whites—are by now, at this point in history, either the colonialists or their cultural descendants and not those who were col-onized. We Latin Americans, or the Canadians or the Americans, are not the "wretched of the earth"—just as Fanon wasn't—but rather the aggressors, the beneficiaries of a hellenistic culture that for almost 3,000 years has exercised a unifying influence on the planet that could be brutal, regrettable, or beneficial (depending on who makes the assessment) but whose centrifugal force no one seems to be able to escape.

What happened to America's black revolutionaries in the 1960s when, drunk with their "blackness," they went to Africa in search of their roots? They imme-diately discovered that they had nothing in common with the Africans, except for the color of their skin and some physical traits. What would have happened to Japan, Korea, or Indonesia if in each of those countries a local Fanon had per-suaded their societies of the intrinsic virtues of their native culture? What about Singapore, which was a poor British colony until about the time when Fanon's book began to circulate and today is an empire with a $21,000 per capita income? What would it have become if it had renounced that very Western idea of progress as its goal, or science and technology as a way of reaching this goal, or the market economy as the framework where these transactions are conducted? What would the United States have become if, instead of viewing itself as a Europe that emigrated to the New World, determined to improve itself, it would have become bogged down in the resentful anti-West indigenous rhetoric that our idiots can't stop muttering in Latin America? It's true that the colonizations were carried out with appalling violence, and no one can hide the horrendous crimes committed on behalf of "superior" cultures. Once the dominant culture has taken root, once its values and view of the world predominate, it is neither possible nor beneficial for us to try and turn back history so that our social mentality can regress to some mythical origin that no one is now capable of elucidating. And if this system were reestablished, the only thing that it would achieve would be to condemn us to eternal backwardness and frustration.

Did Fanon ever consider that those Arabs, grievously colonized in Algeria by the French, were themselves cruel colonizers in the past? Did he realize that the Islamic Jihad unleashed at the beginning of the eighth century against North Africa erased from the map, subjugated, and enslaved numerous indigenous communities, and that this crime lasted much longer than the one committed by the Europeans? Was Ethiopia better off never having been colonized by Europeans (except for an Italian episode that barely left any traces) than Kenya or Nigeria? If the African situation seems to be muddled, can't our Latin American idiot understand that if his language, his institutions, his religion, his way of building cities and feeding himself, his entire being and routine have been molded by Europe, including his way of interpreting reality, how can he expect to escape from this world? Where does he plan on running away to? To the Incan Empire? To the bloody Aztec theocracy? To the fragile Arawak culture lost in the Amazon jungle? How much are our own pocket-size "Fanons" prepared to give up? Latin American *Fanonism* is so ridiculous that it's sad to have to refute it.

Guerrilla Warfare
Ernesto ("Che") Guevara, 1960

Ernesto Guevara was born in Rosario, Argentina, in 1928 and killed in Bolivia in 1967, where he was trying to establish a new guerrilla faction that would have turned Latin America's jungles and mountains into a huge Vietnam. He was an adventurous doctor whose life embraced the delirious political vision that for thirty years excited our most illustrious idiots. Posing for the photographer Korda, his image was transformed into the ultimate poster-boy in which he appears with a fiery, romantic glance as if he were a revolutionary Christ photographed after the moneylenders had been driven out of the temple of the socialist homeland.

During his Argentine childhood he briefly and uneventfully flirted with Peronism. It was there, however, in the midst of Perón's populist/nationalist/anti-imperialist chaos, that he must have acquired his first conceptual distortions, probably without noticing it. After graduating from medical school, he traveled half the continent on motorcycle and in 1954 was taken by surprise with the fall of Arbenz in Guatemala, a country he had visited because of the political attraction that the Guatemalan general and his newfound revolutionary experiment held for him, which were in fact the result of democratic elections.

From Guatemala he went to Mexico, where he met Fidel Castro, a talkative Cuban exile who, after leaving prison (due to the political amnesty granted him by Batista after having served less than a fifth of the time he was sentenced to for attacking two military barracks), was planning an expedition to overthrow the Cuban dictator. Che had his first contact with the Soviet KGB (the Mexican police provided him a business card from a·USSR "diplomat," today a retired KGB general), signed up for Castro's expedition, and landed in Cuba in early December 1956.

A brave, methodical man, intellectually better prepared than his political leader, he soon became the third-in-command. The second was Camilo Cienfuegos, and Castro had both of them—Camilo and Che—create another guerrilla front in the province of Villas, in the middle of the island, not so much to harass the government as to compete with other independent guerrillas in Sierra Maestra who were already operating in the area: the Student Revolutionary Directorate (Directorio Revolucionario Estudiantil) troops led by Rolando Cubelas and Faure Chomón, and the Second Escambray Front (Segundo Frente del Escambray) organized by Eloy Gutiérrez Menoyo.

When the battle had ended—actually just a hodgepodge of insignificant skirmishes, ambushes, and shoot-outs—and Batista had fled the country early on the morning of January 1, 1959, Guevara was already one of Castro's closest men. After the first few months he was named president of the National Bank and then minister of the Department of Industry, and in both jobs he proved to be just as altruistic as he was incompetent, a combination that tends to be fatal in managing public affairs.

In the mid-1960s—after completely failing in administration—Guevara took his first guerrilla strides outside Cuba, fighting with the Angolans against the Portuguese, but that experience (which no one talks about) was disastrous, although it did work up his appetite for other more domestic adventures. In 1965, determined to create "two, three, one hundred Vietnams in Latin America," he disappeared from the scene, and Castro publicly announced that Che, patriotically and voluntarily, was leaving Cuba to carry out *independent* revolutionary expeditions. It was the Cuban government's way of securing a plea of innocence. It was later said, quietly, that Fidel preferred to have Che out of Cuba, since there were serious disagreements between them on how to lead the country and on its relations with the USSR.

Shortly thereafter rumors began to spread about his presence in different places on the continent—he traveled through various countries with a shaved head and false documents—until he was found in Bolivia. In the end, a patrol of the Bolivian army, headed by Captain Gary Prado, captured him alive after a short battle, but the military officers decided to execute him after the usual interrogation without a trial. They cut the fingers off the body to verify his fingerprints and buried him in a nameless grave. His campaign diary survived, however, and ended up in Castro's hands. From then on the legend of Che and his iconography have been steadily reproduced.

The importance of that well-known book *Guerrilla Warfare* is how it came to be a practical and theoretical manual of subversion, with more than a million copies distributed in the Third World. The point of departure for Che's short booklet, written in the didactic prose of a preschooler's primer, was three axioms from his Cuban experience: first, guerrillas can defeat regular armies; second, one doesn't have to wait for an insurrectionary climate to exist, since guerrilla *"focos"* can create these conditions; and third, the natural arena for this type of battle is in the countryside and not in the cities. The heart of revolutionary guerrilla warfare is in the rural areas.

From these dogmas, Che explains the general strategy, the "hit and run" tactics, the creation of guerrilla units, types of armaments, organization, health, the role of women, and the support that urban guerrillas should provide. Che—the Clausewitz of the Third World—wants all communists in underdeveloped areas to be able to create their own homemade revolution without suffering any setbacks. The edition we are commenting upon was published by Era in Mexico in 1968, under the title *Obra revolucionaria* ("Revolutionary Work"). It contains a hagiolatrous prologue by Roberto Fernández Retamar, an esteemed Cuban poet who began fighting in the Catholic ranks and ended his life as a political organizer in the rigid, pro-government culture of Castroism.

This booklet's biggest flaw, which cost Che his life as well as the lives of thousands of Latin American youths, is that it elevates the incident of the struggle against Batista to a universal level, ignoring the true reasons that produced the downfall of that dictator. Castro and Che, who want to see themselves as heroes of Thermopylae, have never admitted that Batista was not a general determined to fight. Rather, he was a stenographer sergeant who rose to the rank of general after the revolution of 1933 and whose main goal was to get rich while in power, along with his cohorts. For example, Batista didn't want to end Castro's guerrilla warfare after Castro landed at Granma. Instead, he let the survivors organize themselves and stockpile supplies for almost a year of very little military activity, just so that he could approve "special wartime budgets" that were going to end up in the pockets of the most corrupt military men. This was to such an extreme that when a private died in "combat," they didn't even bother to take him off the payroll so that the officers could continue collecting the deceased's salary. Naturally, with a level of corruption of this nature, good army officers and soldiers were becoming demoralized to the point of paralysis or conspiracy with the enemy. This being the case, and after losing the support of the United States (which had declared an embargo on the sale of arms to Batista at the beginning of 1958), the dictator decided to escape early one morning, with his army apparently intact and only one city (Santa Clara) in the hands of the enemy. The guerrillas didn't overthrow him. He overthrew himself.

This experience, of course, could not be repeated in any other country, not even in Nicaragua, where in 1979 Somoza was unseated due to the covert and united actions of Cuba, Venezuela, Costa Rica, and Panama, aided by the dictator's loss of credibility and Carter's naivete. But it wasn't the result of a "domestic" confrontation between the National Guard and the guerrillas. Without the obvious international solidarity for the guerrillas—in the form of weapons, fighters, training, money, safe havens, and diplomatic support—along with Somoza's political isolation, Che's manual wouldn't have helped at all!

Revolution in the Revolution?

Régis Débray, 1967

In the 1960s, Régis Débray, born in Paris in 1941, was a young French journalist with a sociology degree, incredibly mature for his age, seduced by Marxist ideas and even more by the Cuban revolution and the photogenic spectacle of a Caribbean island paradise governed by courageous bearded men who were preparing their final attack against the American imperialist fortress.

With a talent for prose and a crazy head inclined to shrewd analyses, he was received in Havana with open arms. Cuba was a nursery for men of action, but there was a scarcity of theoreticians capable of rationalizing their actions or simply even thinkers who were able to justify them reasonably well. Che, for example, had published his famous manual *Guerrilla Warfare* and was preparing to put this into practice in the South American arena, but the battle that was about to begin left a dangerous flank exposed: What were the communist parties and traditional Marxist-Leninist organizations going to do? Not only that, it was necessary to explain the break from the old script (written by Marx in the nineteenth century and completed by Lenin in the twentieth century) from a theoretical perspective. Hadn't we agreed that communism would come as a result of class struggle, goaded by worker-based revolutionary leaders organized by the Communist Party?

This is what *Revolution in the Revolution?* is about. It's not an abstract intellectual exercise, but an extremely important and deliberate revolutionary design, revealed with complete naivete in the following quotation: "It would not be hypothetical to say that when Che Guevara reappears [he got "lost" preparing the uprising in Bolivia], he will head the guerrilla movement as its indisputable military and political leader." Débray, simply put, was just another soldier in the guerrilla war, although his work wasn't ambushing the enemy but justifying the guerrilla's actions, "rationalizing" their heresies, writing in newspapers, spreading the revolutionary message, and making room for his comrades in the annals of the developed world. He was, using the former Cold War jargon, a "fellow comrade" completely conscious and proud of his work.

He did have some experience. In 1964, under the pseudonym "Francisco Vargas," Débray published an extensive piece ("A Guerrilla Experience") in the magazine *Révolution* in Paris, where he described his visit with Venezuelan revolutionaries, who at that time were trying to destroy that country's newly emerging democracy after the defeat of Pérez Jiménez (1958). It was this lengthy article that earned him Castro's trust, Castro being the mastermind behind and the material accomplice to the Venezuelan fighters to whom he not only sent arms and money but also his most beloved disciple: Captain Arnaldo Ochoa (executed many years later, in 1989, as a ranking general when he no longer proved to be sufficiently trustworthy).

In any case, if Che was about to initiate his great (and final) adventure, and if this was going to provoke anger, rejection, or indifference in the local communist parties—devoted to and dependent on Moscow—it was necessary to precede this with a type of Cuban revolutionary grammar lesson: *Revolution in the Revolution?* This little Frenchman says three fundamental things of comfort and benefit to Havana and to further glorify Che. First, he warns that revolutions in Latin American must start from a rural military *"foco,"* which in time will spawn a political vanguard. This is the theory called *"foquismo."* Second, he affirmed that when the order of the factors is reversed—that is, first creating the political vanguard and later trying to generate the revolutionary *foco*—then the political organization becomes an end in itself and the armed battle will never take place; third, he identifies the targeted enemy: Yankee imperialism and its local leaders.

This nonsense, a veritable conceptual amplification of Guevara's manual, didn't help him much. A patrol of poorly armed Indians ended the bombastic theory of *foquismo* with one clean shot. Débray was captured by the Bolivian army after a visit with the guerrillas, which was organized by Guevara, and was convicted of military uprising, despite his claims of innocence based on a journalistic excuse. He did admit, however, to having been on night watch, claimed that he hadn't shot at anyone, and insisted on his legal rights, which, by the way, he never defended for his despised bourgeoisie adversaries. Fortunately his captors didn't mistreat him more than slapping him around a bit, and within a few months, due to international pressure, he was pardoned and excused from the long sentence placed on him. After returning to Paris, he slowly and gradually evolved until he became, much to his regret, a man profoundly hated and scorned by his Cuban friends. Débray had come to understand that within a revolution there is no other revolution, but rather a sheer bloody madness that signifies the death of thousands of hopeful youths enamored of political violence.

Los conceptos elementales del materialismo histórico ("Elementary Concepts of Historic Materialism") Marta Harnecker, 1969

In 1969 there appeared a great Marxist vulgate published in Latin America, descending from the hand of a Chilean writer, Marta Harnecker, who has lived in Cuba since the 1970s following the overthrow of Salvador Allende. In 1994 the Mexican publisher Siglo XXI produced the fifty-ninth printing of "Elementary Concepts," a fact that attests to the resilient vitality of this work (and the heroic obstinacy of the Marxists), despite the defeat of communist countries and the predictable discredit inflicted on Marxist studies in 1989.

The author arrived in Cuba for the first time in 1960, though at that time she was not a believer in Marxism but a leader of Santiago de Chile's University Catholic Action. She was what was at that time called a "progressive or leftist Catholic," imbued with ideals of justice, a reader of Jacques Maritain and Teilhard de Chardin. However, despite the admiration that the Cuban political process awakened in her—as it did with many Western intellectuals—her emotional and intellectual ties to communism and her sudden discovery of the Great Truth didn't surface from that life experience but from the classes she began taking in 1964 from Louis Althusser at the École Normale in Paris. This isn't an insignificant observation—we'll return to it later—because it demonstrates the great paradox that many Marxist intellectuals suffer: while they apparently cling to a Marxist interpretation of reality taken from the books, they ignore the concrete examples they actually experience.

"Elementary Concepts" is nothing more than a good summary of the non-philosophical aspects of Marx's thinking. It's a pedagogical text written to educate Marxists in a couple weeks of heavy reading. It's "everything you wanted to know about Marxism but were afraid to ask" in one volume. Given its didactic nature, it includes summaries, questions, lofty statements, discussion topics and a short bibliography. It's clearly written and tries to establish the Marxist view of the world into three great themes: the structure of society, the classes it consists of, and historical "science." Anyone who can digest these three hundred pages of small type is ready to carry out the work that Marx and Ms. Harnecker desire from all Marxists: to change the world. To change it, of course, by way of a violent revolution that would take down bourgeoisie governments, install proletariat dictatorships, and establish the basis of a just, efficient, brilliant, and prosperous universe.

In a certain way, "Elementary Concepts" complements and improves upon the incredibly well-known *Elementary and Fundamental Principles of Philosophy* (classes given by Georges Politzer in 1936 at the Workers' University in Paris, later collected by his disciples in book form), which has been reproduced thousands of times as the leading text for those entering into the conceptual entanglements of the author of *Das Kapital*. However, Harnecker's book perhaps became part of a new very vogue trend in the 1960s and 1970s: the *re-reading* of the classics. In other words, a re-reading by intellectuals, headed by Althusser himself, who went directly to the sacred texts to find an understanding that wasn't grasped by previous interpreters. To tell the truth, however, there isn't a single new alternative reading in this Chilean's text that justifies her efforts of examining some of Marx's and Lenin's texts in order to uncover . . . the very same readings found by previous exegetes.

However, and despite a truly independent standard that the author wants to pass along, the Siglo XXI edition of "Elementary Concepts" includes an interview in which Harnecker, not completely revealing her purpose, laboriously tries to clearly present four events related to her past that evidently torment her, or perhaps create some difficulties for her in the orthodox Cuba where she lives. First, she's no longer Catholic; second, she is not Maoist (something which she was accused of being in the past for her defense of the Chinese leader's insurrectionary theory); third, she doesn't share the criticism about the USSR that her professor Althusser expressed in his time; and fourth, she wants it to be understood that she completely agrees with the Muscovites' (from the Moscow of that time) point of view.

It's interesting that Ms. Harnecker, so punctilious in wanting to separate herself from her professor Althusser's anti-Sovietism, didn't do the same for the French philosopher's uxoricide, given that the worst thing about the author of *Reading "Capital"* is not that he criticized the Soviet dictatorship but that with his own hands he strangled his unfortunate wife, Elena, something impossible to overlook in someone who has apparently spent his entire life fighting for the freedom of his fellow man.

In any case, there's a painful contradiction that should affect Harnecker in this divorce of one's actual life from his intellectual vision (that is, if her conscience suffers from incongruity the way that it tends to affect normal people). In the two decades in which she has resided in Cuba, she has been able to see, and verify, the growing physical and moral degradation that the society suffers, the failures of centralized planning, the horrors of political police, the government's lack of scruples, the constant lies, the double morals practiced by the people, and the runaway increase in hunger and prostitution. In short, she has seen the terrible calamities that Marxism causes when one practices what her book insists will bring wealth and happiness to the people.

The author of "Elementary Concepts" cannot even hide behind the justification that, despite living in Cuba, she doesn't know what goes on, because her husband, the father of her daughter, is no one else than General Manuel Piñeiro (known as "Red Beard"). He's the man who for more than three decades, from the American Department of the Central Committee of the Communist Party, skillfully led all subversive operations carried out in Latin America by Castroism. Piñeiro and presumably his wife know up to the very last detail of the government's crimes, the drug trafficking, the numerous violations of international rules and decency that the Cuban government has carried out, always on behalf of a mythical revolution that is difficult to defend by any moderately informed person.

How does Harnecker's biography comport with her work as a pedagogue of the ways to cultivate happiness in the world? Maybe Elena, Althusser's wife, asked her husband the same question. God only knows why she was strangled by Ms. Harnecker's favorite professor.

One Dimensional Man
Herbert Marcuse, 1964

If Fanon launched his attack on the West from Third World trenches (which considerably weakened its effectiveness outside the colonized countries), something completely different happened when capitalism received fierce criticism from within the bowels of its own advanced societies. Of all the criticism, none was more echoed in the 1960s and 1970s—the golden era of the Latin American idiot—than that hurled by the German philosopher Herbert Marcuse, settled in the United States.

Marcuse was born in Berlin in 1898. In 1934 he left behind the European uprisings of Nazi-fascism and moved to the United States, a country where he acquired fame as a professor of philosophy and an original thinker. The first book that cat-apulted him to fame was *Eros and Civilization* (1955). But the book that turned him into a veritable guru of the intellectual left during the late twentieth century was *One Dimensional Man,* which appeared in English in 1964 and in Spanish in 1968 under the prestigious imprimatur of the Mexican publishing company Joaquín Mortiz. Barely a year later, Joaquin Mortiz released the fifth and defini-tive edition, this time slightly revised. Marcuse died in 1979, when the United States was experiencing double-digit inflation, the USSR was at the peak of its power, and the American society was atoning for its Vietnam problem, and it wasn't very crazy for one to think—as Revel painfully warned from Paris—that the era of democracy was coming to an end. Marcuse, who was delighted with this fail-ure, never realized that the situation to come was going to be very different.

Before Marcuse, two social analysts had, quite effectively, taken a harsh inventory of the Western model, although focusing primarily on the United States: sociologist C. Wright Mills and Vance Packard, that clever disseminator of sociological observations. Three of Packard's books instantly turned into true bestsellers: *The Hidden Persuaders, The Status Seekers,* and *The Waste Makers.* All three showed a society grossly manipulated by economic powers, irrational in its consumption and deteriorating from the values it fostered. It was impor-tant to succeed at all cost, even if we had to participate in the rat race, trying to climb up the corporate ladder to acquire symbols of social hierarchy that would allow us to . . . keep on climbing.

To this outrageous ideological family—visited by economists like the Swiss Gunnar Myrdal and the American John Kenneth Galbraith—Marcuse added two monumentally influential names and analysis methods from his early Euro-pean training: Marx and Freud. Marcuse was a Freudian and a Marxist, a hereti-cal combination that has already been observed, for example, in such figures as Erich Fromm. By guiding his ruminations through these two mediums—psy-choanalysis and dialectic materialism—he created true celestial music, rich and seductive, for the intellectuals who wanted to crucify the model of Western coexistence and desired something more than flimsy propaganda pamphlets. Marcuse contributed to the "Great Rejection" philosophy.

This is what the *One Dimensional Man* is about: the rationalization, from the Marxist and Freudian perspectives, of a severe attack on "the ideology of advanced industrial society"—as the book's subtitle states. According to Mar-cuse, this ideology alters the profound nature of human beings, alienating them and turning them into poor conformist beings, spellbound by the amount of goods that the devious production apparatus makes available to them, while secretly depriving them of the freedom to choose because, in the end, "the tech-nological society is a system of domination."

Marcuse, who lived in the United States, arriving right at the height of the Great Depression and having seen the system's formidable economic recuperation in his thirty years of U.S. residency, could not base his criticism on "the poor versus the rich" argument, since he was witness to the prosperity of the middle class. He therefore had to reformulate his attack from a different angle: we cannot expect a class confrontation to destroy the system (as Marx prophesied) because "the people [this one-dimensional herd] are no longer the ferment of social change but have become [oh, no!] the ferment of social cohesion." In other words, what Marcuse sadly realizes is that the technological society has upset the mechanism of social change—from quantitative to qualitative, according to Marxist jargon—by anesthetizing the workers to the point of turning them into a blind mechanism of a scientifically and technologically advanced system that dictates its own dynamics.

How to escape this terrible *fatum?* By admitting that true totalitarianism is present in the advanced societies of the West, where private property prevails, separated from individual interests, and by searching for the true moral freedom—that capitalism has taken away from the people—via government-controlled means of production: "Since the development and utilization of all available resources for the universal satisfaction of vital needs is the prerequisite of pacification, it is incompatible with the prevalence of particular interests which stand in the way of attaining this goal. Qualitative change [what Marcuse advocates] is conditional upon planning for the whole against these interests, and a free and rational society can emerge only on this basis."

He later adds, just to make sure there was no misunderstanding—using the most preposterous reasoning—the following paradox: "Today, the opposition to central planning in the name of a liberal democracy which is denied in reality serves as an ideological prop for repressive interests. The goal of authentic self-determination by the individuals depends on effective social control over the production and distribution of the necessities (in terms of the achieved level of culture, material and intellectual)."

Who is going to head the Great Rejection of the "totalitarianism" of the liberal democracies? Obviously "the substratum of the outcasts and outsiders, the exploited and persecuted of other races and other colors, the unemployed and the unemployable. . . . Their force is behind every political demonstration for the victims of law and order." This is the revolutionary seed that will destroy that unjust system that turns its people into zombies. But while Marcuse was writing his desperate defense of disobedience and protest, a horrified multitude was escaping beneath all the barbed wires erected in those Marxist paradises, searching for a one-dimensional, or polydimensional, or whatever kind of destiny, but never the one Marcuse's cohorts were imposing on them. It's a shame that Marcuse didn't live to 1989. The images of the demolished wall of his native Berlin would have perhaps made him rethink his book.

How to Read Donald Duck
Ariel Dorfman and Armand Mattelart, 1972

In 1972, Latin American political idiocy was suddenly enhanced by a book founded on a discipline that at that time was far from the ideological battle: "semiotics" (a term that Ferdinand de Saussure used to designate that very theoretical branch of linguistics that deciphers the signs of communication that exist in every society). The work in question had the clever title *How to Read Donald Duck*, which was followed by a somewhat staler and more academic subtitle: *Mass Communications and Colonialism.* Its authors were two young people barely in their thirties. Dorfman was born in Argentina and arrived in Santiago in his adolescence, while Mattelart was of French origin, and both worked in the field of literary research: Dorfman as a member of the Division of Children's Literature and Educational Publications in Quimandú and Mattelart as a professor-researcher in the Academy of the National Reality, affiliated with the Universidad Católica. In a way, this book was the result of a polemic seminar entitled "Subliterature and How to Fight It," which proves the old often-stated dictum: ideas have consequences. Including the bad ones.

What is this text all about? It's essentially about a hardened ideological reading from a communist perspective, published during the tense and radicalized Chile of Salvador Allende's government. Dorfman and Mattelart, both Marxists, proposed to find the hidden imperialist and capitalist message contained within the cartoon stories of the characters originating from the Disney "industry." However, instead of reading Donald Duck, these two intrepid authors, a linguistic Abbott and Costello, wanted to expose this message, showing the evil intentions it masks, to describe this twisted world and vaccinate society against the lethal, silent poison that cheerfully flows from the Yankee nation. And why did these semiotic police carry out this avenging task? It's obvious: "This book did not emerge from the impetuous minds of several individuals, but rather is directed toward a context of war to destroy the enemy of class structure in your land and in my land." Dorfman and Mattelart, ready for action, singing the *Internationale* while holding hands, have broken the chains of ignominy. Bravo.

And what did they find? Donald, without his costume, that get-up that covers him, is, of course, a pathological rogue. He's also perverted because in his little fantasy world there is no sex, no procreation, no one knows who is whose child, because cultivating this type of confusion around the characters' origins actually contributes to the enemy's reprehensible scheme: "Disney," these two horrified researchers say, "masturbates his readers without physical contact. He has created himself another aberration: an asexually sexual world. This is most evident in the drawings themselves, and not so much in the dialogues." Those depictions are sexist and—at the same time—emasculate, where the women are always coquettish and repressed if not slightly stupid and cowardly.

Donald, Mickey, Pluto, and Goofy are not what they seem. They are covert, right-wing agents, disseminated among children to ensure a relationship of domination between the motherland and her colonies. The rich uncle is not an egocentric millionaire duck, and those things that happen to him are not entertaining adventures but a capitalist symbol directed at children to cultivate the rawest and most self-indulgent type of egoism. Duckyland—a metaphor for the United States—is the cruel center of this world, while everyone else—in other words, we—comprise the exploited and exploitable periphery where inferior beings live. There is no denying it: "Disney drives out everything productive and historic in this world, just like imperialism has prohibited everything productive and historic in the underdeveloped world. Disney creates fantasies by subconsciously imitating how the world's capitalist system creates reality and how it wants to continue creating it." No, they're not ludicrous stories concocted to entertain children: "Donald Duck as its leader is promoting underdevelopment and the daily heart-wrenching of mankind in the Third World, this being the object of permanent enjoyment for the utopian kingdom of bourgeoisie freedom. It simulates an eternal party where the only entertainment/repayment is the consumption of the sanitized symbols of the marginal: the consumption of an equivalently unbalanced world. . . . By reading Disneyland one swallows and digests the condition of being exploited."

As was to be expected, stupidity of this caliber was of course destined to become a bestseller in Latin America. In 1993, the twenty-first anniversary of the first edition, this little book had been reprinted thirty-two times to the joy of the Mexican branch of Siglo XXI. And even in our times of healthy skepticism, when it isn't polite to suck your thumb, there's no shortage of prudent revolutionaries who continue to recommend this as undeniable proof of imperial deception and also the intellectual shrewdness of our sharpest and most observant Marxists.

Why does this book fit so perfectly into the Latin American idiot's ideal library collection? Because it was written with a tone of paranoia, and there is nothing that excites our idiots' imagination more than believing that they are the object of an international conspiracy hatched to subjugate them. For these untrusting souls there is always a "gringo" trying to deceive them, trying to steal their brains, fleecing them in financial centers, preventing them from designing automobiles or creating symphonic works, polluting their air, or conspiring with local accomplices on how to perpetuate the intellectual subordination that we Latin Americans suffer from. Yet it's always gratifying to defend one's native culture or folklore against foreign aggression. Why import heroes and fantasies from elsewhere when we can produce them locally (as Velasco Alvarado did, for example, with his imaginative "baby Manuelito" with an Andean poncho and a woolen cap, which he patriotically tried to substitute for the *gringo*'s Santa Claus and his damn reindeer)?

It's interesting that no one has told our militant semanticists that they could just as well have made an ideological reading of Mafalda, finding lesbian tendencies in her because she never let herself be fondled by little Guillermo (or whatever the boy's name is with the shaved head), or accuse Quino of being a CIA agent, since not once did he have his heroine denounce the U.S. presence in the Panama Canal. What would have happened if our shrewd interpreters were confronted with the Batman figure? Could it be that in that imperfect Yankee world one can defend justice only from the bottom of a cave and wearing a mask? And Superman, our chaste hero, defender of all laws (except for the Law of Gravity), isn't he maybe just a poor homosexual; just like the Lone Ranger who is always accompanied by the Indian whom, undoubtedly, he sodomizes? What kind of revolutionary or Marxist reading could we get from *Sleeping Beauty* or *Little Red Riding Hood*? Have you ever seen a more obvious demonstration of bourgeoisie values at their worst in that gluttonous and heartless grandmother who sends the little girl out into the perils of the forest? God! How can one be so stupid and not die in the process?

Dependency and Development in Latin America
Fernando Henrique Cardoso and Enzo Faletto, 1969

This short manual (scarcely two hundred pages long), read by many Latin American college students and prescribed as "required reading" by many Latin Americanists, was written in Santiago, Chile, in 1966 and 1967 in the shadow of the Economic Commission for Latin America (the famous CEPAL), and its cepalian origin is clearly seen in it. Its authors are two prestigious sociologists, one of them being Fernando Henrique Cardoso, who today is no less than the president of Brazil. However, it's very likely—given Cardoso's government programs—that in the thirty years which have passed between the time he wrote the book and his electoral victory there has been a profound change in his understanding of Latin America's economic reality. All in all, the first thing that this essay exudes is a cold rationality far removed from the dogmatic pamphlet. It is evident that its authors were not set on testing their hypothesis at any cost, but rather on finding a reasonable explanation for Latin America's relatively obstinate backwardness. Except that what they presented—and what is still being repeated by many people—is simply erroneous.

On the surface, this successful book—twenty-seven printings had already been made by Siglo XXI of Mexico by 1994—sought "to establish a dialogue with economists and planners to identify the social and political nature of the development problems in Latin America." In reality, their ultimate objective was much larger: to find out why the principal hypothesis of the most influential Latin American economist of the 1940s and 1950s had failed. An explanation had to be found for the collapse of Argentine Raúl Prebisch's development theory, a school of thought based on two premises that actual experience would completely discredit in the end. The first premise was the industrialization of Latin American countries by using temporary tariff barriers that would allow them to substitute foreign imports; the second was how the economy's giant "modernization" efforts had to be planned and even financed by the government, since local bourgeoisie economies lacked the means as well as the social mentality needed to accomplish this great leap forward.

In the mid-1960s, despite some relative success in Mexico and Brazil, it was already known that the CEPAL recipe had not produced the desired results, and it was obvious that the development policy had not succeeded in narrowing the economic distance that separated countries like the United States and Canada from their southern neighbors. Also, in certain nations—Argentina being the best example—the application of this therapy was counterproductive. Why? Where had the economists' predictions failed? Could it be that the basic problem was of a political nature, and wouldn't it have been better to examine it with instruments not related to economics? This is where Cardoso and Faletto offer something that falls like April showers on the moribund CEPAL thinking of that time. They give a "sociological" explanation that rationalizes, in one fell swoop, the two debated problems of why Latin America is considerably further behind the developed countries and, above all, why the industrialization policy of import substitution didn't work as was predicted, since it would have supposedly ended this age-old problem in the course of a single feverishly laboring generation.

Their rationalization has the magical name *dependency,* and consists of the following: "The dependency of underdevelopment socially implies a method of domination, expressed in a series of characteristics in the performance and orientation of the groups which appear either as producers or consumers in the economic system. This situation assumes that in extreme cases the decisions that affect the production or consumption of a given society are taken as part of the dynamics and the interests of the developed economies." In a global economy, the underdeveloped countries make up the "periphery," always subordinate to the "center," the developed countries that determine "the roles the underdeveloped countries will assume in the world market."

It is from this *structural* vision that Cardoso and Faletto try to describe how dependency is established between the center and the periphery. This method of analysis leads them to construct a behavior model in which a type of mechanical coordination of wills prevails in the society and where chance, individuals, or irrational desires are not figured in. Nor is there even the slightest sign of individual liberty in making decisions. The entire work is weighted down by a mechanistic and reductionist understanding of historical evolution. A typical paragraph would resemble this one: "It is possible, for example, that traditional dominating groups may oppose the premise of handing over their powers of control to the new social groups emerging from the industrialization process, but they can also negotiate an agreement with them, thereby altering the renewing results of development on the social and political plane." There are no people here, just machines.

It's no wonder that these two sociologists, educated in the 1950s, are predisposed to this structuralist conception tinted with Marxist pseudoscience, because throughout almost the entire century two academic trends have competed for supremacy within that discipline: the Webers and the Marxists, and at that time, and even until the 1980s, the Marxists had dominated. From this we can then deduce that if Cardoso and Faletto had written their book today, they would have probably looked to *culture*, as Weber proposed, for the profound reasons explaining our ills, as Lawrence Harrison brilliantly showed in his book *Underdevelopment Is a State of Mind.*

In any case, after the undeniable success of the Asian "tigers" or "dragons," it is no longer possible to continue believing that developed nations—the mythical center—impose dependency on underdeveloped countries, or the periphery, simply because there are societies that at a certain moment in their history—Switzerland, for example, after 1848—begin doing things in a way that leads them toward growth and progressive development. And there are societies that remain trapped by their own mistakes. This can be shown in the comparison between the Chile of the reviled "Chicago boys" and Velasco Alvarado's or Alan García's Peru.

In 1959—and this is another very fitting example—there were two distant islands that distinctly resembled each other in their political circumstances: Cuba and Taiwan. Both were previously threatened by a huge and adversarial giant. Both belonged to the underdeveloped world, although Cuba had a level of prosperity, education, and health infinitely greater than that of the Asian island. What has happened these many decades later? The Taiwanese—who fortunately had never heard of the theory of dependence—worked, saved, invested, and researched until they became an economic power of world importance, without anyone trying to stop them. The rest is, well, nonsense.

A Theology of Liberation
Gustavo Gutiérrez, 1971

The 1960s was a decade marked by rebellions and "commitments" in practically every Western nation and in almost every social sector. Singer-songwriters "protested" against injustices; pacifists against wars; hippies against the consumer society; and students against mediocre universities. Every group, every social class, every union raised its fist furiously and threateningly against the general, vague, and abstract power, as well as the specific power in the fields where they carried out their own particular work. It was the era of the first dawning of guerrilla warfare and the French "May" of 1968. The world had not felt such a revolutionary spasm since 1848.

Naturally, the Catholic Church was not far from this atmosphere, and especially in Latin America, a continent shaken by poverty, political instability, and recurring acts of violence. Its involvement began to surface at the same time, in 1959, that John XXIII convened the Vatican II Council—the Church's great congress of princes and thinkers that would substantially change the direction of this institution. When the Council began, the Church's primary function was to *guide* the flock to peacefully conquer Heaven. When it ended, several years and many documents later, the Church had declared itself a *pilgrim,* in other words, society's companion in the struggle to build a fairer and more equal world. In 1967, the Pope issued his encyclical *Populorum progressio.* Rome had, somehow, secularized its immediate objectives. Shortly before this, already embracing the fighting spirit, the priest Camilo Torres had died alongside a Castro-communist Colombian guerrilla, of female persuasion, in battle.

After Vatican II, in August 1968, the second plenary meeting of the Latin American Bishops' Council (CELAM) took place in Medellín and the consequent *aggiornamento* of the pastoral mission. For this magnanimous event the Church requested collaboration from the best intellectual minds to be found on the continent, a group that undoubtedly included the then young Peruvian Gustavo Gutiérrez with an undergraduate degree in psychology from Louvain, a doctorate in theology from Lyon, and a professorship at the Universidad Católica in Lima. It was for this occasion that Gutiérrez began to organize his thoughts in a document that he already called "liberation theology," a text that he later expanded upon until its final publication in 1971 under the title *A Theology of Liberation.* Since then, few books of thought that have appeared in Latin America have reached the level of influence and penetration of this one.

In order to understand this book, it is very important to remember what its purpose is: to give theological support to a specific new form of action, based on Catholicism's own sacred books. The Church couldn't simply change its pastoral mission. It couldn't turn its global mission around 180 degrees without providing any explanation for itself and its believers as to why it will no longer be complacent and—as often happened—an accomplice to power, but now will oppose and rebel against it. After all, since all of the Church's legitimacy was based on the "divine revelation" given by the Scriptures, the acts of those who subscribe to those beliefs had to change to accommodate the new readings of the texts or risk creating grave contradictions.

Gustavo Gutiérrez created this dilemma. He searched the sacred books and found a suitable reading for converting *the poor* into the historical subject of Christianity. They were in Genesis, in Psalms, in different biblical passages, in anecdotes in the New and Old Testaments. It became perfectly possible, without committing heresy, to state that the Church's principal mission was to rescue the poor, not only from their material deficiencies but also from their spiritual ones. For Gutiérrez, the *liberation* concept was much more than just feeding the hungry or giving the thirsty something to drink: it was necessary to create a selfless creature of solidarity—like Che's and Castro's "new man," whom he mentions—stripped of all vile worldly ambitions.

The situation gets complicated when Gutiérrez goes from theology to economics and puts forth the conventional analysis of Marxist leftists to his Church in order to accomplish this change. The Peruvian priest says: "Poor countries are becoming ever more conscious that their underdevelopment is nothing more than a by-product of other countries' development, based on the type of relationship that they currently have with them. And, therefore, their own development will not happen unless they fight to destroy the domination that the rich countries hold over them." This immediately causes Gutiérrez to assume a Marxist-Leninist perspective of social conflicts and propose a drastic, possibly violent, solution: "Only a radical break from the present state of things, a profound transformation of the property system, the access of the exploited classes to power, or a social revolution that breaks this dependency, will allow us to enter into a different society, a socialist society."

So, Leon XIII's old definition—"communism is inherently evil"—was eliminated, and Christians were tacitly cheered on to show their commitment to the poor by allying themselves with communists in the universities, in political parties, and in guerrilla factions. If an armed battle had to be carried out against a degrading model of society, the Church wasn't going to organize this venture, but it would join or support those who would. It was common that from religious seminaries or educational centers there emerged movements that quickly evolved into armed combat and terrorism, as happened with Spain's Basque ETA and Uruguay's Tupamaro. This was clearly seen in Nicaragua and El Salvador, countries where the influence of liberation theology, irresponsibly managed by certain Jesuits and Maryknolls, led many youths toward violence and some clergymen to martyrdom, killed by soldiers or paramilitary fighters fanaticized by hate.

Rectifying this bloody madness—something that Pope Wojtyla seems to want—is not easy. In addition to encouraging armed conflicts and giving moral legitimacy to a good portion of terrorists and killers, the liberation theology movement created radicalized "grass-roots communities" (especially in Brazil) that no longer respond to the Church's guidance but to the sermons of semi-heretical theologians like Leonardo Boff—uselessly censured by the Vatican in 1985. The rebellion has in fact ended up affecting discipline in the institution itself.

Twenty-five years after publishing his famous book, Gustavo Gutiérrez, true to his word, remains a humble parish priest in a poor Lima shantytown, caring for those who request his help, with the little energy he has left. Those who know him cannot doubt his fundamental honesty and integrity. Those who have carefully read his book cannot ignore his tremendous, painful, and—surely unintentional—bloody mistakes. In the end, his theology has helped neither the poor nor the Church.

Open Veins of Latin America
Eduardo Galeano, 1971

Any self-respecting bibliography that reviews the Latin American idiot's essential library must conclude with *Open Veins of Latin America* (here translated by Cedric Belfrage), by the Uruguayan Eduardo Galeano ("el Trucha" to his friends), born in Montevideo in 1940. There is no better compendium of the errors, arbitrariness, or simple nonsense populating the heads of our most errant radicals than this. Nor is there any book of its genre that can boast of so many reprintings, translations, and praise. In short, there is no single work in Spanish that deserves—as does this one—to be considered as the Latin American idiot's bible or the great soap opera of political thought.

The title, purely lyrical, is already an eloquent sample of what is to come. Latin America is an inert continent, lying unconscious between the Atlantic and the Pacific, victim to the empires and villains who suck the blood out of its veins, in other words, from its immense natural resources. The image is so plastic and so melodramatic that a progressive group of Argentine musicians have even written a protest song dedicated to it, whereas the Círculo de Lectores edition of this book from Colombia, illustrated by Marigot, displays on its cover an enormous U.S. flag in the shape of a knife ruthlessly disemboweling a bleeding South America. Lovely.

What the hell is this Latin American idiot's *vade mecum*? It's an educational book. It's the definitive book explaining why Latin America has lower levels of development than Western Europe and the United States. And each *important* statement made by its author is italicized so that the reader first understands the subtle intelligence of its author and second can better retain the profundity of the reflection or the specific information, and thus reap the fruits of Galeano's God-given intelligence provided us in his impassioned and hard-hitting paragraphs.

The book's structure also betrays it as a revolutionary handbook. In the prologue, the contents of the work are summarized. One can read the prologue and ignore the rest since it's all spasmodically said in the first twenty pages. Past that, he just includes examples to buttress the statements that come gushing forth. These examples are given concerning the natural wealth that the imperialists, since the time those Spanish predators set foot on the continent, have stolen from us: gold, silver, rubber, cocoa, coffee, beef, bananas, sugar, copper, petroleum, and other animal, vegetable, and mineral products that could be used to feed the insatiable foreign Moloch.

The second part of the book attempts to describe the reasons that explain Latin America's failures in its efforts to escape the customary misery that overwhelms its masses. Sometimes the guilty are the British, other times the Americans, but there are always the local traitors. The book is a constant memorial to victimization and the identification of the villains who savagely torment us: those who import our raw materials; those who export goods, machinery, or capital to us; those multinationals that invest and those that don't invest; and international credit organizations (IMF, Inter-American Development Bank, World Bank, USAID). Foreign aid is a trick to suck us dry even more. If they loan us money they are trying to financially ruin us. If they don't loan us money they are trying to strangle us: "the investments that turn Latin American factories into mere cogs in the giant corporation's machinery do not in any way alter the international division of labor. There is no change in the system of intercommunicating arteries through which capital and merchandise circulate between poor countries and rich countries. Latin America continues exporting its unemployment and poverty: the raw materials that the world market needs, and on whose sale the regional economy depends. Unequal exchange functions as before: poverty wages in Latin America help finance high salaries in the United States and Europe."

Are there any good guys in this horror film? Of course. And it's important to know who the heroes of this pillar of Latin American ideological stupidity are. In the past, they were no less than the Jesuit Missions in Paraguay, the creators of a totalitarian system where the poor Guaraní Indians had to even schedule their lovemaking to the sound of a bell. Later, in that same ill-fated country, there was the crazed Gaspar Rodríguez de Francia, a dictator who literally closed down the entire nation to all foreign influences, to the point of allowing only two libraries to exist: his own and Father Maíz's. Why is he admired? Because of his efforts in autocratic development, because of his fiery nationalism, because he didn't accept free trade, because of the militarization he imposed, because of the immense role he assigned to the state as a producer of goods, because of the iron-handed discipline he used to subject the Paraguayans for almost three decades, because of his hate of liberalism. Who else is revered? The rancher Rosas, tyrant of Argentina, and also for similar reasons Fidel Castro, who has done just what Rodríguez de Francia did but with more administrative ineptitude. Galeano, however, says the following falsehood without blushing in the least: "The main reason there are shortages in Cuba is the new abundance of consumers: the country now belongs to everyone. Therefore, Cuba's shortages are the inverse of what other Latin American countries are experiencing."

Naturally, this kind of talk can only lead to the most senseless violence, such as that unleashed by his Tupamaro compatriots. Let's look at the paragraph that ends his book: "In the present process of integration we neither re-encounter our origins nor come nearer to our goals. Bolívar prophesied shrewdly that the United States seemed fated by Providence to plague America with woes in the name of liberty. General Motors or IBM will not step graciously into our shoes and raise the old banners of unity and emancipation which fell in battle; nor can heroes betrayed yesterday be redeemed by the traitors of today. It is a big load of rottenness that has to be sent to the bottom of the sea on the march to Latin America's construction. The task lies in the hands of the dispossessed, the humiliated, the accursed. The Latin American cause is above all a social cause: the rebirth of Latin America must start with the overthrow of its masters, country by country. We are entering times of rebellion and change. There are those who believe that destiny rests on the knees of the gods; but the truth is that it confronts the conscience of man with a burning challenge."

There unquestionably exists something that Galeano hates with even greater intensity than the *gringos* or the multinationals or liberalism: truth, common sense, and freedom. He cannot stand them. He doesn't believe in them. He has no respect for them. His only and strongest allegiance is to feed uninformed Latin Americans errors and nonsense until he perfects the legendary ideological stupidity that he has made famous. And that is why his book ends ours. He's earned it.

INDEX EXPURGATORIUS LATINOAMERICANUS

"It isn't having been an idiot that's so bad but persisting to be one."

I believe in political freedom, but freedom in a market economy is like having a liberated fox among liberated hens.
Raúl Alfonsín, Ex-President of Argentina; Buenos Aires, 1983

In the 1990s, *campesino* dignity is again outwitting technocratic arrogance, and despite all odds being against them, the Cañada Indians are leading on the scoreboard and beating Harvard Yuppies.
Armando Bartra, Mexican Anthropologist; Mexico, 1995

Economic reforms, especially those which incorporate measures promoting a free market economy, have exacerbated social tensions and incited protests [in Colombia] in the past few years.
Amnesty International, A Human Rights Organization; Madrid, 1994

We are not alone. Countries in the socialist community are showing us their fraternal solidarity. This is especially true with the Soviet Union, which we consider as our big brother.

I preside over a government that is not socialist, but one which will resolutely pave the way to socialism.
Salvador Allende, Ex-President of Chile; Moscow, 1972, and Mexico City, 1972

We are neither from the left nor the right; our motto: Peru is our doctrine.

The remarkable drive that ancient Peru achieved can be explained by the advanced level of development that its planning had acquired and which has left irrefutable proof. The Popular Action Party has proposed taking advantage of this.

Fernando Belaunde Terry, Ex-President of Peru; Lima, 1980 and 1994

My letter of intent is not with the International Monetary Fund, but with the Venezuelan people.

Rafael Caldera, President of Venezuela; Caracas, 1993

When will the God of Heaven
wish our fate to shift;
let the poor eat bread
and the rich dine on shit.

How is it the tomato's crime
Just to be born upon a vine
if then some whore's *gringo* man
Should come and stuff it in a can
and to Caracas it consign

Anonymous Songs Sung by Leftist Groups in Latin America

We refuse to turn over the fundamental elements of our nation's security and sovereignty, like electricity, basic petrochemistry and satellite communications.

Cuauthémoc Cárdenas, Leader of the PRD—Party of the Democratic Revolution—in Mexico; Mexico City, 1995

Neoliberalism is inherently immoral because it has as its foundation a Godless positivism, putting profits and money as the supreme good . . . "Ave, Caesar, morituri te salutat" (Cheers, neoliberalism, those who are about to die salute you!).

Bartolomé Carrasco Briseño, Archbishop Emeritus of Oaxaca; Mexico, Oaxaca, 1996

The relationship between one part of this industrialization process [in the Third World] and transnational companies brings about serious concerns proving that they are imposing a new form of dependency on our countries in order to turn us into exporters of simple manufactured products, trapped into a network of international production and marketing systems, while continuing to import the material and capital goods that determine the course of development.

The island will first have to sink into the sea before I will abandon Marxist-Leninist principles.

Dear businessmen, I invite you to invest in Cuba. After all, the worst that can happen to you here has already happened: the country has become communist.
Fidel Castro, Cuban Dictator; Havana, 1988, 1989, and 1990

Peace is a right and a duty that must be mandated.

All Colombians have the right to a decent place to live.

It is recognized that all people have the right to recreation, participation in sports and the enjoyment of free time.
Colombia's Constitution; Bogota, 1991

I know that we will see each other again some day/good day, Fidel, good day, Haydée, good day, my "Casa"[1]/my place among my friends and among the streets/my chum, my dear one, my injured yet more alive than ever little caiman/between us I am this word just as others are your eyes or your muscles together we will all go to the future harvest/to the sugar in a time of no empires or slaves.
Julio Cortázar, Argentine Writer; Paris, 1971

When the Soviet Union has seen it necessary, now and then, to send its troops outside its own borders, it always does so not to export revolutions, but to prevent counter-revolutions.
Luis Corvalán, Ex-Secretary General of the Communist Party of Chile; Santiago de Chile, 1986

Selling our state-run companies as a way of saving the country will not be accepted by the left. We cannot let ourselves be carried away with this theory of neoliberalism. The state has an important and dominant role.
Luis Ignacio (Lula) Da Silva, President of the Workers' Party in Brazil; Havana, 1993

Poor Mexico, so far from God and so near the United States.
Porfirio Díaz, Ex-Dictator of Mexico; Mexico, end of the nineteenth century

---

[1]*Translator's note:* Refers to *Casa de las Américas,* the institutional cultural magazine of the revolution.

Unable to please its constituents, Latin American governments first succumbed to military dictatorships and then to neoliberal reforms. Suffocation from high protectionism, subsidized consumption and production, captive markets, and the lack of competition should have been and was corrected. But then, we went from demonizing national governments, to the illusion of expecting everything from the free play of market forces, to the cruel complacency of a social Darwinism in a land of hunger and extreme necessities.

The Zapatista Army is the first guerrilla force of the twenty-first century.
Carlos Fuentes, Mexican Writer; Mexico City, 1994 and 1995

We shouldn't be dogmatic and adopt the so-called democratic system, which in many countries has degenerated into a pseudodemocracy, and that's why we had to fix it with a machete.

I would love it if we had several Shanghais in Peru.
Alberto Fujimori, President of Peru and Author of the 1992 Coup;
Cartagena, Colombia, 1994

It's much more important for Latin America that I be friends with Fidel than break off relations with him.

If it weren't for Cuba, the United States would have already gone all the way down to Patagonia.
Gabriel García Márquez, Colombian Writer; Bogota, 1992, and Havana, 1996

Other governments, other ideologies and other social sectors have said that if the Government receives 100 it should only spend 100. We say that if the Government receives 100, it can spend 110, 115, because that fifteen will be credit for the *campesinos.*

Gentlemen, I confess to you here that I have only one pair of shoes, not because I want to be poor or unusual, but because I don't need any more.

I am not lazy; I am not a man who has never lived off of politics or his own parliamentary salary.
We need the state to participate in more decision-making and leadership roles because there is still a long way to go before it reaches a level of saturation in the nation's economy.

We are going to industrialize our industries in order to defend them from the invasion of foreign goods and resources.
Alan García Pérez, Ex-President of Peru; Lima, 1990, and Bogota, 1992

What Argentina needs is a little more inflation.
Bernardo Grinspun, Argentina Minister of the Economy in Raúl Alfonsín's
Administratio; Buenos Aires, 1984

We should stop being Marxist fuddy-duddies [highbrows] and instead put aside its obsolete message and just stay with its essence.
Luis Guastavino, Ex-Communist Representative,
currently on the Democratic Platform of the Left;
Santiago de Chile, 1990

The net rate of growth that is lauded as wonderful for all of Latin America is 2.5%. . . . We, however, are confidently talking about a growth of 10%, a growth of 10% is what Cuba foresees for the coming years. . . . What does Cuba plan on having in the year 1980? A net per capita income of some $3,000. More than the United States.

We assert that consciousness raising does more in a relatively short time than material stimulus for developing production and we base this on the general development of society in order for it to enter into communism, which then implies that work stops being a laborious necessity and becomes a pleasant imperative.

Many of our intellectuals' and artists' guilt arises from their original sin; they are not true revolutionaries. . . . New generations will be free from original sin. . . . Our job consists of preventing the current generation, disturbed by conflicts, from becoming corrupted and corrupting the new generation. . . . The revolutionaries will come, and then the new man's hymn, with the true voice of the people.
Ernesto "Che" Guevara,
Ex-Argentine-Cuban Guerrilla Fighter;
Havana, 1961, 1964, and 1965

Stalin, Captain,
Protected by Changó; safeguarded by Ochún
To your side singing free men throng:
the Chinaman who breathes with volcanic lungs,
the black man with his white eyes and beard of bitumen,
the white man, with green eyes and whiskers of saffron . . .
Stalin, Captain,
the people who awaken, together with you they'll march on!
Nicolás Guillén, Cuban Poet; Havana, 1947

Each battle that Cuba has carried out against the great imperialist power is important in its significance. There is some room to say that the socialist utopia is not dead.

Tomás Harris, Chilean Poet; 1996, upon learning he had won the Casa de las Américas Prize given by Cuba

Imperialism is the lower or primary level of modern capitalism in precapitalist or industrially underdeveloped countries.

With the anti-imperialist middle class united with the worker and *campesino* masses—these being the conduit of the true movement to political and social economic changes that APRA has organized—the popular alliance of manual and intellectual laborers is taking shape, that unfailing protagonist of our second continent wide emancipation revolution that will not be a class struggle but a struggle of the peoples.

Victor Raúl Haya de la Torre, Founder of APRA and the Peruvian Aprist Party; Lima, 1977

Fidel sits on the side of a tank rumbling into Havana on New Year's Day. . . . Girls throw flowers at the tank and rush to tug playfully at his black beard. He laughs joyously and pinches a few rumps. . . . The tank stops in the city square. Fidel lets the gun drop to the ground, slaps his thighs and stands erect. He is like a mighty penis coming to life, and when he is tall and straight, the crowd immediately is transformed.

Abbie Hoffman, U.S. Activist; United States, 1967

The state will permeate everything.

Ricardo Lagos, Leader of the Socialist Party of Chile and Minister of His Party's Coalition with the Christian-Democratic Party; Santiago, 1991

For us, privatization is more than a legal change from national to private: the change is a usufruct of the collective to the individual.

Juan Manuel López Caballero, Colombian Essayist; Bogota, 1994

Liberalism and Marxism are the same cat but with a different collar.

Javier Lozano Barragán, Bishop of Zacatecas, Mexico and President of the Economic Committee of the Latin American Bishops' Council; Zacatecas, 1996

I support Fidel Castro.
Diego Armando Maradona, Argentine Soccer Player; Madrid, 1992

Neoliberalism has proposed launching a reconquest of the land. That's right: this conquering of the land is not going to be like the Spanish conquest. It is going to be like the conquest of the American West. Thereby implying the physical, cultural, and historical annihilation of the peasants.
Subcomandante Marcos, Leader of the Zapatista Army of National Liberation of Mexico; Chiapas, 1995

The money that has financed the guerrilla warfare has been voluntarily donated by the *campesinos* and workers.
Manuel Marulanda Vélez, Alias "Tirofijo," Leader of the Revolutionary Armed Forces of Colombia; In hiding, 1995

Having eliminated the myth of a national bourgeoisie and the possibility of a reformist movement with the collaboration of this class, any authentic revolution in Latin America has to necessarily place itself in a socialist perspective. Paraphrasing the words of Theodore Petkoff, the revolution will prevail in Latin America as socialism or it will fail as a revolution.
Plinio Apuleyo Mendoza, Colombian Writer; Paris, 1971

We're waiting; bring on the Little Prince.
General Menéndez, Military Commander of the Falkland Islands; Buenos Aires, 1982, at the height of the conflict with the United Kingdom

The end of Batista's dictatorship and the beginning of this beautiful revolution will bring the Cubans a period of liberty and prosperity that the island has never known. Who can doubt our happy destiny?
Carlos Alberto Montaner, Cuban Writer; Havana, February 1959

Slave on the one hand, menial laborer on the other, this is the first thing that the latter remembers on freeing himself. By exploiting this mission of seeing everything so clearly, one day he will see himself liberated by this revolution.
Pablo Milanés, Cuban Singer; from his song "A Song for a United Latin America"

If you see me rich, call me a thief.

I don't aspire to be ushered into [the palace of] Miraflores; what I do strive for is to be carried out on shoulders.
Carlos Andrés Pérez, Ex-President of Venezuela; Caracas, 1977 and 1988

I have traveled throughout Europe; everything there is ancient. The future is in Perón's Argentina.

Tomorrow, St. Perón, let the boss do the work.
Evita Perón, Ex-First Lady of Argentina; Buenos Aires, 1947

Economic calculations don't interest us; we assert social rights for retired housewives; let the actuarial issues be settled by those who come in fifty years.

Man is good, but if he is chaperoned he is better.

First the country, then the Movement, and then the people.

In an organized community everyone has his social role clearly defined by the state.

I will cut off my own hands before signing any decree that accepts foreign capital.

For friends, everything. For enemies, not even justice.
Juan Domingo Perón, Ex-President of Argentina;
Buenos Aires, 1952, 1950, 1949, 1954, and 1955

Human rights, no; humanoid rights.
Augusto Pinochet, Ex-Dictator of Chile;
this statement, originally stated by Admiral Merino,
a member of the Chilean Junta, was adopted by
Pinochet throughout his regime

Peru has two types of problems: those that cannot be solved and those that solve themselves.
Manuel Prado, Ex-President of Peru; Lima, the 1950s

I do not share the theory of neoliberal opportunities, which is the most conservative of them all, and therefore in my government we will promote opportunities *à la colombia.*

The only authentication that I accept, that I ask for, and that I will seek as president of Colombia is that at the end of my term you will say: Samper is authentic because he kept his promise of social development that he made to all Colombians.

Ernesto Samper, President of Colombia; Bogota, 1993 and 1995

I heard the door close behind me and I lost the memory of my aging fatigue as well as the notion of time. Among these men who were wide awake, in full control of their faculties, sleep did not seem to be a natural necessity, just a simple routine that they had more or less freed themselves from . . . all have erased the habitual altering of lunch and dinner from their daily agenda. . . . Of all these serene beings, Castro is the most alert. Of all these fasters, Castro is the one who can eat the most and the one who can fast the longest. . . . [All of them] exercise a true domination over their personal needs. . . . they make the limits of the possible give way.

Jean-Paul Sartre, French Philosopher; Paris, 1961

We should crush the neoliberal trend. We cannot allow the [liberal] party to Plinioapuleyize.

*Horacio Serpa Uribe, Minister of the Interior of
Ernesto Samper's Administration in Colombia, Bogota, 1993*

Today, the Soviet Union is the freest country in the world.

*Volodia Teitelboim, Secretary General of the Communist Party of Chile;
Santiago de Chile, 1989*

The quite poor yet very predatory neoliberalism on the continent, founded on rash dogmatism, appears to foster the notion that Washington is not only a true but also a perpetual and ever-glowing "Pole Star" for Latin America.

*Juan Gabriel Toklatian, Argentine Political Scientist
and Professor Residing in Colombia; Bogota, 1992*

The United States should get its hands immediately out of El Salvador and let that country breathe freely. U.S. out of El Salvador! U.S. out of El Salvador!

*Alvaro Vargas Llosa, Peruvian Journalist;
Washington, D.C., 1984, in front of the White House*

Within ten, twenty, or fifty years there will come to all of our countries, as there is now in Cuba, the hour of social justice and all of Latin America will be emancipated from the empire that plunders it, from the castes that exploit it, and from the forces that today oppress and repress it.

Mario Vargas Llosa, Peruvian Writer; Caracas, 1967

The revolutionary government of the Armed Forces is neither capitalist nor communist but quite the contrary.

Campesino, your boss will no longer feast on your poverty.

Juan Velasco Alvarado, Ex-Dictator of Peru; Lima, 1970—
the second sentence was adopted by Velasco
as the motto for his 1970 agrarian reform,
after he incorrectly attributed it to the eighteenth-
century indigenous leader Tupac Amaru

ABOUT THE AUTHORS

Plinio Apuleyo Mendoza, a writer and journalist, was born in Tunja, Colombia. He is the author of several works, among which are *Años de fuga* (*Years of Flight,* recipient of the 1979 Plaza & Janés Prize for a novel); *The Fragrance of a Guava* (a book of conversations with Gabriel García Márquez); and *La llama y el hielo* (*Fire and Ice,* 1984).

Carlos Alberto Montaner was born in Havana, Cuba. An essayist, narrator, and journalist, he has published two novels, *Trama* (*The Plot,* 1989) and *Perromundo* (*Dog World,* 1972), as well as several books of essays: *La agonía de América* (*Latin America's Agony*), *Fidel Castro and the Cuban Revolution,* and *Libertad: la clave de la prosperidad* (*Freedom: The Key to Prosperity*). He is vice president of Liberal International.

Alvaro Vargas Llosa was born in Lima, Peru. He attended the London School of Economics and has worked as a journalist for various agencies in Spain, the United States, and Latin America. Currently he is a columnist for the Spanish newspaper *ABC* and the Los Angeles Times Syndicate and is about to launch a cultural magazine in Spain. He has published several books: *El diablo en la campaña* ("The Campaign"), *The Madness of Things Peruvian, El exilio indomable* ("The Indomitable Exile"), and *Cuando hablaba dormido* ("When I Talked in My Sleep"). He has also coauthored another book with Mr. Montaner and Mr. Mendoza, *Fabricantes de miseria* ("Manufacturers of Misery").

Michaela Lajda Ames is a translator/interpreter in Spanish and Slovak and has worked for corporations and government organizations on three continents. U.S. born to East European Cold War refugees, her services have been employed in television, publishing, trade shows, agribusiness, and international development.